D1551554

Universal Human Rights
and Extraterritorial Obligations

Pennsylvania Studies in Human Rights

Bert B. Lockwood, Jr., Series Editor

A complete list of books in the series is available from the publisher.

Universal Human Rights
and Extraterritorial Obligations

Edited by

Mark Gibney and Sigrun Skogly

PENN

UNIVERSITY OF PENNSYLVANIA PRESS

PHILADELPHIA

Published by
University of Pennsylvania Press
Philadelphia, Pennsylvania 19104-4112

Printed in the United States of America on acid-free paper

10 9 8 7 6 5 4 3 2 1

Library of Congress Cataloging-in-Publication Data

Universal human rights and extraterritorial obligations / edited by Mark Gibney and Sigrun Skogly.
    p. cm. — (Pennsylvania studies in human rights)
    Includes bibliographical references and index.
    ISBN 978-0-8122-4215-7 (alk. paper)
    1. Human rights. 2. International and municipal law. I. Gibney, Mark. II. Skogly, Sigrun.
K3240.U683 2010
341.4'8—dc22

                                  2009027548

Contents

Introduction

Sigrun Skogly and Mark Gibney

The fundamental principles governing international law are changing dramatically. International law, which traditionally has regulated the conduct between and among countries, has had as its core the respect for state sovereignty. However, the latter part of the twentieth century witnessed fundamental changes to the way in which the international community operates that are based upon a deep interdependence among states and their openness to international actors. This is often labeled the process of globalization. This process has had a significant impact on states' sovereignty and on the way in which international law regulates the interaction among states. This phenomenon includes the way in which international trade law (spearheaded by the World Trade Organization) dictates how member states' trade policies may operate; the way in which international financial law (led by the International Monetary Fund) determines financial policies of member states; and the way in which international environmental law regulates actions with transboundary effects. Thus, international law is no longer restricted to areas of interstate concern but it has also come to regulate states' domestic actions as well. Opponents to this view may hold that states are still sovereign in that they are not forced to take part in these international legal regimes. However, this view fails to take account of the political and economic realities of international relations where the voluntary nature of this regulation for most states (particularly weaker or poorer states) is a legal fiction.

In this new reality, which is prevalent in the practice of international law but still lacking in theoretical recognition, there is one area that is curiously lagging behind: human rights. This is not meant to suggest that international human rights law does not have a strong domestic foundation. In fact, the reason why international human rights law is so "revolutionary" is that it focuses almost exclusively on the "vertical" relationship between the state and the subjects of that state, rather than the "horizontal" relationship between and among nation-states. However, what human rights has almost totally ignored is that in an increasingly interdependent world—where public and private international actors have great influence upon the lives and living conditions of individuals all over the world—it is not sufficient simply to assess what *domestic* governments are doing in terms of human rights; it is equally important to assess the effect of *other* actors: intergovernmental organizations, international private entities, and foreign states as well.

The worldview adopted by rich and powerful states is that what they do in the world—whether through development activities, trade relations, military cooperation, or other foreign relations—will inevitably be beneficial and "good," while human rights violations are the sole responsibility of "other" governments (Mutua 2002). This, however, offers a very simplistic (and convenient) view of the world, and it ignores the manner in which those states that set the international agenda directly and indirectly influence the enjoyment of human rights in third countries.

There has been some reaction against this dominant approach, most notably in the anti-globalization movement or in the rights-based approach to development. In addition, at least a few scholars have called for creating mechanisms for increased and effective accountability on the part of intergovernmental institutions and private international actors. Still, what has been absent is any kind of systematic analysis of the changed realities of how the international community works, which is one reason why the entire human rights enterprise threatens to make itself irrelevant, especially to those who suffer human rights violations. In the words of Margot Salomon, "a rights-based approach to globalization seeks to place international human rights standards and principles at the centre of international economic affairs; to have them successfully inform all cooperative endeavours that may impact on their exercise. However, the international law of human rights will only provide the humanizing force that the negative trends in globalization require of it if it evolves to meet these challenges" (Salomon 2007, 11).

It is time to address this enormous gap in international law and to examine the manner in which foreign states influence the enjoyment of human rights in third countries. What the chapters in this book analyze is neither the "horizontal" nor the "vertical," but rather, the "diagonal" relationship between outside actors (especially Western states) and citizens in other countries. This is not an attempt to take issue with the principle that it is the domestic state that has the primary responsibility for its own population's human rights. What is added, however, is the notion that states should be held accountable wherever their actions may influence human rights enjoyment. The problem is that this idea runs smack into such established international law principles as "national sovereignty" and "jurisdiction." In a wonderful analogy that he develops in his contribution to this volume, Thomas Gammeltoft-Hansen likens the need for new thinking in the realm of human rights to the emergence of quantum mechanics, which arose when classical physics theory was found to be incapable of explaining phenomena at the atomic level. For Gammeltoft-Hansen (and the other authors in this volume), international law is frequently unable to deal with a globalized world where states are increasingly interrelated. It is tempting to add to this that the intellectual appreciation of extraterritorial obligations may well require the development of legal principles that make a "quantum leap" from the traditional territorial confines of human rights law.

In this book we address a variety of issues: What are the theoretical foundations for asserting that states have human rights obligations that go beyond national borders? How do foreign policy decisions—including development assistance, trade relations, and military cooperation—affect the human rights of individuals in third countries? How could states become more accountable for their foreign policies, and are there remedies that could be put in place for victims of the negative effects of such policies? It is indeed surprising that at the same time that international environmental law is developing provisions that call for consultation with affected people in third states in case of possible pollution, it would still be seen as an infringement of state sovereignty if similar provisions were to be introduced in situations of possible human rights violations.

There are some isolated developments within the implementation of human rights that are starting to reflect the concerns described above. Sweden adopted a White Paper in 1998 in which it approved the principle that all Swedish foreign policy should have the overall aim of protecting or promoting human rights. The UN Committee on Economic, Social, and Cultural Rights has started to question states that report to it as to how they ensure that their voting in international institutions, or their design of development policies, takes into account the effect on economic, social, and cultural rights (Sepúlveda 2006). Opposition politicians in the United Kingdom have suggested that the government of the United Kingdom may have been complicit in the violation of the right to be free from torture in connection with the extraordinary rendition of individuals eventually ending up as detainees in Guantánamo Bay (BBC 2009). And finally, several of the United Nations' special rapporteurs have started to develop this idea of extraterritorial obligations in their own work, some of which is explored in this volume.

There is an emerging literature on the theoretical foundations for extraterritorial obligations (Skogly 2006), the interpretation of applicable treaty law (Coomans and Kamminga 2004), and relevant international economic structures and human rights law (Pogge 2007; Salomon 2007;

Rajagopal 2003). Some more specific work in this area has also been done in the field of economic, social, and cultural rights (Skogly 2003b; International Council for Human Rights Policy 2003; Skogly and Gibney 2007). The aim of the current book is to illustrate the implications of extraterritorial obligations on the enjoyment and implementation of specific human rights, with examples taken from civil and political rights as well as economic, social, and cultural ones. Furthermore, we are addressing some larger cross-cutting issues where the extraterritorial effects of states' actions are considered from the perspectives of environmental law and refugee law.

The theoretical challenges in this realm are substantial. Just as there is a need for rethinking the position of sovereignty with regard to international human rights law generally, there is also a need to rethink other key concepts such as jurisdiction, state responsibility, and accountability. Furthermore, the applicability of the tripartite typology of obligations (to respect, protect, and fulfill) in terms of foreign policy needs to be explicitly recognized.

One of the most controversial issues with regard to extraterritorial human rights obligations has been the concept of jurisdiction. What various adjudicatory bodies have been trying to determine is where the domestic state's jurisdiction ends, and where the foreign state's jurisdiction begins. This approach to human rights obligations is built on the traditional notion that jurisdiction is to be equated solely with territory, rather than control over the individuals who suffer as a result of a foreign state's activities.

This narrow approach to jurisdiction (both in terms of linking it to territory and seeing it as one dimensional), is a challenge to viewing human rights obligations in an extraterritorial light. However, what is beginning to become clearer is that one or more foreign states may directly or indirectly exert sufficient control over an individual to influence his or her human rights enjoyment without that foreign state having territorial control where the individual resides. With increased globalization and international interaction involving parties with significantly unequal (economic, military, or other) power, it makes more sense to talk about jurisdiction over individuals or over actions, than necessarily tying it exclusively to territory.

A concept closely linked to jurisdiction is the notion of state responsibility. This is another key concept that needs to be revisited in order to operationalize extraterritorial obligations. In legal terms, state responsibility is triggered when the state has committed an internationally wrongful act, that is, a breach of an international obligation. International human rights treaties contain obligations for states—both domestically and internationally. However, state responsibility for breaches of international human rights law as a result of a state's actions beyond its borders is rarely triggered. This is partially due to the narrow interpretation of jurisdiction as indicated above, and partially due to a lack of effective accountability mechanisms for human rights violations. Yet, the concept of state responsibility could be applied to breaches of extraterritorial human rights obligations if the willingness to use these principles were present. However, what has to be developed further is the notion of diffuse and shared responsibility. The practice of extraordinary rendition provides a number of examples of how different states might be responsible for different human rights violations—all arising out of the same general incident. Thus, what international law has to begin to get away from is the idea that only one state—invariably the territorial state—is responsible for committing human rights violations.

Yet another related issue is the problem of accountability. There are international accountability structures accessible to victims of violations of human rights. However, these are generally related to the domestic state and are dependent upon this state's acceptance of the jurisdiction of the international courts or committees. Due to the inability to hold states accountable for human rights violations in other countries, international law principles of immunity and jurisdiction limited to territory tend to prevail. The issue of immunity also results in limited accountability for intergovernmental organizations (such as the World Bank and other international financial institutions), even though states that have (extraterritorial) human rights obligations make up the membership of these organizations and are collectively responsible for the decisions and policies of these institutions. Again, the development of accountability mechanisms that can respond to the current international interdependent structures and their effect on human rights is essential.

While the intention of the book is to illustrate how extraterritorial obligations are relevant for individual human rights, it is not possible to be exhaustive in such a relatively small collection of contributions. Thus, each author has chosen his or her own theme within the overall focus of extraterritoriality, and the chapters should therefore be read as illustrations as to how individual human rights may be affected by the actions of foreign states. The advantage of this approach is that several aspects of the extraterritorial effects of states' actions are illustrated (such as trade, development assistance, military cooperation, refugee protection) through the assessment of individual human rights. It is likely that much of the discussions on the variety of extraterritorial conduct could be applied to a number of the other rights as well. Consequently, the chapters add a wealth of knowledge to a field in which systematic analysis is still wanting.

What becomes clear throughout the various chapters on the different

rights is that extraterritorial obligations follow the tripartite classification of obligations mentioned above. There is a negative right to respect
human rights in other countries, inter alia through avoiding taking part
in extraordinary rendition, or through avoiding pollution of water or
restricting the water sources for a neighboring country. In terms of the
obligation to protect, states have obligations to ensure that they protect
individuals against human rights violations by third (private) parties. In
an extraterritorial setting, this means regulating the activities of transnational corporations over which they exert jurisdiction in order to avoid
having these entities engage in practices that breach human rights standards in other countries. Examples of this may be the regulation against
the use of child labor, or regulation to ensure human rights compliance
by private security companies. Finally, the obligation to fulfill is a positive obligation to support foreign countries in their quest to implement
human rights within their own domestic setting through measures such
as development assistance that is human rights conducive, or assistance
to develop a human rights infrastructure (functioning judiciary, anti-
corruption measures, and so forth).

In addressing the concept of extraterritorial human rights obligations,
we have found that violations of civil and political rights are understood
more easily than violations of economic, social, and cultural rights.
Without making any value judgment as to the importance of different
sets of rights, or indeed the necessity of addressing extraterritorial obligations equally for all five types of rights, we have found several causes for
the easier understanding of violations of civil and political rights. First, as
the chapters on torture, life, and refugee protection clearly demonstrate,
the direct causation between government action or inaction and human
rights violation may be more easily ascertained. For instance, in terms of
extraordinary rendition (as addressed by Manfred Nowak in Chapter 1),
the extraterritorial effects of human rights violations are very clear and
easy to document. Second, most people still have a better grasp of civil
and political rights than economic, social, and cultural rights. Thus, the
first part of the book focuses on civil and political rights.

In Chapter 1, Manfred Nowak illustrates that the right to be free of
torture, which has traditionally been viewed as operating within national
territorial boundaries, has recently come to be recognized as having significant extraterritorial components. Nowak, who presently is the UN
special rapporteur on torture, analyzes how the obligation to refrain
from torture reaches beyond the borders of states that have ratified relevant human rights treaties (in particular the International Covenant
on Civil and Political Rights and the Convention against Torture and
Other Cruel, Inhuman, or Degrading Treatment or Punishment), notwithstanding the seemingly territorial limitations in these treaties. By

addressing issues such as *refoulement* in refugee law and torture issues relating to the "war on terror," Nowak makes compelling arguments for the further reach of states' obligations.

Taking the point of departure from the fundamental right to life, Barbara Frey (Chapter 2) illustrates the significant human rights problems created by the proliferation of small arms on the international market. Starting with a review of the extraterritorial obligations to protect the right to life as a customary norm as well as a right based in treaty law, Frey, the former UN special rapporteur on small arms and human rights, considers how such obligations are enforceable. This leads to a consideration of emerging customary norms on the specific issue of small arms transfers and their likely misuse. The failure of the exporting state to recognize its own responsibility for the effects of the prevalence of such arms (and the tragic consequences that so often follow from this) are clearly documented and analyzed in this chapter.

Two chapters in the book take inspiration from other areas of international law that are in many respects closely related to human rights. In Chapter 3, Thomas Gammeltoft-Hansen covers international refugee law. He presents the changing reality of refugee law, which continues to move "outward" from the territorial boundaries of the receiving state. Such examples include the US interdiction program off the coast of Haiti, Australia's "Pacific solution" of transferring refugee determinations offshore, and the various policies pursued by European states that have helped move the refugee determination process seemingly all the way back to the country of origin—or something close to this. In this situation, extraterritorial obligations are not only implicated in the important principle of *non-refoulement*, but in a host of diverse human rights issues as well.

In another sister-area to international human rights law, John Knox (Chapter 4) provides an analysis of how international environmental law has dealt with extraterritorial obligations. Knox situates environmental rights within the broader framework of international human rights law, and he elaborates specifically on vertical and diagonal obligations. He neatly sums up the different approaches this way: "human rights law has the advantage of providing rights to individuals, but the disadvantage of not always clearly extending those rights beyond the territorial jurisdiction of their own states. International environmental law (IEL) has the converse strength and weakness." Using this paradigm as a focal point, Knox shows how several international and regional environmental law instruments, as well as the broader principle of non-discrimination in international law, have important implications in the field of human rights.

Returning to the core of international human rights law, Judith Bueno de Mesquita, Paul Hunt, and Rajat Khosla (Chapter 5) address the right to the highest attainable standard of health, building specifically on the work Hunt has carried out in his capacity as the UN special rapporteur on the right to health. Placing extraterritorial obligations within a larger context, including states' behavior in international financial institutions, the chapter focuses specifically on Hunt's experience in assessing the effect of Swedish development assistance on the right to the highest attainable standard of health in Uganda.

The current international food crisis provides the framework for Michael Windfuhr's contribution on the right to adequate food. In Chapter 6, he addresses how national and international policy structures and policy choices have contributed to the current negative state of food availability, and he sets this situation in the context of a right to adequate food. Through the presentation of case studies where external actors have had significant impacts on local peoples' enjoyment of the right to food, Windfuhr illustrates compellingly that the realization and the protection of the right to adequate food should not be limited to territorial boundaries of any state, but that international cooperation is an instrument to achieve the progressive realization of this right.

Virginia Leary (Chapter 7) takes a different approach from the other contributors in this volume. Leary focuses on a single example where a foreign state (the United States) and an intergovernmental organization (the International Labour Organization) worked in tandem in order to help improve workers' rights in another country (Cambodia). In particular, through a case study of the Cambodian textile exports and the ILO, Leary addresses the benefits that may come from external actors' concern over working conditions, including trade union rights, in a national setting in a developing country, although she is also quite cognizant of the tenuous nature of extraterritorial protection of those rights. What is also important about Leary's contribution is that it clearly shows that the issue of extraterritorial obligations is not solely about negative externalities.

Malcolm Langford's chapter on the right to housing (Chapter 8) contextualizes the issue of extraterritorial obligations within the field of international cooperation, with particular reference to international development. Langford does so through the use of two case studies: one on forced evictions, and the other on urban upgrading in international development.

Amanda Cahill (Chapter 9) addresses an important, yet implicit, right in the International Covenant on Economic, Social, and Cultural Rights, namely, the right to water. Her chapter focuses primarily on *General Comment 15*, adopted by the UN Committee on Economic, Social, and Cultural Rights in 2002, and then applies these principles to a detailed discussion relating to the manner in which the United Kingdom's Department for International Development (DFID) addresses and complies with such obligations in its overseas work.

In sum, each one of the chapters that follows challenges, in one way or another, some of the most basic and established principles in international law generally, and human rights law more specifically. This challenge is not an option but a necessity if human rights law is to remain relevant for, and provide a meaningful response to, individuals around the world who face torture, starvation, lack of housing, polluted water, and failure to obtain refugee status or life-saving medicines—often due to actions or omissions on the part of foreign states.

Chapter 1
Obligations of States to Prevent and Prohibit Torture in an Extraterritorial Perspective

Manfred Nowak

The Notions of Territory and Effective Control

The prohibition of torture and other forms of cruel, inhuman, or degrading treatment or punishment (CIDT), that is, the right to the physical and mental integrity of the human being, is one of the few absolute and non-derogable rights under international human rights law, which even ranks as *jus cogens* pursuant to article 53 of the Vienna Convention on the Law of Treaties (Simma and Alston 1992; UN Human Rights Committee 2004). All general human rights treaties dealing with civil and political rights contain a provision on the right to personal integrity, which is sometimes phrased in purely negative terms. For example, article 7 of the International Covenant on Civil and Political Rights (ICCPR) provides: "No one shall be subjected to torture or to cruel, inhuman, or degrading treatment or punishment." In article 5 of the American Convention on Human Rights (ACHR), this negative obligation of states parties is preceded by the positive right of all persons to have their physical, mental, and moral integrity respected.[1] Similarly, article 5 of the African Charter on Human and Peoples' Rights (ACHPR) contains the right of every individual to the respect of the dignity inherent in a human being and combines the prohibition of torture with another absolute and non-derogable right, the prohibition of slavery and the slave trade.

Under contemporary human rights theory, all rights of human beings entail corresponding obligations of states to respect and ensure such rights (Nowak 2003). While *respect* means refraining from unjustified interference, *ensure* entails positive obligations of states to protect and fulfill the respective rights. The obligation to *protect* requires states to avoid human rights violations by private parties, whereas the obligation to *fulfill* means that states shall take all legislative, administrative, judicial, and other measures necessary to ensure that the rights in question are implemented to the greatest extent possible. It may be further divided into sub-obligations to *facilitate, promote,* and *provide.*

In the texts of human rights treaties, these different obligations of states parties are stipulated only in a fairly rudimentary manner. According to article 1 of the European Convention for the Protection of Human Rights and Fundamental Freedoms (ECHR), the high contracting parties have obligated themselves to *secure* to everyone within their jurisdiction the rights enumerated thereafter. Article 1 of the ACHPR requires African states parties to *recognize* the rights and to adopt legislative or other measures to *give effect* to them. Under article 1 of the ACHR, American states parties undertake to *respect* the rights and freedoms recognized therein and to *ensure* to all persons subject to their jurisdiction the free and full exercise of those rights and freedoms. While article 2(1) of the ICCPR also uses the terms "respect" and "ensure," it restricts these obligations to "all individuals within its territory and subject to its jurisdiction."

In *Banković and Others v. Belgium and 16 Other Contracting States,* which concerned alleged violations of human rights during the NATO air strikes on the territory of the Federal Republic of Yugoslavia in 1999, the Grand Chamber of the European Court of Human Rights (ECHR) considered the jurisdictional competence of states parties, as defined by the words "within their jurisdiction" in article 1 of the ECHR, as primarily territorial: "While international law does not exclude a State's exercise of jurisdiction extraterritorially, the suggested bases of such jurisdiction (including nationality, flag, diplomatic and consular relations, effect, protection, passive personality and universality) are, as a general rule, defined and limited by the sovereign territorial rights of the other relevant States" (*Banković v. Belgium,* par. 59). It follows that the phrase "within their jurisdiction" reflects "this ordinary and essentially territorial notion of jurisdiction, other bases of jurisdiction being exceptional and requiring special justification in the particular circumstances of each case" (par. 61). While the European Court held in *Banković* that the bombing of a foreign territory was insufficient to establish a jurisdictional link between the Serbian victims and NATO member states, in its first judgment of 23 March 1995 in *Loizidou v. Turkey* it accepted that, as a consequence of military action on the ground, Turkey exercised "effective control" of an area outside its national territory, that is, the so-called Turkish Republic of Northern Cyprus, and that the obligations of Turkey under article 1 of the ECHR, therefore, also applied to this part of Cyprus (par. 62). Although the court uses the concept of "extraterritorial jurisdiction" in this respect, it only applies the territorial jurisdictional principle to other territory that is outside a state's "own territory" but nevertheless under its effective control.

Similarly, in the case of *Ilaşcu and Others v. Moldova and Russia*, the European Court of Human Rights held the Russian Federation responsible for violations of articles 3 and 5 of the ECHR in the territory of Transdniestria, a separatist region of Moldova. According to the court, the Russian authorities had provided, and continued to provide, military, political, and economic support to the separatist regime of the "Moldavian Republic of Transdniestria" (the "MRT"). Therefore, the court concluded that the "MRT" was under the effective authority of Russia and thus held Russia responsible for acts of torture and unlawful deprivation of liberty. In *Issa v. Turkey*, the court in a further step affirmed that military action—whether lawful or unlawful—of one state on the territory of another could amount to effective control and thus to an exercise of jurisdiction within the meaning of article 1 of the ECHR. Moreover, a state might also be held accountable for violations of rights of persons through agents of one state operating on the territory of another state, thereby putting the person whose rights are violated under its authority and control. In the case in question, however, the court was not satisfied with the evidence linking a Turkish military operation in northern Iraq to the alleged unlawful arrest, detention, ill-treatment, and subsequent killing of seven Iraqi shepherds. In the case of *Öcalan v. Turkey*, the court also accepted that the arrest or detention of a person by agents of a state party abroad in principle falls within the jurisdiction of this state. Abdullah Öcalan, the leader and founder of the Kurdish organization PKK, had been arrested by Turkish security forces inside an aircraft at Nairobi Airport, Kenya. In its first judgment of 12 March 2003, which was confirmed by the Grand Chamber on 12 May 2005, the court held the opinion that after the applicant had been handed over by the Kenyan officials to the Turkish officials he was under the effective authority of Turkish officials and was therefore within Turkish "jurisdiction" for the purposes of article 1 of the ECHR.

Although the obligation of states parties under article 2(1) of the ICCPR to respect and ensure the rights of the covenant explicitly is restricted to "individuals within its territory and subject to its jurisdiction," the UN Human Rights Committee has interpreted this provision in accordance with the object and purpose of the treaty. In the early *Passport Cases*, it held Uruguay responsible for violations of the right to freedom of movement committed by its diplomatic representatives abroad. Furthermore, in *López Burgos v. Uruguay* (Comm. no. 52 [1979]), it accepted the jurisdiction of Uruguay in relation to victims who were kidnapped by its agents in neighboring states. In its *General Comment 31* on the Nature of Legal Obligations, the Human Rights Committee formulated the rule that each "State party must respect and ensure the rights laid down in the Covenant to anyone within the power or effective control of that State Party, even if not situated within the territory of the State Party. . . . This principle also applies to those within the power or effective control of the forces of a State Party acting outside its territory, regardless of the circumstances in which such power or effective control was obtained, such as forces constituting a national contingent of a State Party assigned to an international peace-keeping or peace-enforcement operation" (UN Human Rights Committee 2004, par. 10).

This legal opinion was confirmed only three months later by the International Court of Justice in its Advisory Opinion on the *Legal Consequences of the Construction of a Wall in the Occupied Palestinian Territory*. The court held that the protection offered by human rights conventions does not cease in case of armed conflict, save through the effect of provisions for derogation of the kind to be found in article 4 of the ICCPR, and that international human rights treaties, including the ICCPR, are applicable in respect of acts done by a state in the exercise of its jurisdiction outside its own territory, such as by Israeli acts within the Occupied Palestinian Territory.

To sum up, "extraterritorial jurisdiction," in the sense of a broader definition of territory than a state's "own territory," has been accepted by international case law whenever the authorities of a state party exercise "effective control" over territory or persons outside the state's own territory in the narrow sense. It is irrelevant whether these actions are permissible under international law (for example, sovereign acts by diplomatic or consular representatives, by border officials in customs-free zones, on board a ship or aircraft registered in that state, in the territory of another state with the consent of this state, or by international peace-keeping or peace-enforcement troops) or not (for example, illegal occupation of foreign territory or kidnapping of persons by security agents abroad) (Coomans and Kamminga 2004).

Usually, this general recognition of "extraterritorial jurisdiction" applies to the obligation of states to respect the rights in question. States are held accountable if their occupation forces in a territory under their effective control subject the population to torture or CIDT, or if their security agents torture a person whom they have kidnapped in foreign territory. More controversial is the question to what extent states are required to take the necessary positive measures to *ensure* these rights by means of *protection* and *fulfillment* outside their own territory. While these questions have been addressed in the literature primarily in the context of economic, social, and cultural rights and in respect of international development cooperation (Vandenhole 2007a; Skogly 2006), the following will focus on the specific obligations of states parties under the UN Convention against Torture and Other Cruel, Inhuman, or Degrading Treatment or Punishment (CAT) of 1984. Since the prohibition of torture and CIDT is already contained in other (general) human rights treaties, this special convention contains various additional obligations aimed at the prevention of torture and CIDT, the use of criminal law and justice against the perpetrators of torture, and the guarantee of a right of victims of torture to a remedy and adequate reparation. Most of these provisions fall under the category of obligations to *fulfill.* Some provisions (that is, arts. 2[1], 11–13, and 16) contain an explicit territorial jurisdiction clause, while others do not. For certain provisions, this distinction seems evident, while for others it might lead to difficult questions of interpretation.

Obligation of States to Prevent Torture and CIDT

Article 2 of the CAT requires states parties to "take effective legislative, administrative, judicial, and other measures to prevent acts of torture in any territory under its jurisdiction," and article 16 contains a similar obligation to prevent other acts of CIDT. Article 3 of the original Swedish draft of 1978 had foreseen to prevent torture and CIDT from being practiced within the states parties' jurisdiction. Since this formulation might also cover jurisdiction on the basis of the nationality principle, a French proposal of 1979 to replace the words "within its jurisdiction" by "any territory under its jurisdiction" was accepted. But the delegations in the Working Group of the Commission on Human Rights emphasized that such wording would also cover torture inflicted aboard ships or aircraft registered in the state concerned as well as occupied territories. [2] It follows that the "extraterritorial obligations" outlined above on the basis of the case law of international human rights treaty monitoring bodies with respect to the obligation of states parties to respect the right to personal integrity in principle also apply to the various *obligations to fulfill* this right by means of taking preventive measures as provided for in the CAT. If a state occupies the territory of another state, for example, it must ensure that its occupation authorities both refrain from practicing torture and take necessary positive measures to prevent torture from being practiced.

What are these preventive measures required by the CAT? Typical obligations to prevent torture and CIDT can be found in articles 10 (education and training of law enforcement and other personnel), 11 (systematic review of interrogation methods and prison rules), 12 (ex officio investigation of torture cases), 13 (investigations of allegations by torture victims), and 15 (non-admissibility of evidence extracted by torture in any proceedings). Some of these provisions contain a specific territorial jurisdiction clause while others do not. For example, article 11 restricts the obligation of every state party to keep interrogation methods and prison rules under systematic review to detention facilities "in any territory under its jurisdiction," while article 10 contains a general obligation to include the prohibition of torture in the training of any "law enforcement personnel, civil or military, medical personnel, public officials and other persons who may be involved in the custody, interrogation, or treatment of any individual subjected to any form of arrest, detention, or imprisonment." The latter obligation seems to be based more on the active nationality (personality) principle than on the territoriality principle. In other words, if a soldier of State A, who serves under the command of State B in a UN peace operation in State C, commits an act of torture, the United Nations and State B might be responsible under the broader territoriality principle of effective control outlined above, but State A might also be responsible for having failed to provide anti-torture training to its military personnel in accordance with article 10 of the CAT. But the obligation under article 11 to keep prison rules under systematic review only applies to detention facilities in any territory in which the respective state party exercises effective control, such as detention facilities of the United States in Iraq. Similar conclusions can be drawn from the fact that article 13 contains a specific territorial jurisdiction clause, whereas articles 14 and 15 lack such a provision.

In addition to the specific obligation to prevent outlined above, most other substantive provisions of the CAT also have a preventive effect. This applies to the prohibition of *refoulement* in article 3, as well as to the obligation to criminalize torture and establish broad criminal jurisdiction over perpetrators of torture in articles 4 to 9. For example, the Committee against Torture in *Guridi v. Spain* held that the pardoning by the government and the king of Spain of three members of the Civil Guard, who had been convicted of torture and sentenced by a Spanish court, constituted a violation of article 2(1) of the CAT because the absence of appropriate punishment was not compatible with the duty to prevent acts of torture. In general, many legal safeguards in the context of the right to personal liberty and the administration of justice—such as the right to habeas corpus; prompt access of detainees to lawyers, doctors, and family members; the prohibition of secret places of detention, prolonged incommunicado detention, and solitary confinement—serve the purpose of preventing torture and ill-treatment. Finally, unannounced visits to all places of detention by independent domestic and international bodies and private interviews with detainees, such as provided for by the European Convention for the Prevention of Torture of 1987 and the UN Optional Protocol to the Convention against Torture (OPCAT) of 2002, seem to be among the most effective measures for the prevention of torture and CIDT.

Most of these provisions only apply to the territorial jurisdiction of states in the broader sense (effective control) outlined above. For example, under article 4 of OPCAT, each state party is required to grant the UN Subcommittee on Prevention and the respective national preventive mechanisms access to all places of detention "under its jurisdiction and control." This means, on the one hand, that the authorities have no obligation to provide access to places of detention that are under their jurisdiction but not under their de facto control. If parts of a state's territory are occupied by another state (for example, the northern part of Cyprus or the territory of Kosovo formerly in Serbia), or under the de facto control of insurgent groups (for example, parts of the territory of Sri Lanka), or governed by de facto authorities (for example, the territories of Abkhazia and South Ossetia in Georgia), the respective governments are not required to provide access to the places of detention in such territories. On the other hand, foreign states exercising jurisdiction and control outside their own territories over places of detention, such as the Turkish authorities in the northern part of Cyprus or the U.S. authorities in relation to detention facilities under their control in Iraq and Afghanistan, are under an obligation, provided they become states parties to the OPCAT, to allow visits of the UN Subcommittee on Prevention and the respective national preventive mechanisms.

Torture and Counterterrorism

The prohibition of torture is one of the few absolute and non-derogable rights under international human rights law. This was confirmed by article 2(2) of the CAT: "No exceptional circumstances whatsoever, whether a state of war or a threat of war, internal political instability or any other public emergency, may be invoked as a justification of torture." Nevertheless, in reaction to the terrorist attacks of 11 September 2001, this absolute prohibition of torture came under attack by global counterterrorism strategies under the lead of the United States. In addition to attempts to justify torture for the sake of preventing terrorist attacks and saving lives of potential victims in the so-called ticking bomb scenario, governments also aimed at circumventing their obligations under the CAT by outsourcing torture practices to private security personnel and detention facilities outside their own territory.

The U.S. government even took the official position that its international human rights obligations do not apply to detention facilities established in the context of its "global war against terror," such as Guantánamo Bay, and that article 2 of the CAT was geographically limited to U.S. territory in the strict sense.[3] This position had already been rejected when the U.S. Supreme Court in June 2004 held in *Rasul v. Bush* that the United States is actually exercising jurisdiction at Guantánamo

Bay and that the guarantees of the U.S. Constitution are, therefore, fully applicable to Guantánamo detainees. In relation to the ICCPR and the CAT, the five independent experts of the UN Commission on Human Rights investigating jointly the situation of detainees at Guantánamo Bay in February 2006 clearly arrived at the conclusion that both treaties are fully applicable to the treatment of detainees at Guantánamo (UN 2006b, sec. 1). In May 2006, the Committee against Torture, in considering the most recent U.S. report, confirmed this interpretation and rejected, once more, the untenable position of the United States (CAT 2007). In July 2006, the Human Rights Committee joined the other monitoring bodies and concluded that the United States should acknowledge the applicability of the covenant with respect to individuals under its jurisdiction but outside its territory (HRC 2006). However, the Bush administration never changed its position.

Apart from denying the applicability of international human rights treaties to which the United States is a party to detention facilities outside its territory in the strict sense, the government of the United States has also attempted to justify the practice of torture by other equally dubious legal arguments. The well-known "Bybee Memorandum" of 1 August 2002, which provided legal justification for harsh interrogation methods explicitly authorized by Donald Rumsfeld, the former defense secretary, against suspected foreign terrorists held outside U.S. territory, implied that outside the territory of the United States acts of torture in the context of the "war on terror" might be justified as acts of "self-defense."[4] Even as recently as 2008, President Bush vetoed congressional legislation prohibiting torture by the CIA outside of U.S. territory.[5]

Another method used by the CIA to circumvent the prohibition of torture on U.S. territory was to send suspected terrorists by means of so-called extraordinary rendition flights by privately chartered aircrafts to countries known for their practice of torture, such as Egypt and Syria. In addition, the CIA used secret places of detention. These practices and the role of European states in cooperating with the United States were confirmed by various investigations by the Council of Europe and the European Union (see Marty 2006, 2007; Fava 2007; Council of Europe 2006; Council of Europe, European Commission for Democracy through Law 2006). Often, these unlawful interstate transfers were based on diplomatic assurances by the governments of states known for their practice of torture to refrain from torture in these particular individual cases. In reality, such diplomatic assurances relating to torture are nothing but another attempt to circumvent the absolute prohibition of *refoulement* analyzed in the following section.

The Prohibition of *Refoulement*

The prohibition of *refoulement* in article 3 of the CAT codifies an important principle of general international law, based partly on case law of human rights treaty monitoring bodies, namely, that a state violates the absolute prohibition of torture not only if its own authorities subject a person to torture, but also if its authorities send a person to another state where there are substantial grounds for believing that the person would be in danger of being subjected to torture. The vast majority of individual complaints decided by the Committee against Torture concern article 3, and most violations found by the committee actually were not directed against states practicing torture themselves, but against asylum states where the authorities had rejected asylum requests and then decided to return the asylum seeker to his or her country of origin (Nowak and McArthur 2008, art. 3, ch. 3.3).

Often, the prohibition of *refoulement* is considered as a form of extra-territorial jurisdiction. Strictly speaking, this is not correct. Although the authority deciding on the expulsion, extradition, return, or deportation of a person to another state must base its decision on an assessment of the risk of torture in the receiving state, this decision is taken on the territory of the respective state party. The authorities of the returning states are not held responsible for any act of torture committed by the authorities of the receiving state but for the fact of deciding to send a person to such state despite a substantial risk of being subjected to torture there.

As stated above, in the context of counterterrorism strategies the United States and certain European states resort to the practice of diplomatic assurances from countries known for their practice of torture as a means of circumventing their obligations under article 3 of the CAT, article 3 of the ECHR, article 7 of the ICCPR, and similar provisions.[6] In reaction to the bombings in London on 7 July 2005, the British government concluded three Memoranda of Understanding with Jordan, Libya, and Lebanon that included diplomatic assurances relating to torture and ill-treatment as well as post-return monitoring by nongovernmental organizations (NGOs). The United Kingdom, Sweden, and a few other countries even initiated a discussion at the Council of Europe on the development of guidelines for diplomatic assurances, but the Committee of Ministers in March 2006 decided to stop this exercise after strong criticism by NGOs, the UN Special Rapporteur on Torture, the Council of Europe Commissioner for Human Rights, and the European Committee for the Prevention of Torture.[7] In the well-known cases of *Agiza v. Sweden* and *Alzery v. Sweden*, the Committee against Torture and the Human Rights Committee, respectively, established that two suspected terrorists, who were arrested in Sweden and sent to Egypt by a

CIA rendition flight with the active cooperation of the Swedish authorities, were in fact subjected to torture despite diplomatic assurances received from Egypt and a limited monitoring mechanism established by Sweden. These and similar cases show that diplomatic assurances from states known for their practice of torture are unreliable and ineffective in the protection against torture and ill-treatment and should, therefore, not be resorted to by states eager to expel, "render," or return suspected terrorists or persons considered a threat to national security (Nowak and McArthur 2008, art. 3, ch. 4.5.5).

Another special problem relating to the extraterritorial application of the convention has arisen in the context of the global fight against terrorism and extraordinary renditions. In its second periodic report, the United States asserted that the *non-refoulement* obligation under article 3 did not extend to a person detained outside its territory, such as in Guantánamo Bay. The Committee against Torture rightly rejected this assertion by repeating that the convention protection extends to all territories under the effective control of the state party's authority. It follows that the "rendition" of a person from Guantánamo Bay to Egypt, Jordan, or any other state is subject to the prohibition of *refoulement*. This means, however, that the "rendition" from Guantánamo Bay to any other U.S. detention facility in the territory of the United States, Iraq, or Afghanistan does not fall under this provision. However, article 3 is again applicable to the transfer of a detainee from U.S. or U.K. custody in Iraq to the Iraqi authorities.[8] Otherwise, the United States and the United Kingdom could easily circumvent their obligations by transferring suspected terrorists or other individuals first to their own detention facilities in Iraq or Afghanistan and then handing them over to the domestic authorities without having to assess any risk of torture. Taking into account the object and purpose of article 3, the phrase "another state" in fact needs to be interpreted as "another jurisdiction."

Obligation to Bring Perpetrators of Torture to Justice

One of the most innovative aspects of the CAT is the obligation of each state party under article 4 to "ensure that all acts of torture are offences under its criminal law" and the obligation under articles 5 through 9 to establish various forms of criminal jurisdiction to bring perpetrators of torture to justice and to avoid safe havens for torturers. While most of the obligations discussed so far either do not entail any extraterritorial obligation at all, such as the prohibition of *refoulement*, or only a broader notion of territorial jurisdiction, such as the obligation relating to territory under occupation, the obligation to establish criminal jurisdiction clearly goes beyond (Nowak and McArthur 2008; Ingelse 2001; Boulesbaa 1999).

Under article 5(1), states parties shall take legislative measures to establish their jurisdiction over offenses of torture on the basis of the *territoriality, flag,* and *active nationality principles.* This means that any state party must ensure that its domestic authorities are competent to prosecute any act of torture committed "in any territory under its jurisdiction" (which, again, includes any territory under the effective control of its authorities), on board a ship or aircraft registered in that state, or when the alleged offender is a national of that state. If a state party considers it appropriate, it is also authorized by virtue of article 5(1)(c) to establish the *passive nationality principle,* that is, when the victim is a national of that state. Whenever an act of torture is committed, the territorial state, the flag state, the active nationality state and, if accepted by the domestic code of criminal procedure, the passive nationality state, without any order of priority, shall take the necessary measures to investigate the crime, to arrest the alleged offender, and to bring him or her to justice before its domestic courts. If, for example, an Egyptian intelligence agent on board a CIA rendition aircraft registered in the United States tortures a Jordanian citizen when flying through Irish airspace or refueling at Shannon Airport, then Egypt, the United States, and Ireland are all required to investigate the case and issue an arrest warrant, and Jordan only if it has accepted the passive nationality principle. If the Egyptian intelligence agent is present in Egypt, the Egyptian authorities, pursuant to article 6 of the CAT, must arrest the agent and bring him or her to justice before their domestic courts unless they extradite him to the United States, Ireland, or Jordan on the basis of a respective extradition request (principle of *aut dedere aut judicare* in article 7[1] of the CAT). If the United States, Ireland, and Jordan do not request the agent's extradition, Egypt has no other choice than to submit the case to its own authorities for prosecution.

Since states known for systematic or widespread practice of torture usually do not comply with their obligations to bring their own military, intelligence, or police officers to justice, article 5(2) also establishes an obligation of states parties under the *universal jurisdiction principle.* The only requirement is that "the alleged offender is present in any territory under its jurisdiction," which again is to be interpreted in the broad sense of effective control. In other words, to stay with the above example, if the Egyptian intelligence agent travels to the United Kingdom for medical treatment, the British authorities, as in the case of General Pinochet (*Regina v. Bartle* and *Regina v. Evans;* see also, Brody and Ratner 2000; Burbach 2004; Davis 2003; Byers 2000; Del Carmen Marquez Carrasco and Alcaide Fernandez 1999), must arrest him and bring him to justice before British courts unless they extradite him to Ireland, the United States, Egypt, or Jordan on the basis of a respective extradition request.

Before deciding whether to extradite, the British authorities must, however, make sure that the extradition does not violate the prohibition of *refoulement* and/or lead to impunity. In our case, the only real alternative to prosecution might be extradition to Ireland, but the Irish authorities are not under an obligation to request extradition.

Although the CAT provides for far-reaching extraterritorial obligations to bring perpetrators of torture to justice, in practice states are extremely reluctant to exercise universal or any other form of criminal jurisdiction against torturers. A typical example of a government's resistance to exercise universal jurisdiction is the case of Hissène Habré (Marks 2005, 131–67; Brody 2001; Nowak and McArthur 2008, art. 5, chs. 3.2.2. and 4.1). The former dictator of Chad, under whose regime torture was systematically practiced during the 1980s, has resided in Senegal since he was overthrown by Idris Déby in 1990. In 2000, Chadian victims and NGOs filed a criminal complaint in Dakar that even led to his arrest and an indictment by a Senegalese judge, but he was soon released from house arrest because the Senegalese authorities had failed to enact the necessary legislative measures to establish universal jurisdiction. After Belgium in 2005 had requested his extradition, the Senegalese authorities still preferred to place him at the disposition of the president of the African Union. Only in 2007 did the Senegalese National Assembly adopt legislation to implement its obligations under the CAT. This occurred only after the Committee against Torture, in a landmark decision of 17 May 2006 (*Guengueng v. Senegal*), found violations of articles 5(2) and 7 of the CAT, and the Assembly of Heads of State and Government of the African Union, on the basis of a recommendation by the ad hoc Committee of Eminent African Jurists on 2 July 2006, explicitly requested Senegal to prosecute Habré. The criminal proceedings instituted against Habré under the universal jurisdiction principle are still pending.

A best practice example, in contrast, is the *R. v. Zardad* case before British authorities. Faryadi Sarwar Zardad, a former warlord and perpetrator of torture in Afghanistan, was arrested in London where he had sought asylum in 1998. The British authorities, above all the Crown Prosecution Service, had invested over three million pounds to collect evidence in Afghanistan before he was brought to trial in 2004. The authorities in Afghanistan and the United States cooperated in accordance with their mutual judicial assistance obligation under article 9 of the CAT. On 18 July 2005, Zardad was convicted in the London Central Criminal Court (Old Bailey) for conspiring to torture and other crimes committed against Afghan nationals in Afghanistan between 1991 and 1996 and was sentenced to imprisonment for twenty years (see Nowak and McArthur 2008, art. 5, ch. 4.9).

The Right of Victims of Torture to a Remedy and Reparation

Article 13 of the CAT requires each state party to ensure that any victim of torture "in any territory under its jurisdiction" has the right to complain to, and have his or her case promptly and impartially examined by, its competent authorities. On the basis of the facts established in accordance with article 13, further action may or shall be taken with a view to bringing the perpetrators to justice under criminal law and/or providing victims with reparation under civil law pursuant to article 14.

In contrast to article 13, the wording of article 14 lacks a territorial jurisdiction clause. Each state party shall ensure in its legal system that the victim of an act of torture obtains redress and has "an enforceable right to fair and adequate compensation, including the means for as full [a] rehabilitation as possible." Whereas the original Swedish draft of 18 January 1978 had provided for a right to compensation only if the act of torture was committed by or at the instigation of public officials of the respective state party, a similar active nationality clause was missing in the revised Swedish draft of 19 February 1979. This prompted the Working Group of the Commission on Human Rights in 1981 to insert the phrase "committed in any territory under its jurisdiction" after the word "torture," based on a proposal of the Dutch delegation, but this phrase later disappeared from the text without any clear reason being provided in the *travaux préparatoires* (cf. Burgers and Danelius 1988; see Aceves 2007, 74; Parlett 2007; Byrnes 2001, 537–52). The lack of such a territorial jurisdiction clause, therefore, begs the question whether article 14 contains any extraterritorial obligations of states parties.

From a human rights perspective, the right of victims to reparation can only be directed against a state that can be held responsible for the act of torture. Usually, this is the territorial state, perhaps also the state of nationality of the perpetrator, but certainly not the state of nationality or residence of the victim. If British citizens were tortured, for example, in Saudi Arabia and returned to the United Kingdom, or if Saudi victims of torture committed in Saudi Arabia flee their home country and seek asylum in the United Kingdom, they cannot claim redress and compensation from the United Kingdom, although the British authorities might end up providing medical and psychological rehabilitation to the victims. But should these victims of torture not be provided the possibility of initiating civil (tort) litigation against the state of Saudi Arabia and its individual torturers before British courts?

This raises the difficult question of *universal civil jurisdiction* or other forms of civil jurisdiction going beyond the mere principle of territoriality. The wording of article 14 speaks in favor of such an interpretation. The victim shall have an "enforceable right" to compensation, and each state party shall "ensure" such right "in its legal system." If both the victims and the Saudi perpetrator reside in the United Kingdom, why should the British courts not be competent to conduct this tort litigation?[9] Should the British courts not even accept jurisdiction against the perpetrators of justice who remain in Saudi Arabia? What if the perpetrators have money in British bank accounts or real property in the United Kingdom? If the British courts reject such claims, would the United Kingdom as a state party to the CAT not violate its extraterritorial obligation under article 14 to provide victims with an "enforceable right to fair and adequate compensation" against their perpetrators?

This question seems to have been answered in the affirmative by the U.K. Court of Appeal in 2004 in the well-known case of *Jones v. Ministry of the Interior of Saudi Arabia* (EWCA Civ. 1394) concerning tort litigation by four British nationals allegedly tortured in Saudi Arabia. While the state of Saudi Arabia was entitled to rely on state immunity in respect of torture claims, the judges denied immunity to individual perpetrators of torture in the case, namely, two officers in the Saudi police force. This seems to be in line with the judgment of the International Court of Justice in the *Arrest Warrant* case according to which state immunity can be successfully invoked by diplomatic representatives as well as incumbent heads of state or government and ministers of foreign affairs (see *Democratic Republic of the Congo v. Belgium*; Cassese 2002; Wouters and de Smet 2004). On appeal in 2006, the House of Lords disappointingly failed to do justice to the distinction between state immunity and immunity of individual state officials so painstakingly delineated by the Court of Appeal. Lord Bingham of Cornwall took the firm approach that "the foreign state is entitled to claim immunity for its servants as it could if sued itself (*Jones v. Ministry of the Interior of Saudi Arabia*, UKHL 26)."

While universal criminal jurisdiction against perpetrators of torture constitutes an explicit extraterritorial obligation of states parties in accordance with article 5(2) of the CAT, a respective obligation to provide universal civil jurisdiction is not explicitly laid down in article 14 of the CAT. The *Jones* case and respective state practice illustrate that governments and courts are still reluctant to infer such an extraterritorial obligation from article 14 despite the fact that its wording, and in principle also the *travaux préparatoires*, would allow such broad interpretation. As Luc Reydams (2003) has argued, this seems rather illogical because universal civil jurisdiction is certainly less intrusive than universal criminal jurisdiction. After all, the perpetrator faces only paying damages rather than going to prison; the authorities of the forum state are merely adjudicators rather than actors; and the courts, in accordance with the respective rules of international civil law, would normally apply the civil law of the territorial state rather than its own domestic criminal law. It is, therefore, advisable for states to enact enabling legislation for universal and other forms of civil jurisdiction, similar to the Alien Tort Claims Act of 1789 and the Torture Victims Protection Act of 1991 in the United States.

Non-admissibility of Evidence Extracted by Torture

Article 15 is another provision of the CAT that contains no specific territorial jurisdiction clause. It requires each state party to ensure that "any statement which is established to have been made as a result of torture shall not be invoked as evidence in any proceedings." The purpose of this provision seems to be twofold. First, confessions or other information extracted by torture are usually not reliable enough to be used as a source of evidence in any legal proceedings. Second, prohibiting the use of such evidence in legal proceedings removes an important incentive for the use of torture and, therefore, shall contribute to the prevention of such practice.

Although the "theory of the tainted fruits of the poisonous tree" seems to be firmly established in most legal cultures, the absolute prohibition of using evidence extracted by torture was recently put into question in the context of the fight against terrorism, as was the absolute prohibition of torture as such. The British home secretary argued, for example, that the Special Immigration Appeals Commission, a British superior court established by statute, may use evidence obtained by torture in another country as long as this evidence had been extracted without the complicity of the British authorities. In Germany, Denmark, and other European countries, intensive debates arose about the legitimacy of using information received by foreign intelligence agencies likely to practice torture for the mere purpose of preventing terrorist acts.[10]

This raises the question of the scope of application of article 15 and its possible extraterritorial application. If the police receive credible information indicating that a bomb might soon explode in a railway station, would it have to check whether this information was extracted by torture before starting the evacuation of the railway station? Although the preventive function of the "theory of the tainted fruits of the poisonous tree" could be invoked as an argument for requiring such prior investigation, this would seem both unrealistic and unreasonable. The police have an obligation to act quickly to protect the human rights to life, personal integrity, security, and health of potential victims. In addition to evacuating the railway station and searching for the bomb, the police may also detain suspected persons indicated in the information for the purpose of preventing them from planting such a bomb. But these preventive police actions are not carried out in the framework of any proceedings envisaged in article 15. The phrase "evidence in any proceedings" only refers to the assessment of evidence before a judicial or administrative authority acting in accordance with certain rules involving the taking of evidence laid down in the respective criminal, civil, or administrative procedural code. In other words, purely preventive police actions outside any formal procedure fall outside the scope of application of article 15.

In contrast, administrative decisions in formal extradition proceedings certainly fall under the scope of application of article 15 (see the Committee against Torture's decision in *G. K. v. Switzerland* [2002], sec. 6.10). Similarly, formal detention certificates issued by the British home secretary against ten suspected foreign terrorists under the Anti-Terrorism, Crime, and Security Act of 2001 are clearly administrative decisions arrived at in the course of formal administrative proceedings to which article 15 applies. This holds true even more for the judicial appeals proceedings before the Special Immigration Appeals Commission. Since the information on which the home secretary based his detention certificates was received from the CIA, which entailed a credible risk that it might have been extracted by torture, the British authorities in fact argued that article 15 lacks any extraterritorial application. In other words, both the home secretary and the Special Immigration Appeals Commission took the position that they may receive and use evidence that has or may have been procured by torture inflicted by officials of a foreign state without the complicity of the British authorities. The detention certificates against the ten suspected terrorists were even upheld in 2004 by the English Court of Appeal by a majority of two to one despite the fact that the court acknowledged that the detainees had presented sufficient evidence to prove the use of torture in the gathering of evidence (*A and Others v. Secretary of State for the Home Department*, EWCA Civ. 1123; see also Gasper 2005).

In a landmark judgment of December 2005, the House of Lords unanimously overturned the judgment of the Court of Appeal by holding that the United Kingdom may not use evidence that a foreign state has procured through torture in a judicial proceeding against suspected terrorists (*A and Others v. Secretary of State for the Home Department*, UKHL 71). Lord Bingham, who provided the lead opinion, interpreted article 15 of the CAT as imposing a blanket exclusionary rule that applies to all formal proceedings without any territorial limitation. This extraterritorial obligation deriving from article 15 means in fact that the British authorities, when basing their decisions on information received from foreign intelligence sources and likely to have been extracted by torture, must inquire as to whether there is a real risk that the evidence was obtained by torture. In view of the secret nature of intelligence information, this is, of course, not an easy task, which means that the burden of proof must shift from the applicants to the authorities invoking foreign intelligence information as evidence in formal proceedings. While the minority of the House of Lords rightly argued that in case of a real risk of torture the evidence should not be admitted, the majority opinion, this time provided by Lord Hope, held that evidence should only be excluded if it is established, by means of diligent inquiries into the sources that it is practicable to carry out and on a balance of probabilities, that the information relied on by the home secretary was obtained by torture.

Conclusions

The analysis of the prohibition and prevention of torture and other forms of cruel, inhuman, or degrading treatment or punishment under general human rights treaties and under the UN Convention against Torture shows that the human right to personal integrity and dignity implies a broad variety of state obligations. In addition to the obligation to *respect* this right by refraining from practicing torture and CIDT, most of the specific obligations under the CAT require states parties to take positive legislative and other measures to *fulfill* this right. This applies to the three main clusters of the convention: prevention of torture, bringing the perpetrators of torture to justice, and providing victims of torture with a remedy and reparation.

In the literature on *extraterritorial obligations* with respect to economic, social, and cultural rights and development cooperation, the argument has been advanced that extraterritorial obligations to respect and to protect can be argued to be part of hard law, whereas "legally binding status to the extraterritorial obligation to *fulfill*, and in particular the sub-obligation to provide development assistance, still meets with resistance" (Vandenhole 2007a, 97). This finding cannot be confirmed in relation to extraterritorial obligations deriving from the CAT.

First of all, the notion of "extraterritorial obligations" is in need of interpretation. In the *Banković* case, the European Court of Human Rights rightly stressed that the jurisdictional competence of a state is primarily territorial, and that the exercise of extraterritorial jurisdiction is exceptional and requires special justification. As bases of such jurisdiction, the court referred to nationality, flag, diplomatic and consular relations, effect, protection, passive personality, and universality. At the same time, the court, other treaty monitoring bodies, and the literature use the term "extraterritorial jurisdiction" also in relation to the prohibition of *refoulement* and to the exercise of effective control outside a state's own territory. Strictly speaking, the application of the principle of *non-refoulement* by a state's authorities in extradition or expulsion proceedings has nothing to do with extraterritorial jurisdiction. The authorities are only required to assess the risk of the person concerned to be subjected to torture in another state in case of expulsion, extradition, or return. If this assessment leads to the conclusion that there are substantial grounds for believing that the person would be in danger of being subjected to torture in the other state, the authorities of the state party must refrain from expelling, extraditing, or returning him or her to this state. But the decision and risk assessment is done by the authorities on the basis of their territorial jurisdiction.

Similarly, if the authorities of a state party exercise "effective control" over the territory of another state on the basis of consent or occupation, their obligation to respect and fulfill the right to personal integrity in fact is also based on the notion of territorial jurisdiction. However, if the authorities of a state party, with the consent of another state, arrest a person in the territory of this state, their obligation not to torture the person concerned can be considered as truly extraterritorial despite the fact that it is also based on the principle of effective authority over the person. The same holds true for obligations of diplomatic or consular representatives exercising effective authority over persons outside the territory of their state. Wherever a state exercises effective control or authority over territory or persons outside its "own" territory, in the strict sense, it must comply with all obligations under the CAT, irrespective of whether these are obligations to respect, protect, or fulfill. For example, the United States, exercising effective control over the Guantánamo detention facilities and the persons detained there, is under an obligation to refrain from practicing torture, to train its prison staff accordingly, to keep the interrogation methods and prison rules under systematic review, to protect detainees against inter-prisoner violence, to provide victims of torture with the right to a remedy and reparation, and to bring perpetrators of torture in these facilities to justice and to refrain from sending Guantánamo detainees to another state in violation of the prohibition of *refoulement.*

In addition to these obligations, which are closely related to the territorial jurisdiction of states and the principle of effective control, the CAT requires states parties also to exercise extraterritorial jurisdiction in the strict sense of this term, that is, without any relation to territorial or other effective control. Most importantly, states parties have an obligation to establish criminal jurisdiction and to bring perpetrators of torture to justice on the basis of the flag, the active nationality, and the universal jurisdiction principles. Furthermore, article 5(1)(c) authorizes them to exercise criminal jurisdiction on the basis of the passive nationality principle. While these obligations are spelled out in detail in articles 4–9 of the CAT, the rights and duties of states parties to exercise civil jurisdiction beyond territorial jurisdiction remains highly controversial. According to article 14, they have an obligation to ensure in their legal systems that victims of torture obtain redress and have an "enforceable right to fair and adequate compensation, including the means for as full [a] rehabilitation as possible." In addition to the right of victims to a remedy and reparation against the territorial state, this provision can also be interpreted to contain an extraterritorial obligation of states parties to provide victims with a civil remedy against the individual perpetrators of torture on the basis of the nationality and universal jurisdiction principles.

Finally, article 15 has also been interpreted as implying obligations beyond the principle of territorial jurisdiction. Judicial and administrative authorities of states parties are prevented from invoking information extracted by torture in any proceedings, irrespective of the facts of where and by whom the respective act of torture was perpetrated. This recognition of extraterritorial obligations is particularly relevant in the context of close cooperation between intelligence agencies as part of the global fight against terrorism. If suspected terrorists or other persons are detained, extradited, or brought to criminal justice on the basis of confessions or information provided by foreign officials, and if these persons advance a credible reason that this evidence may have been procured by torture abroad, the competent judicial or administrative authorities must carry out comprehensive inquiries as to whether there is a real risk that the evidence has been obtained by torture practiced by foreign officials abroad. Since it is extremely difficult for the persons concerned to establish acts of torture by foreign intelligence agencies, this rule necessarily implies a shift of the burden of proof to the authorities that invoke the evidence in question. If a real risk of torture cannot reasonably be excluded, the evidence should not be admitted.

Although states parties to the CAT, in particular in the context of counterterrorism strategies, have come a long way in neglecting and undermining the validity of their territorial and extraterritorial obligations, a careful analysis of the different provisions shows that the convention contains a broad variety of obligations to respect, protect, and, above all, fulfill the human rights to personal integrity and dignity that go beyond the traditional territorial jurisdiction. In the age of globalization, these extraterritorial obligations of the CAT become increasingly important and may also serve as a model for other human rights treaties. To some extent, the recently adopted UN Conventions on the Protection of All Persons from Enforced Disappearance and on the Rights of Persons with Disabilities have been modeled on the extraterritorial obligations of the CAT and confirm this global trend.

Chapter 2
Obligations to Protect the Right to Life: Constructing a Rule of Transfer Regarding Small Arms and Light Weapons

Barbara Frey

Small arms and light weapons are among the principal tools used to violate human rights. Cheap, durable, easy to transport, hide, and operate, firearms are the means by which human rights are violated in every conceivable way in every conceivable setting. Firearms are misused by state agents, from police to security forces, to violate a spectrum of civil and political rights through acts of genocide, arbitrary executions, arbitrary arrests, torture, and forced displacement. Non-state actors carry out grievous abuses with firearms, whether they are organized militia, private security forces, terrorists, or criminals. Small arms are also used to violate economic, social, and cultural rights, directly and indirectly. The brandishing of a firearm is enough to break up a cultural gathering, evict a family from its home, or interfere with the right to organize a workplace. The culture of fear that characterizes a community saturated by guns inevitably diminishes access to education, health care, and the ability to meet an adequate standard of living, among other basic human rights.

Despite these arms-related human rights violations, leadership in developing normative responses to the negative impacts of unrestricted arms flows has not come from the human rights community, but instead is centered in the international disarmament community. In December 2006, 153 members of the UN General Assembly voted to take the first steps toward drafting a treaty to establish common international standards for restrictions on arms transfers that contribute to conflicts, displacement, and serious human rights violations (UN General Assembly 2006a).[1] The General Assembly's action is one of several important legal initiatives generated by the disarmament community—including efforts to harmonize standards on marking and tracing, trade, brokering, and end-use verification—to address the adverse impacts on security, human rights, and economic and social development from the unrestricted flow of small arms and light weapons across borders (UN Secretary-General 2008).

The increased international attention on the linkage between arms transfers and human rights violations suggests the need for a more focused consideration of that linkage by the human rights community itself. This chapter will address one part of the human rights analysis: the extraterritorial human rights obligations of states regarding their arms transfers to states or non-state actors where there is a significant risk that those arms will be used to commit serious human rights violations, including violations of the right to life.[2]

International human rights law has developed fairly clear standards regarding the proper use of small arms by state agents, including law enforcement, in their own territories. Human rights jurisprudence on due diligence also suggests that states must prevent foreseeable violations to persons living in their territories by keeping guns out of the hands of those likely to misuse them (Frey 2006, 5–8). This chapter will review an area of less legal clarity: the extraterritorial legal obligations of an arms-exporting state regarding violations of the right to life committed with those arms in another state. The chapter will begin with an overview of the broad-reaching obligations of states to protect the right to life. It will then review extraterritorial obligations to protect the right to life as a customary norm and under treaty law, and how such obligations are enforceable. Finally, the chapter will consider whether there is a customary norm, or rule of transfer, that is emerging to address the more specific issue of small arms transfers based on their likely misuse. Evidence of this emerging rule of transfer may be found in the existing limitations on arms transfers under international law. Those limitations include prohibitions imposed under international security law and international humanitarian law, and by state practice, as exhibited by regional export regimes, and through voluntary steps suggested as part of the arms trade treaty being discussed by states in the UN General Assembly.

The Human Rights Implications of Small Arms Proliferation

Small arms proliferation negatively affects multiple fields of international concern, including security, disarmament, public health, crime control, development, humanitarian assistance, and, of course, human rights (Annan 2000, 52). The category of "small arms" refers to firearms that can be used by a single person, including revolvers and automatic pistols, assault rifles and light machine guns. "Light weapons" can be carried or used by a small crew and include heavy machine guns, portable anti-aircraft or anti-tank guns, and portable launchers of anti-tank missile and rocket systems.[3] There are about 875 million small arms in the world today; 8 million more are put into circulation each year (Graduate Institute of International Studies 2007, 41). An estimated 1,000 people die from gunshots every day and 3,000 more are injured. The five leading conventional arms producers are the permanent members of the UN Security Council. The production and distribution of small arms in the post–Cold War era is quite fragmented and competitive, with at least 1,135 companies in 98 countries manufacturing small arms. The United States, Russia, and China are also the largest producers of small arms, with 21 European countries, Brazil, and Israel qualifying as medium producers (Graduate Institute of International Studies 2002, 20). While small arms proliferation is not a new phenomenon, the increasing globalization of commerce has resulted in more guns getting into more hands with fewer restraints. In today's world, firearms and even military-style weapons are available to almost anyone who has the will to obtain them. It is estimated, for example, that there are between seventy and one hundred million Kalashnikov-style rifles in circulation in the world today (Stohl, Schroeder, and Smith 2007, 6). The AK-47 has become the symbol of modern warfare, used in conflicts in more than ninety countries.

The lethal capacity of firearms has grave implications for human rights protection. Small arms can have a multiplier effect on human rights violations, wreaking havoc in a matter of seconds. Many assault rifles, including the AK-47, can shoot thirty rounds in three seconds. The availability of firearms can therefore escalate small scale violations into large ones—an arrest becomes a shoot-out, a cattle raid becomes a massacre, ethnic tensions spark massive displacement. The presence of a weapon in the home dramatically increases the level of domestic homicides against women. In addition to physical harm, easy access to weapons aggravates poverty, inhibits access to social services, and diverts resources away from human development (UN Secretary-General 2008). The lethal cycle of violence fueled by small arms diminishes the rule of law and undermines the strong fabric of societies in which human rights are protected. The gravity of these impacts from the uninterrupted flow of small arms calls for a serious response from the human rights community.

While small arms are used to violate the entire spectrum of human rights, this chapter will focus on the state's responsibility with regard to firearms under the central, non-derogable tenet of international human rights law, the right to life. Guaranteed by article 3 of the Universal Declaration of Human Rights and article 6 of the International Covenant on Civil and Political Rights (Civil and Political Covenant), the right to life is considered by the Human Rights Committee to be "the supreme right from which no derogation is permitted even in time of public emergency which threatens the life of the nation" (UN Human Rights Committee 1982, par. 1). The right to life is not absolute; lawful deprivation is permitted, though international law is moving toward customary international law status for the abolition of capital punishment. The right is absolute, however, with regard to the state's obligation to protect all persons from arbitrary deprivation of life, and the death penalty may only be imposed "for the most serious crimes . . . pursuant to a final judgment rendered by a competent court" (Civil and Political Covenant, art. 6[2]).[4] The Human Rights Committee has made clear that article 6 imposes both negative and positive obligations on states parties to protect the right to life: "The Committee considers that States parties should take measures not only to prevent and punish deprivation of life by criminal acts, but also to prevent arbitrary killing by their own security forces" (UN Human Rights Committee 1982, par. 3).

The negative obligations of states to prevent extrajudicial, arbitrary, or summary killings have been further developed by detailed rules governing the use of state-sponsored force, including the use of firearms, to prevent arbitrary deprivation of life. The Code of Conduct for Law Enforcement Officials (UN General Assembly Res. 34, 1979) restricts the use of force to situations in which it is "strictly necessary and to the extent required for the performance of their duty" (art. 3). The commentary to article 3 places explicit restrictions on the use of firearms: "The use of firearms is considered an extreme measure. Every effort should be made to exclude the use of firearms, especially against children. In general, firearms should not be used except when a suspected offender offers armed resistance or otherwise jeopardizes the lives of others and less extreme measures are not sufficient to restrain or apprehend the suspected offender." The Basic Principles on the Use of Force and Firearms by Law Enforcement Officials, adopted in 1990 by the Eighth United Nations Congress on the Prevention of Crime and the Treatment of Offenders, further define the limitations on firearm use, setting forth in clear detail the principles of necessity and proportionality that state agents must follow in order to use firearms in a manner consistent with the right to life. These principles have been adopted as domestic standards in many states. Principle 9 provides that "intentional lethal use of firearms may only be made when strictly unavoidable in order to protect life." The basic principles call for extensive state measures to reduce firearm misuse, including training, storage, the obligation to give verbal warnings, and the obligation to report firearms incidents.

The state's positive obligations to prevent arms-related violations of the right to life have been elaborated in increasingly specific terms to include its responsibility to take steps to prevent reasonably foreseeable armed violence, including armed violence by private actors. In *General Comment 31* (UN Human Rights Committee 2004), on the nature of states' general legal obligations under the Civil and Political Covenant, the Human Rights Committee explained the level of due diligence required by states to give effective meaning to the Covenant's rights: "The positive obligations on States parties to ensure Covenant rights will only be fully discharged if individuals are protected by the State, not just against violations of Covenant rights by its agents, but also against acts committed by private persons or entities that would impair the enjoyment of Covenant rights in so far as they are amenable to the application between private persons or entities." The Human Rights Committee and other treaty bodies have increasingly applied the due diligence standard in their comments, views, and concluding observations (Cerone 2002, 63).

The Human Rights Committee has held states parties responsible for violations of article 6 based on the actions of both private actors and third states. In *Jiménez Vaca v. Colombia*, the committee found a violation of article 6, paragraph 1, of the Covenant, in part because the state did not use due diligence in investigating who was responsible for an attempt on the complainant's life, thus preventing him from living safely in Colombia. To meet its obligation under article 2 of the Covenant, the committee found in *Jiménez Vaca v. Colombia* that the "State party is also under an obligation to try to prevent similar violations in the future" (par. 9). To give meaning to the right to life, then, states must take steps to prevent reasonably foreseeable abuses by private actors.

Regarding responsibility for the actions of third states, the committee has applied an increasingly stringent due diligence requirement in extradition cases. In its 1993 decision in *Kindler v. Canada* the committee did not interpret the Covenant to require Canada to refuse an extradition request unless it sought assurances from the United States that it would not impose the death penalty. In 2003, however, in *Judge v. Canada*, the committee held differently; in light of the growing international consensus against the death penalty, the committee held that for states that had abolished the death penalty, extradition to death penalty states amounted to a violation of article 6, the right to life. The Human Rights Committee's progressive interpretation of the positive responsibilities under article 6 indicates that a state party must pay particular attention to actions it takes that may lead directly to violations of the right to life by other actors, whether private actors or third states.

Other human rights bodies of the United Nations have addressed the due diligence standard with particular attention to small arms and light weapons. The UN special rapporteur on extrajudicial, summary or arbitrary executions has declared that "States have a legal duty to exercise 'due diligence' in protecting the lives of individuals from attacks by criminals, including terrorists, armed robbers, looters and drug dealers" (Alston 2006, par. 47). In August 2006, the UN Sub-Commission on the Promotion and Protection of Human Rights endorsed "Principles on the prevention of human rights violations committed with small arms and light weapons" (UN Sub-Commission, 2006), which articulated *inter alia* the due diligence steps states must take with regard to firearms to carry out their "unequivocal role" to protect the right to life. Those steps include enacting licensing requirements to prevent possession of small arms by persons who are at risk of misusing them; controlling the manufacturing of small arms, including marking each weapon with identifying information; and investigating and prosecuting persons who illegally manufacture or transfer small arms (ibid.).

Extraterritorial Obligations of States Regarding Arms Transfers

Given the increasingly expansive nature of states' negative and positive obligations to protect the right to life, what is the nature of a state's obligations under international human rights law to prevent arms transfers into other states where the arms are likely to be used to commit extrajudicial executions? Does a state's due diligence obligation to protect the right to life extend beyond its territorial borders?

The right to life is a peremptory norm of customary law in addition to being a treaty obligation, and states' positive and negative obligations must be evaluated in light of the *erga omnes* interests of the international community in protecting that right. In examining the human rights law context relating to arms transfers, we should consider the specific jurisdictional reach of the mandate of article 2(1) of the Civil and Political Covenant "to respect and to ensure to all individuals within [a state's] territory and subject to its jurisdiction the rights recognized in the present Covenant," but we must also consider binding obligations on states in related fields of international law, including arms embargoes, prohibitions on manufacture, use, and transfer of specific weapons under international humanitarian law, and international criminal responsibility for complicity. These binding extraterritorial obligations—which are fundamentally connected to human rights even if they are implemented by other bodies—have already created a context in which states have a duty not to transfer arms across borders. States must use due diligence to prevent transfers that violate embargoes, specific humanitarian prohibitions, or aid and assist in crimes.

In addition to legally binding obligations imposed by other areas of international law, at least three legal bases support an extraterritorial human rights obligation to prevent small arms transfers to violate the right to life. First, core non-derogable human rights obligations, including the right to life, are *erga omnes* obligations that are owed to the international community as a whole. States have universal obligations to promote respect for human rights globally and they must take meaningful steps to meet those obligations; at a minimum, states are obligated not to act in furtherance of a foreseeable violation of a peremptory norm. States can be responsible primarily for egregious extraterritorial conduct or secondarily for knowingly contributing to wrongful acts by third states. Second, treaty-based jurisdiction may be appropriate when, as in the case of intentional arms transfers to human rights violators, the exporting state takes actions in its own territory knowing that those actions are likely to result in violations in the territory of another state. When states have the effective means to prevent violations to the right to life and fail to do so, they have acted in ways that defeat the object and purpose of the treaty. Finally, there is an emerging rule of transfer, manifested by state practice and *opinio juris*, that prohibits arms transfers likely to result in serious human rights violations. Each of these bases will be discussed below.

Erga Omnes Obligations as a Basis of Extraterritorial Responsibility

Besides its articulation as a treaty-based guarantee, the right to life is a peremptory or non-derogable customary norm, having attained the highest priority in international human rights law through its repeated articulations in international treaties (Genocide Convention 1949, art. 2; Geneva Conventions 1949, common art. 3; Convention on the Rights of the Child 1989, art. 6), regional treaties (African Charter on Human and Peoples' Rights 1982, art. 4; American Convention on Human Rights 1978, art. 4; European Convention for the Protection of Human Rights and Fundamental Freedoms 1950, art. 2), and universally in national constitutions and laws. How far a particular state's responsibility to protect the right to life extends must be considered against the peremptory normative character of the right.

The peremptory nature of the right to life also supports its characterization as an *erga omnes* obligation upon states (Gormley 1985, 120), an obligation that is not limited merely to bilateral enforcement between states, but is instead an obligation "owed to the international community as a whole" (*Barcelona Traction*, 32). This concept, elaborated in dictum in the *Barcelona Traction* case of the International Court of Justice (ICJ) in 1970, before the human rights Covenants had even entered into force, specifically identified "the principles and rules concerning the basic rights of the human person" as examples of these rights of universal character (33). The universal nature of rights identified as *erga omnes* is such that they not only place limits on states from acting or entering into agreements in violation of the rights, but they impose an affirmative duty to protect rights being violated by another state or, at the very least, not to do anything that would further violations being committed by that other state. The ICJ gave this idea expression in *Barcelona Traction* by citing its own advisory opinion in the *Genocide* case (*Reservations to the Convention on Genocide*, 23), in which it noted "the universal character both of the condemnation of genocide and of the co-operation required 'in order to liberate mankind from such an odious scourge.'" The court's logic presumes both a negative obligation not to commit atrocities and a positive obligation to prevent or "liberate" persons from atrocities at the hands of a third party. These obligations are based on the universal recognition of the seriousness of certain kinds of violations.

The classification of human rights as *erga omnes* obligations has been developed further in the years since the *Barcelona Traction* opinion. While the scope and consequences of the *erga omnes* designation are still contested (Tams 2005, 4), states have taken progressive steps to accept a category of universal rights that bind them. The entry into force of the Civil and Political Covenant and the subsequent movement toward what will likely be universal ratification of the Covenant have borne out the ICJ's inclusion of "the basic rights of the human person" as *erga omnes*. This designation applies most clearly to the set of rights specifically set forth in article 4.2 of the Civil and Political Covenant as being non-derogable, including the right to life. The UN Human Rights Committee explicitly embraced the rights contained in the Covenant as *erga omnes* in *General Comment 31* (2004), noting that, in addition to their obligations toward individual right-holders, "every State Party has a legal interest in the performance by every other State Party of its obligations." The mutual legal interests inherent in universal human rights treaties give rise to duties in response to noncompliance with fundamental rights, including the right to life. Evidence of those duties can be found in the universal legal responsibility, for instance, to prosecute those responsible for international crimes, including genocide, war crimes, and crimes against humanity.

Some commentators have argued that serious violations of *erga omnes* obligations, such as "the threat or occurrence of a large-scale loss of life" (International Commission on Intervention and State Sovereignty 2001, 33), support a collective international response, including humanitarian intervention, to protect the rights being violated by the host state. How far the duties of third states extend to protect human rights is open to further discussion, since a broad duty to intervene provokes concerns especially among weaker states that perceive such an argument as a justification for military intervention and occupation. Despite these concerns,

I would suggest that if the concept of an *erga omnes* obligation—owed to the international community as a whole—is to have any meaning at all, it requires a minimum negative duty to refrain from aiding or assisting in extraterritorial violations of those very obligations. Every state owes the international community as a whole the obligation to take measures to prevent actions that foreseeably lead to serious violations of human rights, especially the violation of peremptory norms such as the right to life (Yihdego 2007, 279).

Primary and Secondary State Responsibility

International practice and jurisprudence with regard to *erga omnes* obligations are set forth most clearly in the International Law Commission's Articles on State Responsibility, adopted in 2001. The ILC's articles define state responsibility for internationally wrongful acts. The legal principle undergirding the ILC's articles is that "every internationally wrongful act of a State entails the international responsibility of that State" (art. 1). That principle was derived from ICJ case law, including *Corfu Channel* (1949), *Legal Consequences, Nambia* (1971), and *Nicaragua v. United States of America* (1986). An internationally wrongful act or omission is established under the ILC's articles when there is (a) conduct attributable to the state; and (b) the conduct is a breach of an international obligation (art. 2). State responsibility can be primary (independent) or secondary (derivative). Actions like arms transfers are usually characterized as providing only the means—or tools—to commit internationally wrongful acts, and therefore could be characterized as acts of secondary responsibility. A more accurate characterization recognizes that internationally wrongful acts are often the result of independent conduct involving several states, each of which holds primary responsibility for the violation (Crawford 2002, 145). A state that intentionally acts to transfer lethal weapons into the hands of a state or non-state actors for the purpose of carrying out a pattern of serious human rights violations, such as extrajudicial executions, mass killings, or genocide, breaches its *erga omnes* obligation to protect the right to life, and therefore shares primary responsibility for the violations.

The ICJ's case law provides some guideposts for the level of effective control required to give rise to primary legal responsibility for internationally wrongful acts. The *Corfu Channel* case, in which Albania was held responsible for its failure to notify the United Kingdom of mines laid by a third party, is an example of the independent responsibility incurred by one state, even though another party may have actually laid the mines that caused the harm (Yihdego 2007, 285). The *Corfu Channel* opinion supports the position that a failure to take steps to prevent clear violations offers a basis for primary legal responsibility. The *Nicaragua* case, in contrast, sets a higher standard of proof needed to establish primary responsibility, that is, "effective control of the military or paramilitary operations in the course of which the alleged violations were committed." The court took the view that even if the United States had been shown to play a decisive role in financing, organizing, training, supplying, and equipping the *contras* paramilitary force in Nicaragua, this evidence alone would not support primary responsibility for violations committed by the *contras*. Instead, primary responsibility would require evidence that "the United States directed or enforced the perpetration of the acts contrary to human rights and humanitarian law . . ." (*Nicaragua v. United States of America*, par. 115). Primary responsibility for extraterritorial violations with small arms, then, at least in the context of humanitarian law examined in *Nicaragua*, may require a showing of intent and control by the transferring state, as evidenced by acts of omission or commission.

As for derivate responsibility for breaching human rights obligations, article 16 of the ILC's Articles on State Responsibility defines the elements needed to prove the secondary responsibility of states that transfer arms to third states knowing that they are likely to be used to commit serious human rights violations: "A State which aids or assists another State in the commission of an internationally wrongful act by the latter is internationally responsible for doing so if: (a) that State does so with knowledge of the circumstances of the internationally wrongful act; and (b) that act would be internationally wrongful if committed by that State." To prove secondary responsibility under this standard does not require evidence of intent on the part of the assisting state, merely knowledge of the intended wrongful use by the receiving state. The principle articulated in article 16 is arguably a customary basis for prohibiting arms transfers to states known to commit human right violations (Bethlehem 2003, 5). It serves as an important international legal consensus to guide states in their decisions concerning arms transfers.

The ILC's Articles on State Responsibility provide a framework for enforcing the *erga omnes* obligations of states to prevent the transfer of deadly weapons into the hands of human rights violators. The framework is a useful one for human rights bodies and special procedures that wish to consider the primary or secondary human rights responsibilities of states for human rights violations that take place with their arms but outside their territory. While the human rights bodies have yet to hold arms-transferring states accountable for their actions or omissions, state responsibility for the negative impacts of arms transfers is being tested in other arenas, including regional legal regimes, and is at the center of international discussions taking place in the UN General Assembly to develop a common standard to reduce the negative impacts of arms exports.

International Action to Prevent Arms Transfers That Violate Human Rights

Pressure for restrictions on arms transfers that facilitate human rights violations has been bubbling up from regional regimes since the problem became more visible in the immediate aftermath of the Cold War. While conventional arms sales slowed, controls over existing firearms stockpiles loosened and new small arms production flooded unchecked into regions that were already facing catastrophic violence, including the Great Lakes Region of Africa and former the Yugoslavia in Europe (Koh 2003, 2343). Regional organizations were the first to respond to the destabilizing effects of small arms transfers into their communities. In 1997, the Organization of American States (OAS) adopted the first treaty to curb illicit manufacturing and trafficking of firearms and ammunition. The Inter-American Convention included a relatively weak provision on transfers, focused generally on preventing diversion by requiring states parties to "maintain an effective system of export, import and international transit licences or authorizations for transfers of firearms" (Inter-American Convention 1998, art. 9). Framed to stem "illicit" or non-state transfers, the convention itself did not establish export criteria tied to human rights or humanitarian law obligations, but non-binding model regulations on brokering promulgated by the OAS do incorporate such criteria (OAS Model Regulations 2003, art. 5).

The European Union adopted the legally binding Joint Action on Small Arms to combat "the destabilising accumulation and spread of small arms" and "to help solve the problems caused by such accumulations" (European Union Joint Action on Small Arms 1998, revised in 2002, art. 1.1). The joint action established export controls to reduce dangerous accumulations in recipient states. It is supplemented with the politically binding Code of Conduct on Arms Exports that requires member states to conduct an assessment of each request for exports of military equipment, including small arms, to ensure that such exports are compatible with specific criteria. Under the criteria, states must "exercise special caution and vigilance in issuing licenses, on a case-by-case basis and taking account of the nature of the equipment, to countries where serious violations of human rights have been established by the competent bodies of the UN, the Council of Europe or by the EU" (European Union Code of Conduct 1998, criterion 2). The EU Code of Conduct includes a mechanism for preventing member states from supplying arms if the request for those arms has already been rejected by another member state. The EU Code of Conduct was tested most visibly in 2002 when Belgium approved the transfer of five thousand machine guns to the government of Nepal after other EU member states had denied arms exports based on human rights concerns. After public criticism of Belgium's transfer, the EU Parliament called on member states to halt arms transfers to Nepal as required by the Code of Conduct (Human Rights Watch 2004, sec. 13).

Other regional initiatives have led to binding treaties with specific provisions to screen exports of small arms to keep them out of the hands of human right violators, including the Southern African Development Community Protocol of 2001, the Nairobi Protocol of 2004 regarding the Great Lakes Region and the Horn of Africa, and the ECOWAS Convention on Small Arms of 2006. Non-binding guidelines include the OSCE Document on Small Arms and Light Weapons of 2000 and the Wassenaar Arrangement Best Practice Guidelines for Exports of Small Arms and Light Weapons of 2002. Collectively, these legal developments embody a common global concern, though not clearly a binding obligation, about the protection of human rights in arms-receiving states.

This reluctance to commit to binding human rights obligations regarding arms transfers was evident as discussions on arms trafficking moved to the international level at the beginning of the millennium. Human rights language was deliberately omitted from the Programme of Action (PoA) adopted at the U.N. Conference on the Illicit Trade in Small Arms and Light Weapons in All Its Aspects (Small Arms Conference) in 2001. That omission was a reflection of the conference's controversial decision to address only transfers defined as "illicit," meaning transfers to unauthorized non-state actors. Negotiators presumed state to state arms transfers to be legal, limited only by Security Council arms embargoes and prohibitions against the transfer and use of specific weapons under international humanitarian law. The PoA, a politically binding instrument, expressed the concern of states that small arms transfers "pose a serious threat to peace, reconciliation, safety, security, stability and sustainable development at the individual, local, national, regional and international levels." If the PoA had included human rights in this list of concerns it might have been interpreted as a step toward prohibiting state to state transfers in certain cases, such as when the arms are likely to be used to commit serious violations by state or private actors. Some key states at the conference were not prepared to address state-sponsored gun violations directly in the PoA, instead choosing to focus on the lowest common denominator: guns that land in the hands of political or criminal elements that threaten government control (Koh 2003, 2347). The PoA does include a general requirement that national export controls be "consistent with existing responsibilities of states under relevant international law" (Report of the UN Conference 2001, sec. 2, par. 11). That general reference to international law has been interpreted by many states and nongovernmental human rights advocates to tie core human rights obligations to national export controls, obligations that are not only "relevant" to arms exports but non-derogable in nature.

The Draft Arms Trade Treaty

The more recent actions of the UN General Assembly, noted at the beginning of this chapter, to move toward drafting an arms trade treaty, go a long way to fill the gap left by the PoA, especially with regard to ill-intentioned or irresponsible transfers that are justified as being "legal," and with regard to "legal" transfers that result in serious human rights violations. The underpinnings of the General Assembly resolution to draft an arms trade treaty are "a respect for and commitment to international law" (UN General Assembly Res. 61/89, 2006, preambular par. 1), and the resolution specifically reaffirms respect for international human rights law, in addition to obligations under the UN Charter and international humanitarian law (preambular par. 7). This preambular framework, with its clear inclusion of human rights law, signals that states now recognize human rights as a basis of *obligation* for transferring states, not just a basis for *concern*, as manifested by previous regional export regimes.

The arms trade treaty resolution aims to establish common international standards on the import, export, and transfer of conventional arms. Efforts to develop more specific legal obligations with respect to arms exports are based on the obligations imposed by core principles of international law, in other words, *erga omnes* obligations. In the words of one state in response to the UN secretary-general's request for views on the arms trade treaty, "We believe that, first of all, the arms trade treaty should be based on *global obligations* stemming from such legally binding documents as the United Nations Charter and UN Security Council resolutions" (UN Secretary-General, 2007, Estonia's reply, at 70, emphasis mine). Among those global obligations are human rights commitments that are based in the UN Charter, articles 55(c) and 56, and reflected in arms embargoes explicitly imposed by the Security Council to prevent foreseeable human rights violations in recipient states as part of the Council's authority to maintain peace and security.

Arms embargoes are the most visible and direct limitations on small arms transfers. The UN Security Council may impose mandatory embargoes under its Chapter VII authority to take measures to restore international peace and security. Despite an increase in the use of embargoes, the mandates have been neither consistent nor effective in reducing arms-related human rights violations. Since the end of the Cold War the Council has declared two voluntary and twenty-seven mandatory arms embargoes (Parker 2007, 5) in response to external aggression, civil war, persistent breaches of peace accords, humanitarian crises, serious violations of human rights coups, and support of terrorism.[5] With regard to Rwanda (S/918/1994), Afghanistan (S/1076/1996), and Darfur (S/1556/2004), the UN Security Council imposed arms embargoes specifically to prevent the killing of civilians. Arms embargoes prohibit UN member states from transferring any weapons or materiel to the embargoed destination and additionally require that states enact national measures so that private actors do not transfer weapons or materiel to the embargoed destinations. Embargoes imposed after violent conflict has broken out have been criticized as "late and often blunt instruments" that are not an effective means of stopping conflict (Wood 2006).

International humanitarian law (IHL) also imposes binding limits on how small arms are used in conflicts and prohibits the use of certain weapons entirely. A cardinal principle of IHL requires a distinction to be made between combatants and civilians, and further requires that civilian populations and objects be protected from harm. Small arms that are intrinsically incapable of distinguishing between combatants and civilians are prohibited under this principle. Certain weapons, including anti-personnel landmines, chemical weapons, and biological weapons, have been expressly prohibited for this reason (Antipersonnel Mine Ban Convention 1997; Chemical Weapons Convention 1993; Biological Weapons Convention 1972). Under the principle of distinction, IHL also requires that parties to an armed conflict may only target military objectives, prohibits indiscriminate attacks, and mandates that precautions be taken to minimize civilian losses. A second cardinal principle of IHL is the prohibition of using weapons of a nature to cause superfluous injury or unnecessary suffering. Small arms that violate this second principle are prohibited, including but not limited to expanding bullets, booby traps, and blinding laser weapons. A prohibition on transfer is expressly or implicitly part of the bans on all these weapons.

Given the failure of arms embargoes and IHL restrictions to effectively address the growing problem of arms availability, and the omission of human rights from the PoA regarding small arms transfers, the arms control community turned to the UN General Assembly to create a more coherent and preventive response to the problems created by arms transfers. State consensus on the need to address the linkage between arms availability and human rights developed rapidly as part of the negotiations. Of the ninety-six states offering their views on the feasibility, scope, and draft parameters of the proposed treaty, violations of human rights were the most frequently cited criteria for restrictions on transfers—proposed by sixty-two states (Parker 2007, 11). Other frequently suggested criteria included violations of humanitarian law (fifty-eight states), terrorism (fifty-one states), and regional and international commitments (forty-two states). Given the prevalence of the suggested criteria, Parker concludes, "There is likely to be general agreement that restrictions on transfers that may be used for violations of human rights or by terrorists should be included in an ATT" (ibid.).

Because the UN secretary-general offered no proposed criteria in seeking states' views on the arms trade treaty, the explicit inclusion of human rights in the views of so many states represents a sea change on this issue. Human rights and humanitarian organizations, including Amnesty International and Oxfam, were at the forefront of lobbying on criteria to be included in the resolution. During negotiations on the resolution in the First Committee, these organizations circulated a letter signed by fifteen Nobel Prize recipients. The letter emphasized, "No weapons should ever be transferred if they will be used for serious violations of human rights" (Rizvi 2006, 1). Persistent pressure from nongovernmental organization (NGO) coalitions, such as the International Action Network on Small Arms (IANSA), to include human rights in the arms trade treaty moved states beyond the limited approach taken in the PoA to the point where human rights concerns are central to the discussion of arms export criteria.

The increased scrutiny of the relationship between arms exports and human rights was brought to life in a dramatic fashion in April 2008 when a Chinese cargo ship headed to Zimbabwe carrying seventy-seven tons of small arms and light weapons was turned away from several African ports after a public outcry instigated by South African trade unionists who refused to unload the weapons. Designated the "ship of shame" by African newspapers, the Chinese ship was reportedly loaded with 3 million rounds of ammunition for AK-47s, 1,500 rocket propelled grenades, and 2,500 mortar rounds (BBC 2008b). The attempted transfer of small arms into the tense post-election situation in Zimbabwe became a rallying point for civil society, which was concerned that the arms would be used to carry out state-sponsored human rights violations. The case illustrates increased public interest in preventing transfers to known human rights violators.

Lack of Progress in Human Rights Bodies

In contrast to the increased discussion of human rights as part of the small arms debate in the General Assembly, there has been a troubling lack of attention shown by UN human rights bodies to the issues. Hundreds of nongovernmental organizations, under the umbrella of IANSA, have been laboring for years in the disarmament sessions of the Small Arms Conference, the First Committee, and the UN General Assembly to develop detailed and binding norms to stem the violence caused by easy access to firearms. They have achieved significant success despite the counterpressure of the pro-gun lobby, including the powerful U.S.-based National Rifle Association and its constituent groups in the international arena, and over the forceful objections of the U.S. government (Bolton 2001). Meanwhile, there has been a distinct lack of activity on the topic of small arms and human rights in the Human Rights Council, its special procedures, and the human rights treaty bodies.

The most visible action in the human rights arena regarding arms-related violations took place in the Sub-Commission on the Promotion and Protection of Human Rights, which, in 2002, authorized my study as the special rapporteur on the prevention of human rights violations committed with small arms and light weapons. While the study had to be approved by the Commission on Human Rights (decision 2003/112), no substantive discussion of the topic has ever taken place at the commission, or its successor, the Human Rights Council.

At its final session, in August 2006, the sub-commission endorsed a set of fifteen "principles on the prevention of human rights violations committed with small arms and light weapons" and transmitted them to the Human Rights Council for consideration and adoption (Resolution 2006/22). The principles reassert the primacy of human rights, and particularly the right to life, in states' decisions and policies regarding small arms and light weapons.

The principles are divided into two parts: (a) obligations with regard to state officials; and (b) due diligence to prevent human rights abuses by private actors. The principles in the first part bring together standards from existing codes, especially related to law enforcement. The small arms principles set forth minimum effective measures states must adopt to ensure human rights protections and to prevent state officials from misusing small arms to violate human rights, including

- adopting rules and regulations on the use of force (art. 2);
- strict enforcement of those rules and regulations, including a clear chain of command, and punishment of violations as criminal offences (art. 3);
- procedures for storage and management, and responsible disposal of surplus small arms (art. 4);
- selection and training of law enforcement personnel (art. 5);
- special attention to human rights as part of that training, including alternative means to force (art. 6);
- prior operational planning to avoid use of force and small arms violence (art. 7);
- reiteration of necessity and proportionality criteria regarding use of firearms (art. 8);
- and minimum criteria for investigating allegations of misuse (art. 9).

The second part of the principles establishes states' responsibilities regarding firearms violence by other actors, including non-state actors. The articles in the second part set forth minimum licensing requirements states must enforce to meet their human rights obligations to prevent foreseeable violations to the right to life; minimum requirements to control manufacture of firearms, including marking and tracing of firearms; and state responsibility to develop effective disarmament, demobilization, and reintegration programs particularly in post-conflict situations.

Principles 12 and 14 most directly address the issue of small arms transfers: Principle 14 states that "governments shall prohibit international transfers of small arms which would violate their obligations under international law, including in circumstances in which such arms are likely to be used to commit serious human rights violations." Principle 14 embodies a due diligence standard to prevent actions that will result in foreseeable extraterritorial violations. Under Principle 12, governments are further obligated to investigate and prosecute crimes, including the illegal transfer of small arms. Within the human rights context, an illegal transfer would be one that violates or aids and assists in the violation of a peremptory norm such as the right to life.

The president of the Human Rights Council, Ambassador Luis Alfonso de Alba, recommended that the council adopt and widely disseminate the small arms principles (de Alba 2006–7, 4). He noted that "the right to life, liberty and security of the person and the principle of due diligence are clearly relevant to the Human Rights Council and it is important that States' practices are examined by it to generate higher standards that would have an impact on the promotion and protection of all human rights. The Human Rights Council could provide new impetus to advance practice in three key areas of gun violence and control the arms trade: regulating the *use* of small arms, regulating the *transfer* of guns and ammunition, and advocating *assistance* to survivors of armed violence."

Despite the president's endorsement, the Human Rights Council has not adopted the principles, nor has it taken any action at all to address the deleterious impacts on human rights of small arms availability and transfers. This may be the result of an overburdened agenda due to the reforms that have been implemented in the human rights arenas of the United Nations in the past two years, but more likely it reflects the hesitancy of human rights experts to wade into areas of law—such as security law and disarmament—in which they do not think they are the primary actors and the reluctance of states to assume human rights obligations with regard to the arms trade.

Treaty-based Obligations

The UN human rights treaty bodies have not yet examined the specific question of extraterritorial obligations regarding small arms transfers in their comments, views, or concluding observations. The extraterritorial application of human rights treaties is a pressing subject in this era, which is characterized by global efforts to suppress terrorism. The decision of the European Court of Human Rights in the *Banković* case (2001) set strict jurisdictional boundaries for applying human rights treaty obligations to victims outside the territory and "legal space" of the states parties to the European Convention on Human Rights. The Inter-American Commission and the UN Human Rights Committee have been far more expansive in their approaches to extraterritorial treaty application (Coomans and Kamminga 2004, 4–5). How far human rights obligations extend and how states can be held accountable for extraterritorial violations will continue to be elaborated in light of the issues raised by globalization and its effects upon human rights. My analysis will focus on the extraterritorial reach of the Civil and Political Covenant.

The Human Rights Committee has addressed the adverse impacts of unrestricted availability of firearms on the right to life, though not in connection with extraterritorial obligations. In its *Concluding Observations* to the report of the United States, the committee expressed the following concern: "It also regrets the easy availability of firearms to the public and the fact that federal and state legislation is not stringent enough in that connection to secure the protection and enjoyment of the right to life and security of the individual guaranteed under the Covenant" (UN Human Rights Committee 1995, par. 282). The committee, however, has not considered the positive obligations of states parties with regard to the right to life and security of individuals residing outside their territorial boundaries.

Regarding extraterritorial application of human rights under the Covenant, the Human Rights Committee has begun to build a limited jurisprudence, beginning with *López Burgos v. Uruguay*, to indicate the circumstances in which the Covenant applies to a state's conduct abroad, affecting its own citizens as well as foreign nationals. In *López Burgos v. Uruguay*, the committee held that Uruguay violated the Covenant when its security forces kidnapped and tortured a Uruguayan national who was residing in Argentina. The committee stated that "it would be unconscionable to so interpret the responsibility under article 2 of the Covenant as to permit a State party to perpetrate violations of the Covenant on the territory of another State, which violations it could not perpetrate on its own territory" (*López Burgos v. Uruguay*, par. 12.3). The *López Burgos* case, then, established at a minimum that the committee will hold states accountable for violations against their own citizens even when the violations occur in another state.

In *General Comment 31* (2004) regarding the nature of the legal obligations imposed on states parties to the Civil and Political Covenant, the Human Rights Committee built upon the rule of *López Burgos* to extend the Covenant's protections to non-nationals who are in the "effective control" of a state party. The committee interpreted the Covenant's article 2(1) obligation, "to respect and to ensure to all individuals within its territory and subject to its jurisdiction," as extending to anyone within the "effective control" of the state party even if that person is not situated within the territory of the state party. The committee's comment was prepared largely as a response to states parties that were trying to avoid the obligations of the Covenant in conducting their global military campaign against terrorism. The committee has relied on the principle of effective control to apply treaty obligations in situations of occupation (UN Human Rights Committee 2003, par. 11), and with regard to violations stemming from the conduct of war (UN Human Rights Committee 2006, par. 10). The International Court of Justice endorsed the Human Rights Committee's approach in part in its Advisory Opinion of 2004 on *Legal Consequences of the Construction of a Wall in the Occupied Palestinian Territory*, finding that "the [Covenant] is applicable in respect of acts done by a State in the exercise of its jurisdiction outside its own territory," and citing the facts in *López Burgos* (the abduction of a national in another territory) as an example of such an act. While the ICJ did not go so far as to cite the "effective control" standard of the Human Rights Committee, by citing *López Burgos* it suggested that it is the state's relationship to the victim and not its control over the territory that is central to whether a state is bound to respect the victim's human rights (Cerone 2005, 2).

Any examination of the extraterritorial application of the treaty-based obligations to protect the right to life, then, turns in some part on the relationship between the state and the individuals whose rights are alleged to be violated. Scheinin refers to this as a *relational* or *contextual* analysis regarding jurisdiction, citing the *López Burgos* opinion as the basis of that type of analysis (2004, 73). In the case of arms transfer, an exporting state does not necessarily have any direct relationship with the victims of firearms violations in the importing state. The arms transferor may not have effective control over the victim or over the use of the weapons in the importing state, though it may be aware of the intended use of the weapons. Instead, the exporting state has total control over the weapons themselves, the means to prevent those arms from reaching human rights violators in the first place.

Does effective control over the means used to violate someone's rights provide a jurisdictional basis under the Covenant? Even a restrictive reading of extraterritorial jurisdiction, such as McGoldrick's, recognizes that states parties have obligations for measures they take within their own territories that lead to violations in other states (2004, 52). It is well established that a state party may not deport a person to another state where there is a real risk that the person's core human rights, including the right to life, will be violated (*Judge v. Canada* UNHRC 2003; *Ng v. Canada*, UNHRC 1993; *Soering v. United Kingdom*, ECHR 1989). In taking steps to transfer a human being across boundaries when there is such a risk, the state has been found to have violated its own positive obligations to protect human rights. According to McGoldrick, "Properly understood, the violations of the ICCPR only appear to occur in the territory of another state. In fact, the states parties' obligations are clearly grounded in measures it has taken within its own territory" (2004, 52). When the physical extradition of a person results in foreseeable violations of that person's right to life then, under this line of cases, the transferring state is primarily, not secondarily, responsible for the violations. The situation of arms transfer, however, is not completely analogous to the extradition of a person. The state in the first instance has effective control over the person—a more direct relationship with the victim than in the second case—where the state has control only over the means. In both cases, however, the transferring state is in a position to give effect to the rights.

A broader analytical basis for holding a state accountable under the Covenant was employed by the Human Rights Committee in its response to Iran's state report of 1993. The committee condemned the pronouncement of a death sentence by *fatwa* "without trial, in respect of a foreign writer, Mr. Salman Rushdie." The committee observed that there had been public appeals to execute the *fatwa* even if Rushdie had to be killed outside the territory of Iran. The committee noted that "the fact that the sentence was the result of a fatwa issued by a religious authority does not exempt the State party from its obligation to ensure to all individuals the rights provided for under the Covenant" (UN Human Rights Committee 1993, par. 9). The *fatwa* case was one in which the Iranian state, having no effective control over the individual victim, who was a non-national, took steps within Iran that could foreseeably lead to the death of the individual outside the physical territory of Iran. The state, then, had the effective means only to control the *fatwa* (even though the *fatwa* was pronounced by religious authorities), not to control the manner in which the *fatwa* was carried out. These facts suggest that, in the view of the Human Rights Committee, states parties have an obligation under the Covenant to give effect to the right to life by abstaining from acts that would put a person's life—even the life of a non-national—in jeopardy outside its physical territory. Scheinin singled out this response to Iran, noting that, based on his experience as a member of the Human Rights Committee, the body employed the same approach in contested cases under the Optional Protocol (2004, 74). It is an approach he characterizes as "facticity creates normativity," or a relationship that is initiated by the state creates a parallel obligation. In other words, when a state takes affirmative steps to put the lives of persons outside its territory at risk it creates legal obligations under the Covenant that are proportionate to the risk. This resonates with the undergirding logic of the ILC's Articles on State Responsibility in that every internationally wrongful act of a state entails the international responsibility of that state.

While a state that transfers arms to a known human rights violator may wish to distance itself from the consequences of such a transfer, under the relational analysis illustrated by the Iran *fatwa* case, it has instead taken on human rights obligations commensurate with the risks created by its own actions. Only by preventing the risk can it avoid the obligation. When a state party has the means to prevent the violation of core human rights treaty obligations outside its territory and fails to do so, it is acting contrary to the object and purpose of the treaty and violates the principle of *pacta sunt servanda*, that the treaty must be performed by the parties in good faith. If a state does not wish to incur the risks inherent in transferring highly lethal weapons across borders, the state must carry out at least the same measure of due diligence that is required domestically to protect guns from falling into the hands of those most likely to misuse them. In the words of *López Burgos*, states should not be allowed "to perpetrate violations of the Covenant on the territory of another state, which violations it could not perpetrate on its own territory" (*López Burgos v. Uruguay*, par. 12.3).

Constructing a Rule of Transfers

A state breaches its obligations *erga omnes* and its good faith obligations not to act contrary to the object and purpose of human rights treaties when it fails to prevent small arms transfers to destinations in which the risks of violations are known. International humanitarian law and mandatory UN Security Council arms embargoes have already established some minimum thresholds for arms transfers, and international institutions charged with enforcing laws in those areas have begun to elaborate indicators for determining states' breaches of their obligations (International Committee of the Red Cross 2007). In my study of small arms and human rights, I encouraged the international human rights community to elaborate independently the nature of states' obligations under international human rights law to regulate the availability, misuse, and transfer of small arms. While the UN Sub-Commission's instrument, "Principles on the prevention of human rights violations committed with small arms and light weapons," represents an important start in that direction, in a world teeming with guns much more needs to be done to enforce states' human rights obligations regarding armed violence inside and outside their territories.

I believe that the collective experience in the security, humanitarian, and human rights arenas to establish criteria to prevent small arms transfers is leading toward a rule of transfer. Evidence of this emerging rule can be seen in state practice and *opinio juris*. Evidence of state practice includes the participation of more than 118 states in regional arms exports regimes that include human rights considerations in evaluating arms transfers; responses citing human rights as a criteria in arms exports from sixty-two out of ninety-six states offering views on the proposed arms trade treaty; and the inclusion of human rights concerns, specifically concerns about violations of the right to life, as the basis of UN Security Council arms embargoes. The public decisions of the governments of South Africa and Angola not to offload Chinese arms exports to Zimbabwe in April 2008 also exemplify state practice. *Opinio juris* for such a rule can be found in the express articulation of human rights violations as the basis for Security Council arms embargoes; the reaffirmation of international human rights in the General Assembly's resolution authorizing the drafting of an arms trade treaty; and the adoption by the UN Sub-Commission of the principles on small arms and human rights, including article 14's prohibition against small arms transfers when "such arms are likely to be used to commit serious human rights violations."

Three considerations should be taken into account in constructing a human rights rule of transfer: the seriousness of the violation that results from the transfer; the degree of knowledge of the transferring state regarding likely violations; and the capacity of the transferring state to prevent the violations. It follows that the more serious the violation, the greater likelihood of the transferor's knowledge, and the more capable a state is to prevent the violation, the stronger the argument for holding a state accountable for extraterritorial human rights violations. I address each consideration below.

The Seriousness of the Violations

While this chapter has addressed the peremptory norm to protect the right to life, a rule of transfer is likely only to apply in cases where there is a documented pattern of killings in the state that is receiving small arms. Genocide, war crimes, and crimes against humanity fall well within the categories of armed violence included in such a rule, but systematic patterns of extrajudicial killings should also support a duty not to transfer. Sporadic or exceptional killings are not likely to be seen as supporting a third state's duty to prevent arms transfers. Given the countervailing legal principle that states are entitled to obtain weapons for purposes of self-defense and national security, it would not be reasonable or feasible to establish a low threshold for the obligation to withhold arms. Criteria in existing regional treaties and codes typically frame the duty to prevent transfers only in the case of serious violations. The European Union Code's duty requires vigilance "where serious violations of human rights have been established by the competent bodies of the UN, the Council of Europe or by the EU" (criterion 2[b]). Even human rights NGOs suggest a threshold of gross or serious violations for establishing a duty to prevent transfers, conveying "a sense of scale," evoking the number and gravity of the violations (Arms Trade Treaty Steering Committee 2006, 20). Unfortunately, there are many situations of serious human rights violations in our global community into which arms continue to flow, so a high threshold for withholding arms would still represent a progressive step toward human rights protection.

Transferor's Knowledge

A rule of transfer will also require objective evidence that the transferring state knew or should have known that the firearms were likely to be used to commit serious violations. The EU Code requires documentation by international bodies, including human rights bodies. Given the time lag in such reporting, knowledge should be attributed to states from other reliable sources, including respected NGOs and media reports about imminent human rights crises. States should at least be required to delay transfers until such reports have been confirmed or dismissed. Under the EU Joint Action, knowledge is imputed to all states when one has rejected an export application based on the human rights record of the recipient.

A state's obligation to prevent arms transfers cannot be avoided by a showing of lack of intent to commit human rights violations. It is the intent of the recipient that is relevant, not the intent of the transferor. The standard of proof for international criminal responsibility requires only knowledge: an individual can be convicted for aiding and abetting if he or she knew the intention of the group to commit the crime (Rome Statute of the International Criminal Court 1998, art. 25). The ILC's Articles on State Responsibility apply the same standard to incur state responsibility for aiding and assisting another state in the commission of an internationally wrongful act: that the conduct occurs "with knowledge of the circumstances of the internationally wrongful act" (art. 16[a]).

Ability to Give Effect to the Right

A final consideration in constructing a rule of transfer based on human rights is how difficult it is for the transferring state to give effect to the right to life outside its territory. The obligation to protect rights extraterritorially is highest when the state has the means to realize the right outside its territory and the burden of doing so is not prohibitive. Tomuschat's concurrence in *López Burgos v. Uruguay* is insightful in its analysis on this point. In it, he asserted that the Covenant will not apply in situations in which a state party is "unable to ensure the effective enjoyment of the rights under the Covenant"(*López Burgos v. Uruguay*, Tomuschat concurrence 1981). Tomuschat's examples of those situations included a state unable to realize the Covenant's rights because it is under military occupation and a state that cannot protect its citizens because they are under the control of other authorities. In those cases, states would have "plausible grounds for denying the protection of the Covenant" (ibid.). McGoldrick suggests other grounds for denying extraterritorial jurisdiction under the Covenant based on a state's inability to give effect to procedural obligations, such as the right to an investigation or fair trial, when the victim is located outside the state (McGoldrick 2004, 46). These de facto limitations on jurisdiction offer an important framework for considering the application of treaty obligations, but they do not apparently limit the obligations of states to deny arms transfers to human rights violators, where a state has effective control over the means to commit serious human rights violations and where enforcing the state's human rights obligations would not "be likely to encounter exceptional obstacles" (*López Burgos v. Uruguay*, Tomuschat concurrence 1981).

Conclusion

States have *erga omnes* customary obligations and treaty obligations to prevent serious and foreseeable violations of the right to life beyond their borders. Human rights bodies, including the Human Rights Council, and UN human rights treaty bodies have a crucial role to play in defining states' positive human rights responsibilities regarding the availability, misuse, and transfer of small arms and light weapons inside and outside their territories. The human rights community must be more visible in the discussion already taking place in other parts of the international system to construct a rule of transfer elaborating the specific obligations of states with regard to arms transfers. Human rights experts must ensure, for instance, that the laws and standards in their field are accurately represented in creating new legal instruments regarding transfer. Human rights bodies can play a role in monitoring the impact of small arms transfer and misuse in human rights violations.

The Human Rights Council should adopt the small arms principles recommended by the UN Sub-Commission and should authorize a special procedure to further delineate states' obligations regarding small arms and to monitor and report on small arms violations. The treaty body system offers another important forum for evaluating the obligations of states' parties with regard to human rights violations. At a minimum, treaty bodies and experts must inquire about the role of states parties in arms transfers to states and non-state actors that are known to be committing gross violations of human rights. Treaty bodies must urge transparency in arms exports and remind states of their due diligence responsibilities to protect the right to life by keeping firearms out of the hands of those who are likely to misuse them. While the carnage of gun-related violence continues, the human rights community cannot afford to ignore the linkage between the arms transferred and the harm inflicted.

Chapter 3
Growing Barriers: International Refugee Law

Thomas Gammeltoft-Hansen

Seeking asylum is a right that necessarily entails a relationship between a host state and an individual arriving from another country. In the majority of cases, this relationship is played out in the territory of the host state, after the refugee arrives and utters the magical word "asylum." Yet, over the past decades the locus for this encounter appears to be increasingly shifting. Migration control at the border is being supplemented by a panoply of mechanisms to intercept those traveling in international waters, in the airports of transit countries, or even before departing their country of origin. As a result, today the asylum seeker is more and more likely to meet the migration authorities of the prospected destination state before reaching its territorial frontiers.

The erection of these administrative and physical barriers beyond the territory for those looking to escape persecution raises important questions under international refugee law. To what extent can the protection normally afforded to asylum seekers and refugees be extended to situations where states engage in migration control outside their territories? The argument by some states remains that refugee law does not, and was never intended to, apply outside the territory of the receiving state. In addition, how are protection obligations distributed when extraterritorial migration control is operated within the territory of another state? The simple answer would be to assign responsibility to whatever state within whose sovereign territory migration control is enacted, yet the structure of the international refugee protection regime and differences in protection capacity among states mean that such a solution could result in a de facto "vacuum" in refugee protection.

The present chapter will attempt to come to terms with extraterritorial obligations under international refugee law by means of a two-step analysis. The next two sections will be looking at the specific structure and applicability of the refugee regime to extraterritorial migration control.

First, international refugee law exhibits some specific qualities that set it apart from human rights law in general. Second, the question of geographical application has been contested from the very outset and the conflicting interpretations evident in the drafting history continue to mar refugee law jurisprudence today.

Third, the question of extraterritorial obligations is deferred to a more general discussion on the concept of jurisdiction as applied in human rights litigation. Here, extraterritoriality may be broken down into three different spheres: excision of territory, *terra nullius*, and actions on third state territory. The jurisprudence between these spheres is markedly different and seems to reflect an underlying tension between what might be termed a *traditional* or Westphalian conceptualization and a more *functional* reading of extraterritorial jurisdiction. The two coexist, though their respective fields of application remain contested.

The Refugee and International Law

The fundamental problem of extraterritorial obligations has been outlined at the outset of this volume: How do we reconcile the seemingly universal claim by human rights on the one hand with the practical need for dividing such obligations among equal states and the Westphalian institutional setup delineating their sovereign power along geographical borders on the other? This dilemma remains applicable to refugee rights as well, yet the international refugee regime exhibits a number of particularities compared to general human rights law that makes the question of extraterritorial obligations especially acute.

As outlined in the introduction, despite the fact that human rights law is coached in interstate treaties and universal language, the primary subjects of human rights protection is a state's own nationals (Skogly and Gibney 2002, 782). The major achievement of the human rights movement was to introduce to international law a set of norms that did not concern simply the *horizontal* relationship between states but also a *vertical* obligation between each state and its subjects (ibid.). As the contributions to this volume amply illustrate, human rights obligations are of course not limited to this sphere and may involve an additional *diagonal* relationship between a state and individuals outside its territory, yet intrastate protection remains the starting point.

The international refugee protection regime is, on the one hand, part and parcel of this development. Refugee law must be considered a branch of human rights law and refugee protection has benefited substantially from bolstering and patching claims under specific refugee instruments with obligations derived from general human rights law.

On the other hand, refugee law is distinctive in at least one respect.

Whereas the thrust of the human rights movement is geared toward opening up the black box of the state hitherto so viciously guarded by principles of national sovereignty, refugee law is specific in dealing solely with what might best be termed the *transversal* relationship between the state and the subjects of another state. This relation may still be played out vertically within the host state, yet the fact that it is concerned solely with foreigners and not a state's own subjects means that the refugee regime in certain ways differs from the ordinary modus operandi of the broader human rights regime.

Much of the human rights movement has been geared toward pushing for increased state responsibility in ensuring rights owed to its citizens; the refugee regime, in contrast, takes the starting point that for some individuals the realization of fundamental rights within their country of origin will never be possible. While both the human rights regime and the refugee regime share the same concern to avoid human rights violations, the solution offered under the refugee regime is not state reform, but protection in another state (Hathaway 2007). No onus is put on the obligations of countries of origin under international refugee law; rather, instruments have been explicit in stating that the grant of asylum is not to be considered as an "unfriendly act" toward countries of origin.[1] Thus, where the human rights regime in general is *preventive* and aimed at protection in the country of origin, the refugee regime is by and large *reactive* and *exilic* (Chimni 1999; Okoth-Obbo 1996).

There have been several attempts to overcome this exilic bias. The movement by some scholars to "reconceive refugee law as human rights" naturally involves an extension of protection obligations to states without a direct territorial affiliation to the refugee, to countries of origin for ending persecution, and to more developed states for providing financial support to the countries of first asylum that continue to receive the majority of the world's refugees (Hathaway 1997). Similarly, current policy developments in a number of countries seem to emphasize "protection in the region" or even "in-country protection" as alternatives to asylum in, for example, Europe or the United States.

To some extent these developments might be readily welcomed. For decades, refugee agencies have been trying to get the message across that "refugees are human rights violations made visible" (Moore 1987). A more equitable distribution of the global burden for refugee protection is no doubt needed if greater compliance with refugee protection standards is to be ensured. Yet, the increasing popularity of extraterritorial migration control may also be seen as an attempt to overcome this exilic bias. In this case, however, the result is not increased burden sharing but rather the opposite. As states engage in extraterritorial migration control, obligations otherwise owed under international refugee law are either deconstructed or shifted to those countries that more or less willingly commercialize their national sovereign territory for this purpose.

The basic structure of international refugee law could be argued to provide a certain incentive for doing exactly that. This concerns first the basic mechanism of responsibility assignment. The core of the refugee regime is the *non-refoulement* principle, which establishes the refugee as the exception to the sovereign right of states to exercise migration control and reject foreigners at the borders. Normally, this prohibition is enacted as soon as a refugee or asylum seeker arrives at the frontiers of a given state and in principle obliges the state to undertake a status determination procedure (Fitzpatrick 1996, 229ff; UN High Commissioner for Refugees 2007). In this way, the division of refugee protection responsibilities generally follows territorial borders—whatever country a refugee finds herself in, that state is responsible for not sending her back to persecution.

Second, beyond the *non-refoulement* principle, the bulk of rights under the Refugee Convention of 1951 are not granted en bloc but rather according to a principle of territorial approximation. This means that more and more rights are acquired as the refugee obtains a higher level of attachment to the host state. This incremental approach reflects a concern of the drafters not to extend the full scope of rights in situations where refugees may arrive spontaneously in large numbers (Hathaway 2005, 157). Thus, in particular, social and economic rights may only be claimed when a refugee is "lawfully present" or "lawfully staying" within the territory of the host state.

The combination of these two traits makes the question of extraterritorial obligations particularly important in relation to refugees. The first and most pertinent question is whether states acting extraterritorially are bound by even the most fundamental norm of refugee law, namely that of *non-refoulement*. If this is not the case, no other protection under the Refugee Convention is likely to be accessible. The second question concerns the territorial structure of the broader array of rights under the Refugee Convention: What obligations are effectively owed to the refugee encountered on the high seas or at foreign airports, as opposed to those arriving at the border of the host state? To resolve these issues, the chapter will proceed in two steps. The first sets out from the specific debate within refugee law and attempts to bring clarity to the application, *ratione loci*, of the *non-refoulement* principle under the Refugee Convention. The second refers the issue back to the broader framework of human rights and international law, and here the question of legal obligations in situations of extraterritorial migration control will be discussed by reference to the concept of jurisdiction as it has been applied in different situations by international human rights bodies.

Article 33 Revisited

Article 33.1 of the 1951 Convention Relating to the Status of Refugee stipulates: "No Contracting State shall expel or return (*"refouler"*) a refugee in any manner whatsoever to the frontiers of territories where his life or freedom would be threatened on account of his race, religion, nationality, membership or a particular social group or political opinion." In 1992, the U.S. Supreme Court held that the American interdiction program toward Haitian refugees did not violate the *non-refoulement* principle set out in article 33 (*Sale v. Haitian Center Council*). The Supreme Court argued that the Refugee Convention did not, and was never intended to, apply extraterritorially. The ruling garnered substantial criticism from both scholars and other national courts (Koh 1994; Hathaway 2005, 339). Yet, the *Sale* case in several ways picks up on a much older debate on the *ratione loci* of article 33, and while the Supreme Court's jurisprudence hardly stands undisputed, it does rely in part on arguments forwarded by reputable scholars. The present section cannot detail the vast amount of evidence of each position in this half-century old debate. Yet, some remarks as to the extraterritorial applicability of article 33 are in order since, following the structure of the Refugee Convention, if the *non-refoulement* principle does not apply extraterritorially, not much else under the Refugee Convention does.

An important element in the Supreme Court's ruling concerned the preparatory work of article 33. The Supreme Court put emphasis on a remark made by the Swiss delegate to the Conference of Plenipotentiaries that the word *non-refoulement* could not be understood to apply to refugees arriving at the border, but only to those already present within the territory.[2] The Swiss interpretation was supported by a number of countries and the Dutch delegate argued that clarification of this issue was of "great importance" and asked that it be officially noted that the conference was in agreement with this interpretation before signing.[3] On the basis of these remarks, an early commentator to the convention concluded that "Art. 33 concerns refugees who have gained entry into the territory of a Contracting State, legally or illegally, but not to refugees who ask entrance into this territory. . . . In other words, if a refugee has succeeded in eluding the frontier guards, he is safe; if he has not, it is his hard luck" (Robinson 1953, 163). This interpretation subsequently drew support from Atle Grahl-Madsen, who argued that "even though '*refoulement*' may mean 'non-admittance at the frontier' . . . it is quite clear that the prohibition against '*refoulement*' in Article 33 of the 1951 Convention does not cover this aspect of the term '*refoulement*'" (Grahl-Madsen 1997, 135).

While this conclusion may be reached when relying exclusively on this part of the *travaux*, it should be noted that this was not the only interpretation forwarded during the negotiations. The Ad Hoc Committee responsible for drafting the text emphasized the interpretation that *refoulement* did, as it is customary under French and Belgian law, equally cover instances where a refugee presented himself at the border but had not yet entered the territory.[4] A similar argument may be drawn from the Ad Hoc Committee's considerations as to the wider implications of the *non-refoulement* principle. It was noted that *non-refoulement* did not, in all instances, entail an obligation of admittance, since a state could always redirect a refugee to another state, as long as he or she did not risk persecution there.[5] This would clearly presuppose an obligation by the state toward refugees not yet in its territory, whether standing at the border or encountered elsewhere.

Further, relying on the preparatory work as a primary source does not sit well with ordinary standards of interpretation. Following a more doctrinal approach, the Supreme Court in the *Sale* case also based its conclusion on the wording of article 33.2. Noting that this article exempts states from the *non-refoulement* obligation for the refugee who constitutes a "danger to the security of a country *in which he is*" (emphasis added), the Supreme Court went on to argue that since a refugee on the high seas is in no country at all, if the *non-refoulement* obligation were to apply there, it would create an anomaly where "dangerous aliens on the high seas would be entitled to the benefits of 33.1 while those residing in the country that sought to expel them would not" (*Sale v. Haitian Center Council*, 180). Based on this reasoning, the Supreme Court found it "more reasonable to assume that the coverage of 33.2 was limited to those already in the country because it was understood that 33.1 obligated the signatory state only with respect to aliens within its own territory" (ibid.).

Even though article 33.2 clearly represents a concession to national sovereignty in maintaining the right of states to expel refugees in their territory who are causing security concerns (Legomsky 2006, 689), the argument that this exception entails a territorial limitation of the *non-refoulement* obligation as such seems flawed in its underlying logic. Whereas article 33.2 is an exception to article 33.1, and thus reflects the *ratione loci, materiae, and personae* of article 33.1 and in itself sets out a subgroup of refugees from whom the protection against *refoulement* is waived, it does not conversely follow that article 33.1 is equally limited by the scope of article 33.2.[6]

In addition, the wording of article 33.1 has given rise to several arguments in favor of a more expansive reading. First, as mentioned above, the term *refoulement* does include rejection at the border within French law and the deliberate insertion in the English text next to "return" may be seen as a strong indicator that the broader ambit of the French term should prevail (Council of Europe 1965, 6). Second, there is the argument that the question of *from* where a refugee is returned is irrelevant on a closer reading of the terms employed. Article 33 sets out two proscriptions, one regarding expulsion and one regarding return. As indicated by the use of "or" between "expel" and "return" in the article, these two prohibitions should be read disjunctively. The first, expulsion, clearly refers solely to actions removing a refugee *from* a contracting state. The second prohibition, however, bans actions returning refugees *to* any territories where his life or freedom would be threatened (UN High Commissioner for Refugees 1994, 87).

Looking for the object and purpose of the *non-refoulement* principle, it seems equally hard to support a strictly territorial reading. The preamble of the convention notes the endeavor to "assure refugees the widest possible exercise of these fundamental rights and freedoms" (par. 2), which would support a wider *ratione loci*, at least where differing interpretations are possible from the wording alone. Similarly, several scholars have argued that the "essential purpose" of the *non-refoulement* principle is enshrined in the text itself, namely to prohibit "return in any manner whatsoever of refugees to countries where they may face persecution" (Goodwin-Gill and McAdam 2007, 248). This clearly emphasizes a consequentialist reading, in which it is *to* where, not *from* where, that matters.

At this stage, any continued dubiety as to the geographical scope of article 33 may be dismissed by examining subsidiary sources, such as soft law, state practice, and codification of the *non-refoulement* principle in other areas of international law. The UN High Commissioner for Refugees Executive Committee has made it clear that the protection offered by article 33 was to encompass situations at the border.[7] The Council of Europe has similarly argued that it "seems illogical a priori that a person who has succeeded in crossing the frontier illegally should enjoy greater protection than someone who presents himself legally" and that "no one shall be subjected to refusal at the frontier" (Council of Europe 1968, par. 2). Beyond the frontier, the Executive Committee has further noted that the *non-refoulement* principle must be respected whenever a state engages in interception measures and that states are "to respect scrupulously the fundamental principle of *non-refoulement*, and to make every effort to ensure the safety and well-being of refugees within their jurisdiction."[8] Lastly, the Inter-American Commission of Human Rights specifically rejected the reasoning of the U.S. Supreme Court in *Sale*, and argued that article 33 does indeed apply to persons interdicted on the high seas (*Haitian Center for Human Rights v. United States*).

As for state practice, up until the *Sale* case, scholars have found it difficult to record a single historical precedent for such extraterritorial deterrence mechanisms without some assumption of responsibility—even if only in principle (Hathaway 2005, 337). The UN High Commissioner for Refugees equally noted that, to its knowledge, no other state has resorted to the implementation of a formal policy of intercepting refugees on the high seas and repatriating them against their will (UN High Commissioner for Refugees 1994, 92). Of course, since the *Sale* case one could point to at least some additional examples of interdiction policies. Yet, while the Australian operation of the so-called Pacific Solution has been criticized for violating a number of human rights principles, it notably does not challenge the application of the *non-refoulement* principle to interdictions carried out in international waters, but rather, claims that article 33 is respected by relocating those interdicted to a third country where asylum procedures are provided (Pugh 2004; Kneebone 2006). Similarly, the European Union's interdiction schemes carried out under Frontex's auspices do assume responsibility and subsequent access to EU territory for all persons interdicted in international waters. Lastly, it is noteworthy that up until the Kennebunkport Order of 1992,[9] the United States, not only in practice but also as a matter of *opinio juris*, considered the *non-refoulement* principle to apply to actions undertaken on the high seas (Legomsky 2006, 679).

Thus, despite of the surge in attempts to enact offshore migration control, we may conclude that while some uncertainty as to the application of article 33 to situations at or beyond the border may have pertained at the time of drafting, subsequent state practice and soft law has clearly confirmed a wider *ratione loci* (Goodwin-Gill 1996, 121ff.). This would bring the geographical scope of article 33 of the Refugee Convention in line with the formulations of the *non-refoulement* principle as it has emerged in other human rights instruments. These have been expressed in the interpretation of article 3.1 of the UN Convention against Torture, article 7 of the International Covenant for Civil and Political Rights, and article 3 of the European Convention of Human Rights, all of which emphasize state jurisdiction as geographical scope. While differences *ratione loci* between human rights instruments may remain, a parsimonious interpretation of the Refugee Convention would thus subject the *non-refoulement* principle to the general proposition that as a matter of human rights states remain responsible for conduct in relation to persons "subject to or within their jurisdiction" (Lauterpacht and Bethlehem 2003, 110).

In conclusion, an interpretation of article 33 as applying only within the territory or at the borders is difficult to uphold. While those specifically looking for more restrictive interpretations may find some support in different sources, a balanced and holistic interpretation irrefutably emphasizes "jurisdiction" as the *ratione loci* of a state's obligations. The question, of course, remains how much is gained by this achievement. Not only do other rights under the Refugee Convention carry a narrower application, but the exact interpretation of what constitutes "jurisdiction" when states act extraterritorially also becomes essential if the protection offered by the *non-refoulement* principle is to have any practical significance in these situations.

Refugee Protection and the Concept of Jurisdiction

Moving past the *non-refoulement* obligation, what rights may then be claimed by the refugee encountered by the host state outside as opposed to inside its territory? The immediate answer would have to be: relatively few. As mentioned above, the Refugee Convention follows an incremental structure in which more and more rights are granted according to the level of attachment established between the refugee and the host state. By far the majority of entitlements are thus reserved for refugees who are present in the territory or have some higher attachment to the host state. For refugees who have not physically reached the territory, a state's obligation is immediately reduced to a few core rights under the convention, for which no particular level of attachment is specified. In addition to the *non-refoulement* principle, these include access to courts (art. 16) and non-discrimination (art. 3), as well as the somewhat more specific issues concerning property (art. 13), education (art. 22), and rationing (art. 20). If the analysis of the geographical scope of article 33 set out in the previous section is to be trusted, we may assume, mutatis mutandis, that these obligations are similarly owed anywhere a state is held to exercise jurisdiction (Hathaway 2005, 160ff.).

Compared to the territorial setting, extraterritorialization of migration control thus entails a rather substantial reduction of rights owed. In the ordinary operation of the refugee regime, this is of minor importance as there is a natural progressive transition toward the full extension of the entire catalogue of convention rights; the most fundamental rights are guaranteed when arriving at the border and from here more and more rights are accrued as asylum procedures are initiated, residence is granted, and so on. Yet, where this encounter takes place not at the border but extraterritorially, the progression of rights may be less certain. Thus, in scenarios where extraterritorial migration control is coupled to schemes for extraterritorial asylum procedures in offshore or third country locations, refugees may find themselves stuck at the most basic level of rights.

Similarly, the increasingly popular policies to summarily deflect asylum seekers to designated "safe third countries" may raise additional concerns when coupled with extraterritorial migration control. Most refugee scholars agree that while "safe third country" rules are not explicitly prohibited under international refugee law, such transfers of protection from one state to another do, as a minimum, require the second state to respect the full catalogue of rights already obtained by the refugee in the first state (Hathaway 2005, 333; Legomsky 2003, 612ff.). This means that a refugee arriving at the territory of a more developed country would be entailed to any right owed by that country according to the level of attachment of the refugee as "physically present" even when deflected back to a third state with more derogations to the Refugee Convention or a different interpretation of its obligations. Any shortcomings in this regard may entail the liability of the sending state (see the European Court of Human Rights case *T.I. v. United Kingdom*). Yet, for the refugee who never sets foot on the soil of the controlling state before being deflected en route to a third country, the acting state will only be bound to guarantee that the limited number of rights pertaining to refugees "within the jurisdiction" is guaranteed in the third country.

In addition, a particular problem arises where migration control is carried out by a third state from within the country of origin. This can be the case where many vessels are granted permission to patrol and intercept in the territorial waters of foreign states, where immigration liaison officers operate control in foreign airports, or by the simple denial of visas at consulates, thereby impairing the possibility of exiting the country of persecution (Byrne et al. 2002, 10ff.). In such cases all rights under the Refugee Convention are lost, since refugee status is premised upon having left the country of origin (article 1). By moving control so far forward that it even precedes flight, the very label "refugee" is deconstructed. Instead, those in need of protection are referred to the less robust rights catalogue as internally displaced and to general human rights law, which for the persecuted clearly lacks realization by the home state. An obligation under general human rights law may of course still fall upon the acting state, and it should be noted that similar formulations of the *non-refoulement* principle, such as that flowing from article 3 of the European Convention of Human Rights, does not have such a limitation.

Beyond these scenarios, it is nonetheless still fair in the majority of cases involving extraterritorial migration control to assume that as long as the cornerstone of the regime (*non-refoulement*) is guaranteed, the rest of the rights under the Refugee Convention will eventually unfold. This is in line with the analysis in the previous section and by other scholars who argue that *non-refoulement* applies wherever a state exercises jurisdiction (Davy 1996, 105ff; Plender and Mole 1999, 86; Hathaway 2005, 160ff.).

Yet, this seems to be the end of analysis for many refugee lawyers. It is simply assumed that any exercise of migration control, whether inside, at, or beyond the border, necessarily entails an exercise of jurisdiction. This view, however, finds little support under general international law.

For the purpose of engaging human rights responsibilities, the concept of jurisdiction is bound by a premise of effective control. Within the territory, this control flows from the formal entitlement to exercise sovereign authority. Beyond the territory, however, the test for establishing effective control, at least when states act in regard to foreigners, is substantially more demanding. Not all actions a state undertakes outside its territory appear to bring about such control. Yet, the establishment of jurisdiction is conversely the premise for subjecting such states to relevant obligations under international refugee and human rights law. The fundamental question of this chapter may thus be rephrased: When, if ever, is extraterritorial migration control equivalent to effective control?

The General Basis for Establishing Jurisdiction Extraterritorially

Jurisdiction is the right of a state to prescribe and enforce rules against others (Lowe 2007, 171). Within the Westphalian state system, this power is limited by competing claims to authority by other states and thus normally only exercised within the "sovereign nation cage," horizontally covering the territory and the territorial sea and vertically extending from the "von Kármán line" 50.55 miles above sea level down to the subsoil of national territory ending at the center of the earth (Palan 2003, 97). In this sense, there is a basic presumption against extraterritorial competence. As noted by the Permanent Court of International Justice in the *S.S. Lotus* case from 1927: "Now the first and foremost restriction imposed by international law upon a State is that—failing the existence of a permissive rule to the contrary—it may not exercise its power in any form in the territory of another State" (p. 14).

Yet, although this is the starting point and may cover the vast majority of a state's dealings, it is equally clear that jurisdiction is not limited to the territory. Transnational interactions, whether between states, individuals, or something in between, have entailed a need for a range of subsidiary legal bases for jurisdiction. States have thus been seen to claim extraterritorial jurisdiction over nationals and particularly serious criminals, over certain parts of the high seas (the contiguous zone), and in extreme situations of national security (Lowe 2007, 170ff.).

For the purpose of human rights, the question of jurisdiction is not one of authority but responsibility, regardless of the legal entitlements to a state's actions. When states themselves move outside this "sovereign nation cage," assertions of jurisdiction may generally be conceived of in two ways for the purpose of human rights obligations—as a property flowing from a state's effective control over a defined *territory*, or as a result of a state's exercise of authority or control over an *individual*. The first is clearly derived from the principle of national sovereignty, extending jurisdiction to all geographical areas where a state exercises de facto sovereign control, such as in the case of military occupation. As was shown in both *Loizidou v. Turkey* (see the judgment of merits of 18 December 1996) and *Cyprus v. Turkey* (2001), of the European Court of Human Rights, responsibilities in such situations not only pertain to acts conducted directly by government agents, but also to any act or omission leading to human rights violations conducted within the area where effective control is upheld.

Extraterritorial jurisdiction conceived as effective control over an individual has been established in a number of cases where state agents act inside another state, whether unlawfully or following agreement between those states. In *López Burgos v. Uruguay* (UN Doc. Supp. no. 40 [A/36/40, 6 June 1979]) the Human Rights Committee held that the arrest and subsequent mistreatment of the applicant by Uruguayan Security Forces inside Argentina *did* bring him within Uruguayan jurisdiction. Similarly, the European Court of Human Rights established Turkish jurisdiction in *Öcalan v. Turkey* (first judgment of 12 March 2003), involving the arrest and forcible return of the PKK leader Abdullah Öcalan in the Nairobi airport in Kenya. The argument for asserting jurisdiction in these situations seems to reflect a more universalist principle not to set double standards.

It is important to underline, however, that just as there is a presumption against the competence of states to exert power extraterritorially, so there seems to be one as regards the establishment of human rights responsibility when moving outside the sovereign nation cage. Under both the personal and spatial notions set out above, *extra*territorial jurisdiction is conceived of as *extra*ordinary. Thus, despite the proliferation of extraterritorial state functions in a globalized world, territorial jurisdictional competence has remained the point of departure. In practice, international bodies have thus applied rather high tests in order to establish extraterritorial jurisdiction for the purpose of human rights responsibilities. In the case of extraterritorial jurisdiction conceived as control over a geographic area, this has so far demanded a high degree of structural control over a well-defined area. For extraterritorial jurisdiction over individuals inside a foreign jurisdiction, affirmative case law has similarly been limited to instances involving abduction or physical detention.

In the following, these tests for establishing effective control shall be considered with regard to three distinct spheres. The first sets out by examining not where extraterritorial obligations end, but rather where they start. States excising parts of their territory or designating "international zones" have become increasingly popular, but do they qualify as extraterritorial? Second, the "basic" or "pure" situations of extraterritorial obligations are analyzed, as migration control is moved to the high seas, or *terra nullius*. And third, the more "complex" question of extraterritorial obligations under international refugee law is taken on, namely, those situations where extraterritorial migration control is moved unto the territory of a third state and thus involves the simultaneous potential jurisdiction of the territorial state.

Withdrawal of Authority and Excision of Territory

The first issue to consider is the growing trend to withdraw authority from parts of a state's territory, whether simply de facto or by excising certain geographic areas through national legislation. This may be argued by some to fall outside a discussion of extraterritoriality. Yet, it is a logical corollary of applying the jurisdiction approach in order to delimit, *ratione loci*, state responsibilities toward refugees. If it is submitted that jurisdiction is primarily territorial and flows from a state's effective control over a given geographic area, does state jurisdiction collapse when this control ceases, either because another polity overtakes it or because a state self-imposes restrictions to its territorial sway? The latter situation is particularly interesting, as an affirmative answer would suggest that extraterritoriality can be constructed at will when states declare that part or all of their authority is henceforth withdrawn from a given area.

A number of states seem to think that this is the case and that such withdrawal of authority, whether de facto or de jure, may relinquish them of asylum and refugee protection obligations otherwise owed. This has found various expressions in national policies and legislation. In addition to its interdiction policies on the high seas, the United States has maintained a "wet-foot, dry-foot" policy in regards to Cuban asylum seekers that effectively exempts U.S. territorial waters for asylum purposes. Under the 1995 Cuban Migration Agreement, all Cubans interdicted, whether on the high seas or in territorial waters ("wet-foots"), have thus been returned directly to Cuba, while those who manage to reach U.S. shores ("dry-foots") have been allowed to stay. While the agreement does include a concomitant obligation by Cuba not to subject those returned to reprisals and allow resettlement of those found to have a valid refugee claim, the U.S. oversight mechanisms to ensure their implementation are unlikely to be efficient (Werlau 2004, 11). The radical distinction reached absurd dimensions when, on 5 January 2006, fifteen Cubans clinging on to a bridge in the Florida Keys were repatriated by the Coast Guard with the argument that the decommissioned bridge had been physically cut off from the beach and thus did not constitute U.S. soil (Wasem 2007).

Even more encompassing, yet clearly inspired by the U.S. example, Australia has passed laws to excise more than three thousand islands, certain coastal ports, and northern coastal stretches as well as its territorial waters from its "migration zone" (Kneebone 2006, 697). Under the amended Migration Act of 1958, no asylum claims are permitted outside the migration zone. Asylum seekers who do arrive in these excised territories, dubbed "offshore entry persons," are instead transferred to third countries declared by the minister of immigration to provide effective asylum procedures and with whom Australia holds agreements for offshore asylum processing (Goodwin-Gill and McAdam 2007, 256).

Lastly, several states have claimed that "international zones" or "transit areas" in ports and airports do not form part of the national territory of the state in which they are situated. The United Kingdom has taken the position that an asylum seeker arriving at one of its airports has not reached U.K. territory until he or she encounters the U.K. immigration authorities (Nicholson 1997, 618). With the increased delegation of migration control to private carriers and security companies (Guiraudon 2002), refugees may find themselves unable to access such authorities after their arrival and instead be confined to these international zones effectively under private authority. Thus, the "Sheremetyevo 2" transit zone at the airport in Moscow has been known to hold refugees denied onward flights to western Europe with no access to Russian immigration authorities and thus nowhere to direct asylum claims. The zone is in practice controlled by the carriers, which decide whether onward travel may be allowed or return flights arranged in order to avoid the heavy fines due for flying in unauthorized individuals to an EU country (Nicholson 1997, 598–99).[10]

From the standpoint of international law, however, such arrangements for withdrawing specific exercises of executive power, in this case asylum, from certain geographic areas otherwise regarded as a state's sovereign territory have little merit. The question of international airport zones was specifically dealt with by the European Court of Human Rights in *Amuur v. France* (1996), concerning the detention and subsequent removal of four Somali asylum seekers from the international zone of Paris-Orly Airport. The French authorities held that the international zone was different from French territory. Within the zone no interpreters, legal assistance, or private assistance was allowed and the French Office for the Protection of Refugees denied the applicants access to the asylum procedure on the grounds that it lacked jurisdiction (Bello and Kokott 1997, 148). Nevertheless, the court was quite assertive when concluding that "despite its name, the international zone does not have extraterritorial status" and that regardless of national legislation to the opposite, holding the applicants in this zone made them subject to French law (par.

52). In its judgment, the court put emphasis on the fact that for all other purposes, France exercised sovereign authority in this zone and thus that the protections afforded under both the Refugee Convention and the European Court of Human Rights must be afforded (par. 43).

Yet, even in cases where such authority and control can be seriously questioned, case law seems to support the general presumption that jurisdiction extends to the entirety of a state's formally recognized territory. In *Ilascu and Others v. Moldova and Russia* (2004), concerning acts committed by the authorities of the Moldavian Republic of Transdniestria (a self-proclaimed independent polity not internationally recognized), the Grand Chamber of the European Court of Human Rights held that *both* Russia and Moldova had jurisdiction: Russia by the fact that it asserted decisive influence over the regional regime, Moldova by the fact that it held de jure sovereignty over the area. Notably, it was recognized that Moldova did not exercise effective control over the area, yet that "positive obligations" remained to take all measures within its power to ensure the rights under the convention (par. 331). The establishment of Moldavian responsibility has been substantially criticized as moving past the necessary link between human rights obligations and the actual ability of states to ensure them (Roxstrom et al. 2005, 127), yet the ruling does underline the primacy of formal territorial readings in ascribing human rights responsibility.

From the perspective of refugee rights, these rulings are important in cementing the conclusion that jurisdiction cannot be retracted at will and thus that as a matter of international law situations of extraterritoriality do not arise despite the legal fictions attempted through national policies or legislation. This position finds ample support in the case law of other international human rights institutions. In regard to the U.S. detention of Cuban asylum seekers in Guantánamo, the Inter-American Commission noted that the protections set out in the American Declaration of the Rights and Duties of Man must be extended to any petitioner "present in the territory or otherwise under the authority or control of that state" regardless of domestic laws to the contrary (*Ferrer-Mazorra v. the United States*).

This said, the applicability of international law does not preclude states from installing special border procedures under national law as long as they are consistent herewith. Notably, Australia's Pacific Strategy never challenged its international obligations, but it deterred any refugees arriving in its excised territories to protection in third countries that have been declared safe. Similarly, a number of countries maintain particular expedient asylum procedures for those arriving at international airports or are intercepted within territorial waters, and the EU Asylum Procedures Directive permits special and accelerated procedures for applications made at the borders.[11] States with more developed asylum systems that normally ensure a wide and comprehensive rights catalogue to refugees arriving at their territories remain free to withdraw the application of any or all of these rights in such areas as long as the resultant treatment does not fall short of international obligations. Yet, the risk of falling below this threshold obviously increases the closer a state seeks to approximate its policy thereto. This causes a particular concern for the refugee who, if she even makes it that far, almost inevitably encounters the state within these marginal zones.

In addition, the general principles set out in these cases may inform our onward quest in determining extraterritorial obligations vis-à-vis refugees on the high seas and in foreign territorial jurisdictions. The principal lesson from the *Amuur* case is that states cannot divide their authority according to different competences. Sovereign powers cannot be assumed for one purpose while being excluded regarding others—from the assumption of authority in regard to migration control follows the concomitant responsibilities in respect of asylum seekers and refugees. From the *Ilascu* case it appears that even an actual withdrawal of authority over parts of the territory does not relinquish a state from its obligations under international human rights and refugee law to asylum seekers who might arrive there. Moreover, if the "positive obligations" doctrine is to be trusted, these responsibilities not only amount to respect for the principle of *non-refoulement*, but also to a positive duty to make available the entire nexus of rights owed to refugees physically present in these locations (Hathaway 2005, 171).

Interception on the High Seas

Moving beyond political claims to extraterritoriality within a state's formal territory, the first real situation of extraterritoriality then appears when states act in geographic areas not pertaining to the territorial jurisdiction of any sovereign, also referred to as *terra nullius*. Lacking any examples of refugees attempting to cross the poles, such considerations may in practice be limited to the high seas. Shifting migration control to international waters is not a new phenomenon. With the rise of boat refugees in the 1970s and 1980s, high-sea interception practices quickly became a favored response of coastal states concerned with mass influx. The U.S. interception program of Haitian boat refugees has already been mentioned. Similarly, the Australian Pacific Solution also included interception of unauthorized migrant vessels in international waters (Pugh 2004; Kneebone 2006). In southern Europe, migration control on the high seas has been carried out by Italy in the Adriatic, by France and Greece in the Mediterranean, and by Spain both in the Mediterranean and the Atlantic outside the Canary Islands (Lutterbeck 2006).

In the European context, international interception operations are currently being expanded and have now come under EU auspices with operational activities being coordinated by the European Union's border agency, Frontex. So far, two missions have involved interdiction outside the European Union's territorial waters. One was the "Nautilus Operation" that took place in October 2006, during which patrols were carried out in the international waters off the Mediterranean to prevent migration from Libya reaching Malta, Sicily, or Lampedusa. While this mission was originally conceived to incorporate Libya, thus allowing for EU vessels to patrol within Libyan territorial waters, it was nonetheless hailed as a success with the claim that migrants had been completely prevented from arriving in Malta during the time of operation. The second operation was HERA II, set to curb the migration flow toward the Canary Islands, which has involved an array of airplanes, helicopters, and navy ships. This operation intercepted 14,572 individuals on the high seas during its five months of operation beginning in August 2006 and the mission is being continued, covering both high seas and the territorial waters of Senegal, Mauritania, and Cape Verde (Frontex 2006).

To what extent are states undertaking such interdiction operations on the high seas bound by international law not to return those intercepted claiming asylum or fearing torture or other inhumane treatment? So far national courts and governments have varied somewhat in their interpretation of the jurisdictional implications in such situations. U.S. interdiction policies are clearly based on an exclusively territorial conception of jurisdiction and the application *ratione loci* of the *non-refoulement* obligation. This understanding was upheld by the U.S. Supreme Court in *Sale v. Haitian Center Council*, which not only proposed a strictly territorial reading of the Refugee Convention, but also denied that the United States had jurisdiction when operating Coast Guard vessels in international waters with reference to a general presumption against extraterritoriality emanating from principles of national sovereignty.

Yet, both the reasoning and the conclusions of the *Sale* verdict have been widely criticized as "erroneous" and essentially "political" (Goodwin-Gill 1994; UN High Commissioner for Refugees 1994; Hathaway 2005, 339). Clearly there are exceptions to such a presumption against extraterritorial jurisdiction, and the U.S. Supreme Court soon after overturned it in its litigation involving competition law (Koh 1994, 2418). The U.K. Court of Appeal bluntly concluded that *Sale v. Haitian Center Council* was "wrongly decided; it certainly offends one's sense of fairness" (*R. v. Immigration Officer*). The *Sale* case in this sense provides an excellent example of why national court decisions, even from the highest instance, should not be regarded as final settlements. As Harold Koh has pointed out, even though such cases are considered waypoints in the "complex enforcement" of the otherwise self-executing Refugee Convention, in Europe such decisions are routinely being overturned by the European Court of Human Rights (Koh 1994, 2406).

Looking instead to the jurisprudence of international human rights institutions, the Inter-American Commission issued a report specifically rejecting *Sale* and affirming the applicability of article 33 of the Refugee Convention in situations involving migration control on the high seas (*Haitian Center v. United States*). The report is fully in line with previous case law extending the notion of effective control over individuals in cases concerning international waters. In the so-called *Brothers to the Rescue* case (*Alejandre v. Cuba* 1999), Cuba was never held to control any specific geographic area of international air space or the high seas when it shot down two planes deemed to be outside Cuba's twelve miles of territorial waters. Yet, the commission argued that states' jurisdiction encompasses "all the persons under their actual authority and responsibility" (par. 24, citing *Cyprus v. Turkey* [2001]) and that since an analysis of the facts found that "the victims died as consequence of direct actions of agents of the Cuban state" this was "sufficient evidence to show that the agents of the Cuban state, despite being outside its territory, subjected to their authority the civil pilots" (par. 25).

A single precedent for establishing jurisdiction in situations involving migration control in international waters can also be found in the jurisprudence of the European Court of Human Rights. In the *Xhavara* case, an Italian navy vessel seeking to stop and inspect suspected irregular migrants onboard the Albanian ship *Kater I Rades* ended up colliding with and sinking the ship. The incident became known as the "Otranto tragedy" and eighty-three people are assumed to have died as a result of the collision, though not all bodies could be recovered. Italy operated under a bilateral agreement with Albania that allowed Italian officials to board Albanian vessels wherever encountered, but the collision occurred on the high seas, thirty-five miles off the Italian coast in the Strait of Otranto. The court eventually held the case to be inadmissible due to non-exhaustion of national remedies. Yet, the court did consider Italy to have exercised jurisdiction and in principle held Italy responsible for instigating a full and independent investigation into the deaths under article 2—a requirement that Italy was considered to have fulfilled already by having initialized public manslaughter proceedings against the captain of the Italian vessel (*Xhavara v. Italy and Albania*).

In sum, the presumption that states do incur obligations under international refugee and human rights law when exercising migration control on the high seas is strong. Looking beyond rare examples of strictly territorial interpretations by national courts, international human rights jurisprudence uniformly supports an interpretation that jurisdiction is established when state agents undertake sovereign functions or otherwise assert authority in *terra nullius*. In doing so, both the Inter-American Commission and the European Court of Human Rights seemingly adopted a broader concept of extraterritorial jurisdiction over individuals. While it is fairly likely that bringing intercepted asylum seekers onboard vessels of the intercepting states would reach the threshold of effective control over an individual set by such cases as *Öcalan* or *López Burgos*, the victims of *Xhavara* or *Brothers to the Rescue* were not brought within the physical detention or control of the acting state.

The reasoning in these cases appears to follow what could be termed a *functional* approach to jurisdiction.[12] What matters is not some abstract or generalized test of personal or geographic control, but rather the specific power or authority assumed by the state acting extraterritorially in a given capacity. Jurisdiction in this sense flows from the de facto relationship established between an individual and a state through the very act itself, or the *potential* of acting. As is also evident from *Brothers to the Rescue*, rather than having a general test as a distinct issue of admissibility, the issue of jurisdiction hereby becomes integrated in the analysis of the facts and liability of the state in question.

This approach stands in some contrast to the examples of formal territorialism that may be relied upon in situations of excision and that have been expressed in cases such as *Ilascu*, where the lack of such a relationship was overlooked in favor of official sovereign entitlements. Under a functional conception of extraterritorial jurisdiction, the test becomes entirely case specific. Certain situations involving interception at sea may continue to fall below the threshold for establishing jurisdiction. Yet, a case that on the merits would hold a state responsible under the *non-refoulement* prohibition for actions occurring within the territory could be argued by this fact alone to engage the jurisdiction of states in similar instances occurring on the high seas.

From a human rights perspective, this conclusion may appear somewhat banal, bordering on the tautological. Any other interpretation would simply lead to an unacceptable result. As Louis Henkin noted in relation to the *Sale* case, "It is incredible that states that had agreed not to force any human being back into the hands of his/her oppressors intended to leave themselves—and each other—free to reach out beyond the territory to seize a refugee and to return him/her to the country from which he sought to escape" (Henkin 1993, 1). Similarly, the European Court of Human Rights has asserted that it would be "unconscionable . . . to allow a State party to perpetrate violations of the Convention on the territory of another State, which it could not perpetrate on its own territory" (*Issa v. Turkey*)[13] and thereby establish a "gap or vacuum in human rights protection" (*Cyprus v. Turkey*). Yet, not only may such a functional test of jurisdiction be markedly different from the simple presumption of jurisdiction in the territorial context, as we shall see it is also challenged by this very presumption as the locus is moved from *terra nullius* to the sovereign territory of another state.

Migration Control within a Foreign Territorial Jurisdiction

Compared to the practices of excision or interception in international waters, migration control within a third state's territorial jurisdiction encompasses a much wider range of policies. From the control performed at visa consulates, over the deployment of immigration liaison officers, to interception in foreign territorial waters, policies to bring the different layers of migration control closer and closer to the sites of departure have expanded substantially over the last years (Boswell 2003; Gammeltoft-Hansen 2007). The role and responsibility of these activities vary substantially. More than twenty-two European and North American countries have deployed immigration liaison officers to the vulnerable and hard to patrol border lands between Russia and Ukraine (Gatev 2006, 10). While according to EU guidelines such officers "do not carry out any tasks relating to the sovereignty of States," they clearly have the competence to advise and support national border guards and in some instances expanded authority to access police and border records (ibid.).

In other instances, authority is asserted more directly. Under the juxtaposed controls scheme, the United Kingdom thus controls demarcated zones at the ports of Calais, Dunkerque, and Boulogne where, pursuant to agreements with France, British migration law is enforced without modifications. Under the most recent amendments the actual control may even be outsourced to private contractors.[14] Similarly, in extension of the Frontex interception mission outside the Canary Islands, bilateral arrangements were made to allow interception not just on the high seas but also inside Cape Verdean, Senegalese, and Mauritanian territorial sea, contiguous zone, or air space.

Shifting migration control to third country territories may thus be equally characterized as processes of outsourcing and privatization rather than merely extraterritorialization. For the purpose of determining extraterritorial legal obligations, this raises a number of additional challenges. First, the question of establishing international responsibility of states aiding and abetting another state or private party in committing acts violating international refugee law is somewhat distinct from that of establishing responsibility for acts conducted by the state's own agents in an extraterritorial locus. The former question is largely beyond the scope of this chapter, yet recourse may no doubt be found in the International Law Commission's Articles on State Responsibility.[15]

Second, as a practical issue, accessing dealings and agreements conducted between states for the purpose of migration control is often cumbersome. Much foreign policy is cloaked in secrecy, and trade-offs for entering into arrangements regarding migration control may involve a number of different policy areas ranging from development aid and trade concessions to pure diplomacy (Gammeltoft-Hansen 2006). Establishing the exact authority granted to states exercising migration control inside a third country may thus be a complex and tricky endeavor.

Last, clearly categorizing a particular situation as one or the other may be difficult, and creative labeling itself becomes a strategy for avoiding extraterritorial obligations. In the case of the Frontex missions, Senegalese immigration officers are thus brought on board European ships and argued by Frontex to be formally in charge of rejecting migrants' passages to international waters. Consequently, any vessel intercepted within the territorial waters of the cooperating states is turned back either to its port of departure or to a port within the territorial waters where the interception occurred. During 2006, 3,665 persons were intercepted in these zones and directly returned. No possibilities to initiate asylum claims were given (Frontex 2006).

These issues notwithstanding, the first question to ask is whether the jurisdictional assessment changes when migration control is moved onward from the high seas to the territory or territorial waters of a third state. For the cases where migration control is established extraterritorially by asserting authority over a well-defined geographic area, the presumption of jurisdiction would be strong. Extraterritorial jurisdiction in the spatial sense could be argued to apply in the case of the U.K. juxtaposed control scheme where a defined zone is clearly appropriated for enforcing U.K. domestic law. Similarly, cases where the actual control is followed by a transfer of asylum seekers to defined camps or enclosures located outside the territory are likely to fulfill the criteria. As part of the U.S. interception of Haitian boat refugees, four thousand Haitians were at one stage directed to the American naval base in Guantánamo, where they were promised "safe haven." When they were subsequently forced back to Haiti, several refugee organizations considered this to constitute *refoulement* (Legomsky 2006). In 2003, the United Kingdom proposed a similar model whereby all asylum seekers intercepted in the Mediterranean or at the borders of an EU country would be sent back to "transit processing centres" in countries such as Morocco (U.K. Home Office 2003). Even though the plan was never realized, several scholars have argued that the operation of such centers would in all likelihood entail obligations under the European Convention of Human Rights (Noll 2003).

Other cases may be less straightforward. International law has traditionally described a ship exercising government functions as "float-ing territory"[16] and the argument could be made that naval intercep-tion in, for example, Senegalese territorial waters on this basis could entail jurisdiction. Yet, the presence of Senegalese immigration officers on board Frontex ships is clearly a move to underline not only that this is Senegalese territorial jurisdiction, but also that the actual denial of onward passage is conducted by Senegalese authorities.[17] Similarly, the granting or denial of visas to asylum seekers, though an act normally conducted from within a consular facility where the sending state holds certain immunities from the jurisdictional competence of the territo-rial state, has generally been held as insufficient to constitute *refoulement* under the Refugee Convention, both for lack of a sufficient causal link and for lack of authority (Noll 2003, 552–53; Goodwin-Gill 1996, 252; but see Lauterpacht and Bethlehem 2003, 112).

In these and other situations, the applicability of refugee law will in-stead have to rely on the possibility of establishing extraterritorial juris-diction in the personal sense. As noted above, this does find support in certain cases involving the apprehension or abduction of an individual in a third country. Both the *López Burgos* and *Öcalan* cases were reasoned by a concern to avoid "double standards" between the territorial and extraterritorial loci. According to the Human Rights Committee the "ju-risdiction test" thus "does not imply that the State . . . cannot be held accountable for violations of rights under the Covenant which its agents commit upon the territory of another State, whether with the acquies-cence of the Government of that State or in opposition to it" (*Lilian Celiberti de Casariego v. Uruguay*, UN Doc. CCPR/C/OP/1, par. 10).

On first look, this principled assertion seems to support a more ex-pansive reading of the jurisdiction concept, similar to that forwarded in the case law regarding actions in international waters and airspace. Yet, other case law emphasizes a rather high test for the level of con-trol a state needs to assert vis-à-vis an individual in order to establish extraterritorial jurisdiction in the personal understanding. Notably, to the surprise of many, the admissibility decision of the Grand Chamber of the European Court of Human Rights in *Banković and Others v. Belgium and 16 Other Contracting States* did not find that the killing of relatives of the applicants by NATO smart bombs was enough to establish effective control. Similarly, while extraterritorial jurisdiction over a certain area of Iraq was in principle established when Turkish forces entered into Kurdish Iraq, the court in *Issa* dismissed the case on the basis that it could not be established that the shooting down of Iraqi shepherds oc-curred within the zone in which Turkish armed forces had jurisdiction (pars. 74 and 81).

How are we to interpret this seeming contradiction? The criterion applied is perhaps best illustrated by the ruling of the House of Lords in *Al-Skeini v. Secretary of State for Defence*. The case concerned six deaths of Iraqi civilians. Five of them had been shot by U.K. armed forces or caught in cross fire during British patrols. The last claimant, Mr. Mousa, had been detained at a British military base in Basra at which he was brutally beaten and died from his wounds. Yet, according to the House of Lords only this last case fell within the jurisdiction of the United Kingdom. As regards actions taking place in the territory of a foreign state, it thus appears that a distinction can be made between cases where states exercise complete and physical control over an individual, such as in the case of arrest or physical detention, and situations that only *result* in violations of human rights on foreign soil or territorial waters, even when these instances are so important that they infringe the right to life (art. 2).

Under such a reading, it becomes harder to establish jurisdiction when a state operates migration control within the territorial jurisdiction of a foreign state. Does rejection of onward passage by an immigration officer entail effective control in the personal sense? Does turning back a ship in foreign territorial waters? As mentioned above, an argument could be made in cases where officials of intercepting vessels physically board ships or detain those on board, but it is more doubtful whether merely denying onward passage or escorting vessels back is sufficient to meet the test of extraterritorial personal jurisdiction. Failing these tests, jurisdiction conflicts are resolved by returning to the basic territorial principles for dividing responsibilities.

The "Double Standard": Between a Territorial and a Functional Reading of Extraterritorial Jurisdiction

In the above, we set out to see how the concept of jurisdiction was applied in three distinct spheres. For situations involving excision of territory and claims of non-responsibility in "international zones," the case law is unequivocal. States are not free to withdraw jurisdiction from certain parts of their territory, and even in cases where effective control is doubtful the presumption of jurisdiction may remain based on a formal territorialist reading. In the second sphere, state actions undertaken in *terra nullius*, the approach to jurisdiction has been quite different. The emphasis has not been on testing effective control *strictu sensu*, but on establishing a meaningful jurisdictional link based on the actual relation between the state and the individual in the given situation. The interpretation in these cases has been rather embracive and the guiding principle clearly a concern to avoid "double standards" in the adjudication of human rights.

For cases where extraterritorial actions occur within the realm of another territorial sovereign, however, yet another approach is taken. In this sphere, the two lenses applied above are seemingly interpolated. The aim to avoid a "gap or vacuum in human rights protection" (*Cyprus v. Turkey*, par. 78) in such situations remains, yet it is tempered by the conflicting concern that stresses the sovereign nation cage as the primary basis for establishing jurisdiction. The result is the exceedingly abstract and seemingly arbitrary "effective control" test employed in cases such as *Banković* and *Al-Skeini*. In this line of reasoning, jurisdiction is neither taken as a given nor necessarily linked to the question of state responsibility; instead it becomes a separate test in which the conflicting basis for territorial jurisdiction has to be overcome in order for the "exceptional" situation of extraterritorial jurisdiction to materialize (*Banković*, par. 59–61).

The law on jurisdiction is geared to avoid overlapping or competing claims to jurisdiction by several states. For situations involving extraterritorial control over a geographic area, this conflict is easier to resolve, as a sufficient degree of structural and/or military authority would normally exclude the presence of similar control being exercised by the territorial state within that area. In cases involving control or power exercised over an individual, the test becomes more difficult. The personal notion of jurisdiction does not exclude the presence of a territorial state holding simultaneous jurisdiction. From the case law above, the result seems to be a retreat to a micro-variation of the territorial interpretation where jurisdiction is only asserted when the individual is under the exclusive and full physical control of the state in question, which effectively nullifies any competing authority. Anything short of this threshold is defaulted back to the jurisdiction of the territorial state.

From the perspective of the refugee and other human rights victims, the regrettable thing about this jurisprudence is that it effectively ends up doing exactly what it set out to avoid. A double standard is clearly created where states remain free to engage in human rights violations on foreign soil that would in principle entail responsibility for similar conduct at home, and likely also if carried out on the high seas. The "vacuum in human rights protection" thus persists both as a matter of law and as a matter of realization and may be a key reason that international cooperation regarding migration control is growing increasingly fashionable.

None of this resonates well with the *telos* of international refugee law. Recalling the words of Louis Henkin during the drafting of article 33 of the Refugee Convention, it should not matter whether a state encounters the refugee before or after he crosses the frontier: "the problem remains the same . . . he must not be turned back to a country where his life and freedom could be threatened".[18]

At the core of the present interpretation is a seeming inability to escape principles of national sovereignty. For the purpose of jurisdiction this seems to entail at least two dogmas. First, jurisdiction is conceived to be *exclusive*. This can be derived from the *S. S. Lotus* quote above establishing the principle *par in parem non habet imperium*—a state has no authority within another state. Regardless of the fact that in most situations of extraterritorial migration control permission is granted by the territorial state, the jurisdiction litigation seems adamant to avoid conflicting claims. As a result, the test of effective control becomes a question of either-or, with any doubt cast in favor of the territorial state.

The second dogma is that jurisdiction is conceived to be all inclusive or *total*. As professed by the European Court of Human Rights in the *Banković* case, "Article 1 does not provide any support . . . that [jurisdiction] can be divided and tailored in accordance with the particular circumstances of the extra-territorial act in question" (par. 75). This view is equally derived from a territorial conceptualization of jurisdiction and has been readily transferred to cases involving spatial extraterritorial control (see, for example, *Loizidou v. Turkey*; *Cyprus v. Turkey*; Roxstrom et al. 2005, 84).

However, the question is whether these two creeds can continue to be upheld in an increasingly globalized world. As for *exclusivity*, the proliferation of auxiliary legal bases for jurisdiction makes coexisting and competing jurisdictional claims unavoidable. While in the majority of cases such conflicts may be resolved by deferral to territorial primacy, this may not always be the preferred solution (Lowe 2007, 181). Indeed, non-exclusive approaches to jurisdiction are already reflected in several areas of international law. The European Union could be described as an example of a functionally limited polity essentially operating within the same geographic area as its sovereign Member States that demands us "to conceive of autonomy without territorial exclusivity" (Walker 2003, 23). Finally, while one may disagree on the premise for asserting Moldavian jurisdiction in *Ilascu*, it does set an important precedent for establishing double jurisdiction.

In regards to the question of *totality*, the conclusion that extraterritorial jurisdiction must in all cases encompass the entire rights catalogue owed seems equally flawed. Again, the European Union and its member states spring to mind as an example where authority is clearly divided and tailored along different competences and subject matters. Similarly, there is no logical reason to assume that the extent of obligations cannot change and be adapted to the circumstances as a state moves outside its territory. The Refugee Convention itself is an example that rights may be afforded incrementally, taking heed of state concerns that not all obligations may be realizable as soon as state responsibility is triggered.

In contrast to the conception flowing from national sovereignty, the case law concerning state actions in *terra nullius* is illuminating and provides another pathway to the problem of extraterritorial jurisdiction. Within a *functional* conception of extraterritorial jurisdiction, the deciding factor is not "the place where the violation occurred, but rather the relationship between the individual and the State in relation to a violation of any of the rights set forth in the Covenant, wherever they occurred" (*López Burgos*, par. 12.2). This approach applies the basic principle of human rights law that power entails obligations (Lawson 2004, 86). In the words of Cassel, summarizing the jurisprudence of the Inter-American Commission: "Where a State can kill a person outside its territory, it exercises sufficient control over that person to be held accountable for violating his right to life" (Cassel 2004, 177). Importantly, however, this does not amount to holding states responsible for human rights violations all over the globe or extend the entire nexus of convention rights to any individual wherever the state encounters her; the extent of obligations follows from the functional relationship established.

In addition, a non-exclusive approach to jurisdiction does not necessarily entail that in practice the state acting extraterritorially must in all cases take on a protection burden. In the words of the UNHCR's Executive Committee, "The State within whose sovereign territory, or territorial waters, interception takes place has the primary responsibility for addressing any protection needs of intercepted persons."[19]

This principle would seem to suggest that to the extent that full and effective protection can be guaranteed by the territorial state, this would be the preferred party to take on protection obligations. However, crucial in this interpretation is the establishment that where this is not the case an underlying responsibility is borne by the state exercising extraterritorial jurisdiction for ensuring that protection obligations are met, and this may involve initiating asylum procedures and relocation to the territory of the acting state where refugee rights cannot be guaranteed by the territorial state.

Between these two fundamentally different conceptions of extraterritorial jurisdiction, it remains to be seen whether human rights litigation will continue to cling to notions of national sovereignty or whether a functional conception, more in line with progressions in other areas of international law, will eventually find its way even in cases involving extraterritorial acts committed on a foreign state's territory. It is as if there is a fundamental barrier that is hard to move past, a conceptual history that makes it cognitively difficult to conceive of jurisdiction not tied to territorial claims.

In essence, the relation between territorial and functional conceptions of jurisdiction may be much like the relation between Newtonian physics and quantum mechanics. Quantum mechanics was developed because classical physics theory had become inapt in explaining phenomena at the atomic level and dissolves the distinction between waves and particles, light and matter, much like a notion of functional jurisdiction dissolves the distinction between each polity's exclusive sphere of authority assumed under the territorial conceptualization of jurisdiction.

Yet, as Niels Bohr was acutely aware, even though the phenomena he wanted to explain fell outside of existing theory, the very description of his theory, and of the experimental setups, would have to conform to the language and rules of traditional physics for others to accept it (Bohr 1957, 88). Thus, the distinction between matter and light has survived in everyday usage, and matter and light are seen as epistemically distinct categories. Despite wide acceptance, quantum mechanics has remained what has been termed a "border theorem." That is, it is a conceptual framework mainly employed to describe highly abstract physics, yet one that does not replace classical physics theory but merely limits its field of application (Rozental 1955, 327).

Similarly, the language of national sovereignty and its associated norms of territorial exclusivity in both competence and responsibility are unlikely to falter with the advent of offshore migration control or similar problems of extraterritorial obligations. As long as the world still consists of sovereign states, territorial jurisdiction will remain the epistemic starting point and remain apt as the normative framework to guide the majority of situations where state actions are carried out and effected within the respective national boundaries. When confronted with the growing exception of extraterritoriality, this is the backdrop for any judiciary. It will thus remain a challenge for both national and international courts to develop a concept of jurisdiction that fits our global age while still couching it within the language of national sovereignty and territorial principles.

Chapter 4
Diagonal Environmental Rights

John H. Knox

Environmental rights are "diagonal" if they are held by individuals or groups against the governments of states other than their own. The potential importance of such rights is obvious: governments' actions regularly affect the environment beyond their jurisdiction, either directly (by taking actions themselves, from building dams to bombing cities) or indirectly (by financing, authorizing, regulating, or failing to regulate private actors). Those who live in and rely upon the environment affected would like to be able to exercise rights against the governments causing them harm. Although international law has not adopted a comprehensive, uniform approach to such rights, human rights law and international environmental law (IEL) have begun to develop some possible bases for diagonal environmental rights.

Human rights law operates primarily along a vertical axis, setting out individuals' rights against their governments and the corresponding duties owed by the governments, but it may also be diagonal, giving rise to duties on the part of states that extend beyond their own territories. As the chapters of this book illustrate, the scope and extent of diagonal human rights are often controversial. Environmental rights face additional difficulties. With the exception of two regional treaties, human rights agreements do not include a free-standing right to environmental protection. Tribunals have recognized that environmental protection implicates particular human rights, including the rights to life, health, and property, but the nature of the protection required by those rights has clarified only gradually, on a case-by-case basis. To the extent that human rights require environmental protection when aligned vertically, it would be logical to conclude that they require the same degree of protection whenever they may be aligned diagonally. As the first section of this chapter explains, however, human rights law provides few precedents to support that conclusion.

Compared to human rights law, international environmental law provides a clearer and more specific set of duties with respect to environmental protection. Moreover, most IEL has an extraterritorial focus, in that it requires states to regulate actions within their control that could harm the environment beyond their territory. The problem with grounding diagonal environmental rights in IEL is that, in contrast to human rights law, most IEL operates along a horizontal axis: its duties are owed by states to other states, not to private actors. If the challenge for human rights law is to extend rights from the vertical axis to the diagonal, the challenge for IEL is to derive diagonal rights from horizontal ones.

One way to achieve this result would be for violations of horizontal IEL duties to give rise to claims not only by affected states, but also by private actors within those states. Compliance mechanisms open to individuals and groups are very unusual in IEL because governments are reluctant to grant private parties the right to pursue remedies for violations of state-to-state obligations. Still, private actors do have access to some IEL compliance mechanisms. In addition, IEL has established other bases for diagonal environmental rights. It has developed a principle of non-discrimination, which provides that each state must give non-residents affected by transboundary harm rights equivalent to the rights its residents have under its domestic environmental laws. The disadvantage of this principle is that it provides no floor: if domestic law does not provide vertical rights, it need not provide diagonal rights, either. Combining the non-discrimination principle with minimum vertical rights would establish the securest possible basis for diagonal rights. The 1998 Aarhus Convention exemplifies this approach. Although the scope of the Aarhus Convention is limited to certain procedural rights, and its membership to states in Europe and North America, it illustrates how international law may establish diagonal environmental rights.

Diagonal Environmental Rights within Human Rights Law

The most important human rights instruments—the 1948 Universal Declaration of Human Rights and the two 1966 covenants on human rights—do not mention a right to environmental protection, undoubtedly because they were drafted before the dawn of the modern environmental movement. Two regional agreements adopted more recently include environmental rights, but only in very general terms. The 1981 African Charter on Human and Peoples' Rights provides that "[a]ll peoples shall have the right to a general satisfactory environment favorable to their development," and the 1988 San Salvador Protocol to the American Convention on Human Rights states that "[e]veryone shall have the right to live in a healthy environment."

The most detailed effort to add free-standing environmental rights to human rights law came in 1994 when Fatma-Zohra Ksentini, a special rapporteur appointed by a sub-commission of the UN Human Rights Commission, prepared a draft declaration on human rights and the environment. After stating the basic right of all persons "to a secure, healthy and ecologically sound environment," the Ksentini Declaration sets forth many related rights, including "the right to freedom from pollution," "the right to protection and preservation of the air, soil, water, sea-ice, flora and fauna, and the essential processes and areas necessary to maintain biological diversity and ecosystems," "the right to safe and healthy food and water adequate to their well-being," and "the right to information concerning the environment" (Ksentini Declaration, principles 2, 5, 6, 8, 15). In one provision, the declaration specifically recognizes the problem of transboundary harm, stating, "All persons have the right to freedom from pollution, environmental degradation and activities that adversely affect the environment, threaten life, health, livelihood, well-being or sustainable development *within, across or outside national boundaries*" (principle 5, emphasis added.) The Human Rights Commission did not adopt the declaration, however, and governments have not shown interest in recent years in drafting another instrument that recognizes a right to environmental protection.

Nevertheless, even in the absence of a clearly stated right to a healthy (or satisfactory, or ecologically sound) environment, environmental rights have continued to emerge within human rights law, as international bodies have found such rights to be derived from, contained in, or implicated by existing human rights, such as the rights to life, health, property, and privacy. The most important of these interpretations have come from the three regional human rights systems. The European Court of Human Rights has held that by preventing individuals from enjoying their homes, severe environmental pollution may violate Article 8 of the European Convention on Human Rights, which protects the right to privacy (*Guerra and Others v. Italy*, par. 60; *López Ostra v. Spain*, par. 51). The African Commission on Human and Peoples' Rights has read the obligations imposed on states by the right to health, together with the African Charter's right to a satisfactory environment, as "ordering or at least permitting independent scientific monitoring of threatened environments, requiring and publicising environmental and social impact studies prior to any major industrial development, undertaking appropriate monitoring and providing information to those communities exposed to hazardous materials and activities and providing meaningful opportunities for individuals to be heard and to participate in the development decisions affecting their communities" (*Social and Economic Rights Action Center for Economic and Social Rights v. Nigeria*, par. 55). And the Inter-American

Commission on Human Rights has found that environmental degradation may violate the rights to life, to personal safety and integrity, and to property, among other rights (Inter-American Commission on Human Rights 1997; *Maya Indigenous Community of the Toledo District v. Belize*, par. 193–94; see Shelton 2003, 20–21).

Deriving environmental rights from existing human rights has real advantages. Relying on existing rights often seems entirely appropriate, since environmental harm can damage individuals' lives, health, property, and other interests protected by human rights law. Practically, this approach allows environmental advocates to bring complaints to existing mechanisms for monitoring human rights without having to convince governments to adopt instruments defining new environmental rights. In the absence of effective domestic remedies, human rights tribunals may be courts of last resort for those victimized by environmental degradation (Boyle 1996, 63; Shelton 2003, 1–2). Moreover, advocates can use human rights law as a basis for developing important participatory rights specific to environmental protection, such as rights to receive information about the environmental consequences of actions, to participate in decision-making affecting the environment, and to have access to remedies for environmental harm (Boyle 1996, 59–61).

Basing environmental interests on human rights has limits, however. Human rights are inherently anthropogenic; they are *humans'* rights. Human rights law is ill-suited to protecting values not easily expressed in terms of human interests, including the conservation of biological diversity when such conservation does not directly benefit humans (Handl 1995, 117). With respect to environmental degradation that does harm humans, human rights institutions are not well-designed to provide prospective, detailed regulation. Standard-setting bodies in the human rights field usually operate at a high degree of generality, leaving details to be developed later. Governments have shown no interest in using those bodies to develop environmental regulation, instead creating agreements and institutions outside the human rights framework to address specific problems such as ozone depletion, climate change, marine pollution, and the loss of biological diversity.

Nevertheless, environmental human rights play an important role in ways other than establishing prospective regulations. First, by reviewing actions that harm the life, health, property, or other protected interests of individuals, and identifying which actions violate general, reasonable norms, human rights tribunals develop a common law of environmental protection. That law may complement regulatory environmental treaties, just as nuisance law and other tort doctrines complement environmental regulatory statutes. Second, by justifying and clarifying individuals' rights to participate in the domestic avenues through which environmental laws are created and enforced, human rights law supports a fairer and more effective regulatory process.

In both of these respects, one can make a strong policy argument that human rights law should establish extraterritorial obligations. It is difficult to see why a state that has caused environmental harm that rises to the level of a violation of human rights should avoid responsibility for its actions merely because the harm was felt beyond its borders.

With respect to participatory rights, while foreign nationals do not have the full range of rights that the nationals of a state possess (for example, they have no rights to vote or to run for election to office), it does not follow that they should not have rights equivalent to those of nationals to receive information about environmental policies that affect them and to receive the same access to domestic remedies for environmental harm.

Unfortunately, the extent to which human rights law applies to extraterritorial environmental harm remains unclear. First, because environmental rights stem from a range of human rights that are recognized by different instruments, they are subject to the range of approaches those instruments take to jurisdiction. The Universal and American Declarations and the African Charter contain no explicit jurisdictional limitations, and the International Covenant on Economic, Social and Cultural Rights (ICESCR) can even be read as envisaging extraterritorial obligations. But the International Covenant on Civil and Political Rights (ICCPR) and the European and American Conventions limit at least some of their protections to individuals subject to (or within) their jurisdiction, leaving ambiguous how far their protections extend beyond their *territorial* jurisdiction (Coomans and Kamminga 2004, 2).

Second, the tribunals and quasi-tribunals charged with interpreting these treaties have not clarified whether and how they apply to extraterritorial environmental harm. Almost every environmental claim brought to a human rights tribunal has been vertical, in that the complainants have been nationals of the government against which they were complaining. More generally, tribunals have not developed a clear jurisprudence on the extraterritorial effects of actions taken internally, the situation most likely to give rise to diagonal environmental claims. Occasionally, a state causes environmental harm through its direct operations in another state, but the most common type of international environmental degradation is transboundary: the source of the degradation is within a state's territory and the resulting harm is felt outside it, as in the case of air or water pollution that crosses a border. Even when a corporation based in one state causes environmental harm through its conduct in another, so that the *polluter* as well as the *pollution* is extraterritorial, the claim against the home state is typically that it has failed to act within its own territory to regulate the extraterritorial conduct of the corporation.

Decisions of the European Court of Human Rights and the Inter-American Human Rights Commission suggest that under certain circumstances, a state may be responsible for the effects of its actions on the human rights of individuals beyond its territory. For example, the Inter-American Commission has stated that "a party to the American Convention may be responsible under certain circumstances for the acts and omissions of its agents *which produce effects* or are undertaken outside that state's own territory" (*Saldano v. Argentina*, par. 17, emphasis added). Similarly, the European Court has said that "in exceptional circumstances the acts of Contracting States performed outside their territory, or *which produce effects there*, may amount to exercise by them of their jurisdiction within the meaning of Article 1 of the Convention" (*Ilascu and Others v. Moldova and Russia*, par. 314, emphasis added).

These statements leave unclear which effects would give rise to such extraterritorial jurisdiction, or how individuals affected by extraterritorial harm would be subject to the jurisdiction of the state where the harm originates. One approach to answering these questions might be to rely on decisions of the European Court and the Inter-American Commission holding that the obligations of a state extend extraterritorially to areas over which it has "effective control," and to argue that extraterritorial harm caused by the state places those affected by it under the state's authority or control.

This argument would have a greater possibility of success in the Inter-American Commission system than before the European Court of Human Rights. In *Banković and Others v. Belgium and 16 Other Contracting States*, the European Court rejected the argument that the NATO bombing of Serbia in 1999 amounted to "effective control" of the places bombed, saying, "the applicants' submission is tantamount to arguing that anyone adversely affected by an act imputable to a Contracting State, wherever in the world that act may have been committed or its consequences felt, is thereby brought within the jurisdiction of that State for the purpose of Article 1 of the [European] Convention. The Court is inclined to agree with the Governments' submission that the text of Article 1 does not accommodate such an approach to 'jurisdiction'" (*Banković v. Belgium*, par. 75). If dropping bombs on a city does not amount to effective control of its occupants, allowing pollution to move across an international border almost certainly would not. In contrast, the Inter-American Commission has held that by shooting down an unarmed plane over international waters, agents of the Cuban government "placed the civilian pilots . . . under their authority," thereby satisfying the jurisdictional requirement of the American Convention (*Alejandre v. Cuba*, par. 25). Although this is an easier standard to meet, it remains unclear whether the Inter-American Commission would view extraterritorial pollution as a similar exercise of authority over those affected by it.

Rather than arguing that extraterritorial pollution effectively takes control of or authority over those affected by it, one might emphasize that in the case of transboundary environmental harm, the actions in question are not truly extraterritorial at all. The source of the harm is, after all, within the territory of the originating state; only its consequences are felt extraterritorially. Perhaps for this reason, Dominic McGoldrick has written that cases where the state takes measures within its own territory that have an extraterritorial effect "are interesting but not that problematic. Properly understood, the violations . . . only appear to occur in the territory of another state. In fact, the [state's] obligations are clearly grounded in measures it has taken within its own territory" (McGoldrick 2004, 52). But the cases McGoldrick cites in support of this statement all concern individuals who are clearly within the jurisdiction of the state at the time it takes the measures in question: for example, individuals contesting the decision of a state to deport or expel them to another state where their human rights might be violated. The language of the jurisdictional provisions in the ICCPR and the European and American Conventions suggests that the key question is not whether the *actions taken by the state* are within its territorial jurisdiction, but whether the *individuals affected by those actions* are within its jurisdiction. If so, the fact that the state has territorial jurisdiction over the sources of transboundary environmental harm may be beside the point.

Another approach would be to rely, to the extent possible, on obligations that do not appear to be constrained by jurisdictional limits, such as those in the African Charter. The most promising treaty in this respect may be the ICESCR, which not only includes no jurisdictional limit, but actually requires each party "to take steps, individually *and through international assistance and co-operation,* especially economic and technical, to the maximum of its available resources, with a view to achieving progressively the full realization of the rights" (ICESCR, art. 2(1)). The Committee on Economic, Social and Cultural Rights (CESCR), the expert body charged with overseeing the ICESCR, has relied on this language in stating that parties have extraterritorial obligations with respect to several rights with environmental implications, including the rights to health, water, and food. But the scope of extraterritorial duties with respect to the environment remains unclear. Moreover, developed countries have resisted the idea that they have any concrete extraterritorial obligations under the ICESCR at all. Unlike the ICCPR, the ICESCR has no quasi-tribunal able to apply its obligations to particular complaints from individuals. Although a protocol to the ICESCR has been adopted that would give the CESCR that authority, it would authorize the committee to receive complaints only from individuals or groups "under the jurisdiction" of the state party against which the complaint is directed, hampering the committee's ability to clarify the extraterritorial scope of the ICESCR even after the protocol enters into force.

Although the American Convention does include a jurisdictional limit, it may not be as sweeping as it first appears. The Inter-American Commission has said that the jurisdictional provision of the American Convention "was largely patterned" on that of the European Convention (*Saldano v. Argentina*, par. 17), but the agreements differ in an important respect. Article 1 of the European Convention states simply, "The High Contracting Parties shall secure to everyone within their jurisdiction the rights and freedoms defined in Section I of this Convention." Article 1(1) of the American Convention says, "The States Parties to this Convention undertake to respect the rights and freedoms recognized herein and to ensure to all persons subject to their jurisdiction the free exercise of those rights and freedoms." By its terms, its jurisdictional limit applies only to the second clause of article 1(1), not to the first. The obligations to respect rights and to ensure their free exercise has been interpreted, especially in the context of the ICCPR, to impose different duties: the former requires each state party to *respect* rights by not violating them itself, and the latter requires each party to *ensure* them by taking positive steps to secure them from interference, including interference by private actors (Knox 2008, 21). A reasonable interpretation of the American Convention would be that the *respect* clause requires parties not to violate human rights through their own actions, wherever those violations might be felt, while the *ensure* clause is limited to the protection of persons subject to the jurisdiction of the parties, however that might be determined. In environmental cases, this interpretation might allow claims for transboundary harm directly caused by the government itself (for example, pollution from government-owned sources), but not necessarily claims for its failures to protect against harm from other sources (for example, pollution from private corporations).

The following two sections describe two ways advocates of environmental human rights have sought to avoid these interpretive tangles entirely. The first approach, illustrated by the Inuit climate change petition to the Inter-American Commission, is to combine a claim of extraterritorial harm with a claim of internal harm. As long as the environmental damage is of the same type and arises from the same sources, success on the vertical claim should have a beneficial effect on the extraterritorial victims, even if their diagonal claim is denied. The second approach is to take the issue to a body with more flexibility than human rights tribunals. In the early 1990s, advocates asked the UN Human Rights Commission to examine the effects on human rights of toxic waste from developed countries being dumped in developing countries. The commission, an institution more legislative than judicial, appointed a special rapporteur who has made extensive recommendations to the states of origin.

The Inuit Petition on Climate Change

In December 2005, the Inuit, an indigenous people residing in the Arctic and dependent on subsistence harvesting for their way of life, filed a petition with the Inter-American Commission arguing that the United States was violating their human rights by failing to restrict its contributions to global warming. The petition detailed the effects of climate change upon the Arctic and tied those effects to violations of specific human rights of the Inuit, including their rights to life and health, to residence and movement, and to use and enjoy their traditional lands and personal property. The petition based the rights primarily on the American Declaration of the Rights and Duties of Man, because the United States is not a party to the American Convention on Human Rights, the other instrument monitored by the commission.

The petition was filed by Sheila Watt-Cloutier, the chair of the Inuit Circumpolar Conference, on behalf of all Inuit of the Arctic regions of the United States and Canada, with the assistance of Earthjustice and the Center for International Environmental Law (CIEL). To the extent that the petition raised claims of Canadian residents against the United States, it was a diagonal case rather than a vertical one, and thus it implicated the potential difficulties with jurisdiction described above. Attorneys from Earthjustice and CIEL explained, in a paper prepared one year before the petition was filed, that they thought it would be "prudent" to include at least one claimant from the United States "to ensure that the petition is accepted." At the same time, by including claimants outside U.S. territory, the petition "would test the premise that any person or group, regardless of citizenship or national residence, ought to be able to petition the IACHR for redress for human rights violations by an OAS Member State" (Wagner and Goldberg 2004, 2). As filed, the petition pursued both ends. In addition to formally claiming on behalf of all Inuit in Canada and the United States, it listed over sixty Inuit petitioners by name, including fifteen residents of Alaska. The aim was to sidestep jurisdictional obstacles.

The Inter-American Commission neither dismissed the petition on jurisdictional grounds nor accepted it. Instead, the commission informed the petitioners in November 2006 that it would not be able to process the petition because "the information provided does not enable [the commission] to determine whether the alleged facts would tend to characterize a violation of rights protected by the American Declaration." The commission did not explain its reasoning; perhaps it felt uncertain as to the chain of causation between the actions of the U.S. government and the harm experienced by the Inuit. In 2007, at the request of the Inuit Circumpolar Conference, the commission invited representatives of the Inuit to provide testimony to the commission, outside the context of the petition procedure, on the effects of global warming on the Inuit and other vulnerable communities and the implications of those effects for their human rights. The representatives provided the requested information and asked the commission to be the "institutional conscience of the Americas" on this issue by issuing a report recognizing a link between global warming and human rights, calling on nations to take steps to reduce the risk of more egregious violations, developing a plan to monitor the effects of warming on indigenous communities, and assisting countries unable to meet their responsibilities under human rights law. As of May 2009, the commission had not responded to these requests.

The Human Rights Commission Special Rapporteur on Toxic Dumping

In the late 1980s, African governments and environmental advocates became increasingly concerned about the transboundary movement of toxic substances to poor countries. They raised the issue in the negotiations that culminated in the 1989 Basel Convention on the Control of Transboundary Movements of Hazardous Wastes and Their Disposal, but as concluded, the Basel Convention addresses only hazardous waste, does not prohibit trade in that waste, and in any event cannot completely prevent unlawful dumping. In 1995, the Basel parties adopted the "Basel Ban," an amendment to the convention that would prohibit all trade in hazardous waste between developed and developing countries. The amendment has not yet entered into force, however.

African governments also took the issue of toxic dumping to the UN Human Rights Commission on the ground that it violated the right to health and other human rights. Beginning in 1990, the commission adopted a series of resolutions affirming that illicit traffic and dumping of toxic and dangerous products and wastes constitute a serious threat to the rights to life and health of every individual. In 1995, the commission appointed a special rapporteur to investigate the effects of the illicit dumping of toxic products in developing countries on the enjoyment of human rights. As part of her mandate, the rapporteur was asked to gather information on toxic dumping and make recommendations on adequate measures to control, reduce, and eradicate it. The first rapporteur was Fatma-Zohra Ksentini, who had the year before submitted the declaration on human rights and the environment described above. Developed countries opposed the appointment of the special rapporteur, arguing that the issues should be addressed in other forums, including under the auspices of the Basel Convention (Dennis 1998, 119). Nevertheless, the mandate has been continued and expanded (see Gwam 2002).

In addition to the rights to life and health, the rapporteur has identified a host of other human rights that may be infringed by toxic dumping, including "such fundamental rights as the right of peoples to self determination and permanent sovereignty over natural resources, the right to development, the rights to . . . adequate food and safe and healthy working conditions, freedom of expression, the right to form and join trade unions, the rights to strike and to bargain collectively, the right to social security and the right to enjoy the benefits of scientific progress and its applications" (Special Rapporteur to the UN Commission on Human Rights 2001, par. 58). The commission has listed rights to clean water, food, adequate housing, and work as among those threatened (UN Commission on Human Rights 2005a, par. 4).

The principal sources of toxic dumping are usually private actors such as corporations. States may be responsible under human rights law for failure to prevent such actors from, or failure to punish them for, taking actions that interfere with the enjoyment of human rights (Knox 2008, 18–27). The reports of the rapporteur and the commission resolutions make clear that the states responsible may include not only those with territorial jurisdiction over the endpoint of the illicit traffic or dumping, but also the states where the movement of the toxic substances begins, which are often the home states of the enterprises that cause it to take place. Implicit in their view of human rights law is that the states of origin may owe extraterritorial obligations to those harmed (or potentially harmed), and the victims of toxic dumping may claim a violation of diagonal rights, not just vertical ones.

The rapporteur has recommended that countries of origin hold transnational corporations accountable for their actions (where those countries apply stricter environmental standards than the country where the dumping takes place), prosecute and punish the perpetrators of criminal offenses, no longer produce for export chemicals that they have banned for their own markets, and provide non-resident victims access to the same administrative and judicial remedies that residents would receive (Special Rapporteur to the UN Commission on Human Rights 1998, par. 100; 2003b, par. 106, 112). The commission has repeated some of these recommendations, including that developed countries ban the export of toxic substances that are banned in their own countries (UN Commission on Human Rights 2005a, par. 10).

The mandate thus illustrates how a human rights body may support diagonal environmental rights. The success of this approach should not be overstated. Developed countries have consistently opposed the mandate, indicating that they do not necessarily accept the view that human rights law requires them to take steps such as banning for export toxic substances that are banned in their own countries. Even the special rapporteur has been reluctant to read human rights law to require developed countries to extend their extraterritorial jurisdiction. In a report made in 2003 after a trip to the United States, the rapporteur encouraged the U.S. government "to facilitate the prosecution of United States corporations whose subsidiary entities in Mexico are responsible for failing to deal with imports of toxic and dangerous products and wastes in accordance with United States, Mexican or international law," but recommended only that the government should cooperate with Mexican authorities, facilitate the enforcement of Mexican judgments, and "*consider* extraterritorial jurisdiction in these matters" (Special Rapporteur to the UN Commission on Human Rights 2003a, par. 72(c), emphasis added). Nevertheless, developed countries have accepted that they have some responsibilities in this area. In particular, they joined in the declaration adopted by the 1993 World Conference on Human Rights stating that toxic dumping potentially constitutes a threat to human rights and calling on "all States to adopt and vigorously implement existing conventions relating to the dumping of toxic and dangerous products and wastes and to cooperate in the prevention of illicit dumping" (Vienna Declaration, par. 11).

Diagonal Rights within International Environmental Law

As a basis for diagonal environmental rights, human rights law has the advantage of providing rights to individuals, but the disadvantage of not clearly extending those rights extraterritorially. International environmental law (IEL) has the opposite strength and weakness. The orientation of most IEL is extraterritorial, in that it requires each state to take steps to protect the environment beyond its own territory. Its touchstone is expressed in Principle 21 of the 1972 Stockholm Declaration, which says that states have "the responsibility to ensure that activities within their jurisdiction or control do not cause damage to the environment of other States or of areas beyond the limits of national jurisdiction." Many environmental treaties build on this idea. They address an enormous variety of extraterritorial harms, from air pollution that crosses a boundary between two countries, to global problems such as the loss of biological diversity, ozone depletion, and global warming.

With few exceptions, states' obligations under IEL are horizontal, not vertical: they are formally owed to other states, not to individuals. In this respect, IEL comports with the traditional view of international law, in which states are the only actors on the international plane, and individuals harmed by a foreign state's violation of international law have no direct recourse against it. Nevertheless, individuals do have some rights in IEL, including some diagonal environmental rights. The following sections describe three examples of such rights: (a) rights to enforce compliance with horizontal, state-to-state obligations contained in environmental treaties; (b) rights arising from obligations on the part of states not to discriminate against non-residents; and (c) diagonal rights extending from vertical rights created by environmental treaty.

Enforcement of Compliance with Horizontal Obligations: The North American Agreement on Environmental Cooperation

Although most environmental treaties set out horizontal rights and duties, many of their *benefits* run diagonally. Those most affected by extraterritorial environmental harm are neither residents nor nationals of the state with territorial jurisdiction over the source of the harm. One could argue that the foreign residents affected by such harm are the real parties in interest in any dispute arising under such treaties, and to that degree they have diagonal interests implicit in the treaties. If those interests were expressed as rights, then IEL would give rise to diagonal environmental rights. Such a conversion could occur if the individuals had rights to enforce the treaties against the states that are party to them. This would not require amending the treaties to set out new *substantive* rights on the part of the individuals, but rather allowing them to have access to procedures that promote compliance with existing horizontal obligations.

Environmental advocates have long argued that allowing individuals and groups to pursue claims against states under environmental treaties would not only be fairer, since it would allow those most directly affected to pursue claims, but would also make the treaties more effective, since states rarely bring legal claims against one another for violations of their obligations under IEL (Sands 1989, 411; Barratt-Brown 1991). States may fail to bring claims because they want to avoid attracting attention to their own environmental record and establishing a precedent that could be used against them, or because they fear reciprocal damage to other interests (Wirth 1994, 779). Even states that sincerely want to promote compliance may find international adjudication of claims too slow, expensive, inflexible, and backward-looking to address complex environmental problems. As a result, they may prefer less confrontational, more "managerial" approaches to compliance, which emphasize building capacity, clarifying unclear obligations, and monitoring performance (Chayes and Chayes 1995, 205). States have incorporated such managerial mechanisms into IEL and use them more frequently than formal claims procedures. But the same concerns that cause states to resist bringing claims that might draw attention to their own records or cause damage to other interests might also prevent states from using these mechanisms when it would otherwise be appropriate to do so. Here too, then, one can argue that individuals and groups should have access to them (Knox 2001, 10, 26–27).

One of the few compliance mechanisms in IEL that may be triggered by individuals and groups is the submission procedure of the North American Agreement on Environmental Cooperation (NAAEC). The NAAEC resulted from a U.S. proposal for a supplemental agreement to the North American Free Trade Agreement (NAFTA) to address the concern that lowering barriers to trade and investment would attract U.S. companies to Mexico to take advantage of relatively low environmental standards. In fact, while Mexican environmental law was weaker than U.S. law in some areas, on the whole its laws as written were comparable to U.S. laws; the problem was in their lack of enforcement (Magraw 1995, 583, 615). The NAAEC therefore includes commitments by the parties to "effectively enforce" their domestic environmental laws (North American Agreement on Environmental Cooperation [herewith cited parenthetically as NAAEC], art. 5(1)). To make clear that governments could not weaken this obligation by lowering their domestic standards, the agreement also requires each party to ensure that its laws provide for high levels of environmental protection and to strive to continue to improve those laws (art. 3).

To oversee and facilitate implementation of these obligations, and to further regional environmental cooperation generally, the NAAEC created the Commission for Environmental Cooperation (CEC), which includes a council composed of the environmental ministers and a secretariat of international civil servants. The NAAEC created a state-to-state dispute resolution procedure, which in principle could lead to fines or trade sanctions for parties' persistent failures to effectively enforce their own environmental laws, but in practice it has never been invoked. The agreement also established a procedure that allows any person or nongovernmental organization (NGO) "residing or established in the territory of a Party" to file a submission with the secretariat claiming that any of the NAFTA states is failing to effectively enforce its environmental laws. Because the NAAEC does not require that the submitter be in the territory of the particular state party that is the subject of the submission, it opens the door to diagonal as well as vertical complaints (Knox 2001, 80).

The secretariat reviews every submission to determine whether it meets set criteria and whether, in light of any response from the party concerned, the submission warrants developing an investigative report, known as a "factual record." If so, the secretariat requests authorization from the council, which may provide it by a two-thirds vote (NAAEC, arts. 14–15). This complaint-based monitoring procedure resembles both formal adjudication, in that it allows claims against governments to be brought to an independent body, and "managerial" compliance mechanisms, in that the resolution of the procedure is not a binding decision but rather an investigative report, which may nevertheless persuade a state to bring itself into compliance. As of May 2009, the procedure has received more than sixty submissions. (Information about the procedure and documents relating to specific submissions may be found at the website of the Commission for Environmental Cooperation, http://www.cec.org.)

Perhaps surprisingly, given the presence of many instances of controversial transboundary pollution in North America, none of these submissions is purely diagonal: none has been filed solely by a non-resident submitter and none solely concerns extraterritorial harm. However, many of the submissions have been filed with the participation of submitters both inside and outside the territory of the state complained against. Some of this participation appears to result from cross-border solidarity between environmental groups with similar interests, or concern by groups in one state for the internal consequences of environmental harm in another. But other submissions complain of the extraterritorial as well as the internal effects of failures to enforce environmental laws, and thus raise diagonal as well as vertical claims.

Most of the diagonal claims have not resulted in factual records. The NAAEC procedure is designed to promote effective enforcement of domestic laws, and domestic environmental laws are generally concerned with environmental effects within the territory of the state, not outside it. National air and water pollution laws in North America do include provisions that address transboundary pollution, but often in terms that leave a great deal of discretion to the regulatory agency, so that it is difficult to argue convincingly that the provisions have not been effectively enforced. For example, a 1999 submission from a coalition of Canadian and American environmental groups, which concerned airborne emissions of dioxin and mercury from incinerators in the United States into the Great Lakes, argued inter alia that the United States was failing to effectively enforce sec. 115 of the U.S. Clean Air Act, which provides that whenever the EPA administrator has reason to believe that air pollutants emitted in the United States cause or contribute to air pollution "which may reasonably be anticipated to endanger public health or welfare in a foreign country," he or she shall notify the governor of the state where the emissions originate. The notification triggers an obligation on the state to address the problem by amending the implementation plan through which it implements the Clean Air Act. The secretariat decided that a factual record was not warranted largely because its reading of U.S. case law convinced it that the "EPA's flexibility regarding when, whether and how to implement § 115 is very broad" (*Secretariat Determination* [*Great Lakes,* 2001], at 22). A later submission, concerning the effect of emissions from coal power plants in Ontario on eastern Canada and the northeastern United States, alleged that Canada was failing to enforce the equivalent provision of the Canadian Environmental Protection Act (CEPA). The secretariat concluded that like sec. 115, the relevant CEPA provision "appears to provide a considerable degree of discretion to the [Canadian] Environment Minister," and noted that "nothing in the Act indicates that Canada has a clear obligation to require a pollution prevention plan or recommend regulations" (*Secretariat Determination* [*Ontario Power Generation,* 2004], at 10). In the absence of such an obligation, the secretariat again decided that a factual record was not warranted.

Another approach is to look to domestic environmental laws that protect against internal pollution or other environmental harm, but that if effectively enforced would also reduce transboundary harm. (This approach resembles that taken by the Inuit petition, except that here the search is for domestic laws, rather than domestic plaintiffs.) In 2004, another coalition of environmental groups filed a submission alleging that the United States was failing to enforce the Clean Water Act with respect to mercury emissions from coal power plants throughout the United States, thereby degrading rivers and lakes across the country. The submitters focused on provisions of the Clean Water Act protecting U.S. waters, but the Canadian submitters were obviously motivated in part, at least, by the belief that better enforcement of those provisions would improve the quality of transboundary bodies of water.

Submitters have also tried to address transboundary issues by claiming that the parties are failing to effectively enforce environmental treaties, which, unlike domestic laws, are primarily directed at preventing transboundary harm. For example, the *Great Lakes* submission also asserted that by failing to reduce pollution from the incinerators, the United States was not complying with its obligations under two bilateral agreements with Canada, one on the Great Lakes and one on the transboundary movement of hazardous waste. Similarly, a 2006 submission argued that Canada and the United States had failed to prevent the possibility of transboundary pollution from Devils Lake in North Dakota, in violation of the 1909 Boundary Waters Treaty between the two countries. In both cases, the secretariat dismissed the submissions. It underlined that the scope of the procedure was limited to enforcement of domestic environmental law and concluded that the agreements in question were international obligations that had not been transformed into domestic law by implementing statute or regulation (*Secretariat Determination* [*Great Lakes*, 1999], at 5; *Secretariat Determination* [*Devils Lake*, 2006], at 7).

By alleging failures to enforce legislation implementing an environmental treaty, a submission may avoid both of these problems: the submission concerns domestic law, and the law addresses the transboundary concerns that are the subject of the treaty. In 1999, environmental groups from all three NAFTA countries filed a submission complaining that the United States was failing to enforce its law protecting migratory birds with respect to logging operations, and in 2002 a U.S. environmental group joined several Canadian groups in submitting a complaint alleging a similar failure on the part of Canada. The submissions focused not on the treaties between the countries on the protection of migratory birds, but on the domestic statutes implementing those treaties. In both cases, the submissions were deemed admissible and resulted in factual records. Their success was limited, however. In the first case, the Council of Ministers approved preparation of the investigative report only after greatly narrowing its scope, from logging operations throughout the United States to just two specific examples cited in the submission. The result was to undermine the utility of the report almost entirely (Wold et al. 2004). In the second, the council required the submitters to provide much more detailed information before it agreed to approve preparation of the report, delaying the completion and publication of the report until 2007, five years after the submission was filed.

The record of the council's role in deciding whether to authorize and publish reports under the NAAEC supports the arguments of those who are concerned that, left to their own devices, governments will resist giving private actors a role in promoting compliance with state-to-state obligations under environmental treaties. Despite the weakness of the NAAEC reports—they are not legally binding and cannot even reach a legal conclusion as to whether a government has failed to effectively enforce its laws—governments are so easily embarrassed by them that they have exercised their control over the procedure to delay and narrow the reports. And in almost every other environmental treaty, governments have refused to accept even this degree of public participation in compliance mechanisms, even less confrontational "managerial" mechanisms (Pitea 2005, 212; Kravchenko 2007, 19–23).

The Principle of Non-discrimination and the Espoo Convention

Another basis within IEL for diagonal environmental rights is the principle of non-discrimination. As first developed in the 1970s by the Organisation for Economic Co-operation and Development (OECD), the non-discrimination principle would require "each Country [to] ensure that its regime of environmental protection does not discriminate between pollution originating from it which affects or is likely to affect the area under its national jurisdiction and pollution originating from it which affects or is likely to affect an exposed Country" (Organisation for Economic Co-operation and Development 1986, 152). The OECD concentrated on the principle's procedural aspects, recommending in 1976 that the rights accorded persons affected by transboundary pollution should be equivalent to the rights of residents of the country where the pollution originates with respect to *information* concerning projects that may give rise to a risk of transboundary pollution, *participation* in hearings concerning proposed decisions that could lead to such pollution, and *access to remedies* for abatement of or compensation for such pollution (Organisation for Economic Co-operation and Development 1977, 19).

The concept has been influential in the development of transboundary environmental law. The International Law Commission, composed of independent legal experts who propose new legal instruments to the United Nations, has included the principle of non-discrimination in all of its proposed drafts of environmental instruments, including a convention on the law of non-navigational uses of international watercourses, articles on the prevention of transboundary harm, and principles on the allocation of loss in the case of transboundary harm. Only the first of these proposals has been adopted by governments as a treaty, however, and it has not yet entered into force. Regional efforts have been more successful. In 1979, a joint working group of the American and Canadian bar associations proposed a draft treaty on equal access; although the governments did not adopt it, the draft did lead to a model statute providing for equal access on a reciprocal basis that has been enacted by seven states, including Michigan, and four provinces, including Ontario. And the UN Economic Commission for Europe has included the principle of non-discrimination in several of its treaties, notably the 1991 Convention on Environmental Impact in a Transboundary Context, known as the Espoo Convention, which now has forty-two parties, including Canada, the European Union, twenty-six of the twenty-seven EU member states, and fourteen other European countries.

The Espoo Convention illustrates how the principle may provide a basis for diagonal rights. The treaty requires parties to prepare an environmental impact assessment (EIA) before undertaking certain types of projects likely to cause a significant transboundary impact, and it sets out in detail the criteria a transboundary EIA must meet. Many of Espoo's obligations are state-to-state: the state within whose jurisdiction a proposed project is to take place must notify affected states of the proposed project, give them information about the project and its possible transboundary impacts, and take due account of their views before authorizing it. But Espoo also provides that the public in affected states have rights, including the same opportunity as the public of the state of origin to participate in the EIA procedure. More specifically, the non-residents must be notified of the proposal and provided the EIA documentation prepared by the state of origin, they must have the opportunity to submit comments to the state of origin on the proposal and the EIA documentation, and their comments must be taken into account in the final decision on whether to permit the proposed activity (Espoo Convention, arts. 2(6), 3(8), 4(2), 6(1)). Since the domestic EIA laws of most Espoo parties already provide their own residents such rights, Espoo effectively applies the principle of non-discrimination to domestic EIA laws (Knox 2002, 301–5). It ensures that individuals in states potentially affected by projects in another state have the same rights to participate in the EIA procedure of that state as do the residents of that state, thereby expanding the vertical rights held by those residents into diagonal rights.

Vertical Environmental Rights and the Aarhus Convention

The advantage of the non-discrimination principle developed by the OECD is that the rights it provides to non-residents extend as far as the rights provided to residents. But the corollary is that when residents have few or no environmental rights, so do non-residents. There is no ceiling to the rights, but also no floor. As the first section explained, human rights treaties provide a floor for certain vertical rights in the environmental context. Independently of human rights law, environmental treaties have also begun to develop vertical rights.

In 1992, the UN Conference on Environment and Development adopted the Rio Declaration, principle 10 of which states that "[e]nvironmental issues are best handled with participation of all concerned citizens." Principle 10 identifies the same three avenues of participation addressed by the 1976 OECD recommendation: access to information concerning the environment; the opportunity to participate in decision making; and effective access to judicial and administrative proceedings, including proceedings for redress and remedy. But while the non-discrimination principle says that non-residents should receive whatever level of these rights residents receive, principle 10 suggests that "all concerned citizens" should enjoy a minimum level of participation. It thus establishes a foundation for minimum vertical rights. Its extension to non-citizens remains unclear, however. Although the Rio Declaration was not a legally binding treaty, principle 10 became a focal point for efforts to recognize participatory rights in binding environmental agreements. Major post-Rio environmental treaties often include provisions requiring the parties to make certain environmental information available to the public (for example, the Rotterdam Convention, art. 15(2); the Cartagena Protocol, art. 23; and the Stockholm Convention, art. 10). Like principle 10, however, these treaties typically do not clarify whether the information should be provided to non-residents.

Treaties that set forth minimum rights *and* make clear that those rights apply without discrimination to non-residents provide the strongest basis for diagonal environmental rights. The most important example of such a treaty is the Aarhus Convention on Access to Information, Public Participation in Decision-Making, and Access to Justice in Environmental Matters, which was adopted by the member states of the UN Economic Commission for Europe in 1998. As of May 2009, it has forty-two parties, including the European Union, twenty-six EU member states, and fifteen other European states. As its name suggests, the Aarhus Convention provides detailed requirements with respect to each of the three areas of public participation identified by principle 10 of the Rio Declaration: access to information, participation in decision making, and access to legal remedies. Although it refers to states' obligations, rather than individuals' rights, its effect is to create obligations that are owed by the states parties to the public. Indeed, as Svitlana Kravchenko has written, it "is the first multilateral environmental agreement that focuses exclusively on obligations of nations to their citizens and nongovernmental organizations" (Kravchenko 2007, 1).

The obligations the Aarhus Convention sets forth are concrete and specific. For example, it requires governments to respond to requests for environmental information (which is defined broadly) unless an excuse listed in the agreement is met; it makes clear that requesters do not have to state their interest in the information; and it requires information to be provided within one month unless its volume and complexity justify taking up to two months. Moreover, it sets out detailed requirements for governments to collect and disseminate environmental information in the absence of such requests, and equally detailed requirements with respect to public participation in decisions on specific projects, broader plans and policies, and legal instruments. Its provisions on access to justice focus primarily on cases involving requests for information and public participation in specific projects; within those areas, the Aarhus Convention requires that members of the public have access to independent and impartial bodies with the power to review the decisions in question and provide effective remedies.

Article 3(9) of the convention makes clear that all of these obligations must be met "without discrimination as to citizenship, nationality or domicile." The effect is to create specific diagonal environmental rights of non-nationals and non-residents to receive environmental information, participate in environmental decision making, and have access to remedies. In addition to its specific requirements on access to justice, the Aarhus Convention includes a more general obligation for each party to ensure that members of the public have access to legal procedures to bring claims against public authorities and private persons for violations of its domestic environmental law, as long as the plaintiffs "meet the criteria, if any, laid down in its national law" (art. 9(3)). Although this language is not completely clear, the "criteria" clause seems to be limited to requirements of standing, not to determining whether such remedies may exist at all (Stec and Casey-Lefkowitz 2000, 130–32). A separate question is whether states could use such criteria to discriminate on the basis of nationality or residence. On its face, this language does not override article 3(9), which by its terms applies "[w]ithin the scope of the relevant provisions of this Convention." As a result, the Aarhus Convention would require "equal access" to justice in environmental cases generally, not just with respect to cases concerning access to information and participation in decision making regarding specific projects.

In addition to requiring that states recognize diagonal rights in their domestic law, the Aarhus Convention creates new diagonal rights on the international plane, through its compliance mechanism. Like the NAAEC, the Aarhus Convention is one of the very few exceptions to the general reluctance of states to allow public participation in IEL compliance mechanisms. The first meeting of its parties, in 2002, adopted a procedure that allows citizens and NGOs (as well as states parties and the convention secretariat) to make submissions concerning compliance to an eight-person committee of independent experts. After conducting an investigation, the committee may make findings and refer the matter to the meeting of the parties, which in turn may make recommendations, issue declarations of non-compliance, and even suspend a non-complying party's rights under the convention (Kravchenko 2007, 30–31). The decision of the parties creating this compliance mechanism lists the only requirements that submissions must meet to be admissible. For example, they must not be anonymous or "manifestly unreasonable." The list does not require submitters to be nationals or residents of the state of which they complain (Wates 2005, 183). And any such requirement would be inconsistent with the spirit, at least, of article 3(9).

Although most of the cases brought to the compliance committee to date have been vertical, brought by individuals and NGOs against their own governments, one case illustrates the potential for diagonal claims. In May 2004, the Biotica Ecological Society, an environmental organization in Moldova, filed a submission with the committee alleging that Turkmenistan had enacted a new law that introduced severe restrictions on environmental NGOs, including, among other things, a prohibition on the participation of non-citizens. (The submission and documents pertaining to it are available at http://www.unece.org/env/pp/compliance/C2004-05/DatasheetC-2004-05v30.06.05.doc). The committee accepted the submission without finding it necessary to address the fact that the submitter was based outside the state complained against. The committee held that the exclusion of non-citizens violated article 3(9) of the convention, and that other provisions of the law violated the requirement that parties to the convention provide appropriate recognition and support of environmental organizations. The second meeting of the parties, in June 2005, endorsed those findings.

The Aarhus Convention can be seen as the culmination of the approaches to diagonal environmental rights described in this chapter. Like human rights treaties, it requires its parties to respect specific rights of individuals, while it also incorporates the IEL principle of non-discrimination. And, like the NAAEC, it establishes a compliance mechanism open to diagonal claims as well as vertical ones. As a result, the Aarhus regime not only requires its member states to provide diagonal as well as vertical environmental rights in their domestic law; it establishes a new international procedure to promote those rights.

Chapter 5
The Human Rights Responsibility of International Assistance and Cooperation in Health

Judith Bueno de Mesquita, Paul Hunt, and Rajat Khosla

As a result of globalization, the actors and processes affecting the right of everyone to enjoyment of the highest attainable standard of physical and mental health (the "right to the highest attainable standard of health" or "right to health") are increasingly internationalized. This is particularly the case in low-income countries, where the right to health is influenced, positively and negatively, by international debt relief efforts, trade agreements, humanitarian and development assistance, and the national health policies of, and pharmaceutical research and development carried out in, high-income countries.

During the twentieth century, the health of people across most parts of the world steadily improved. However, progress has significantly slowed in recent years, particularly in low-income countries, where there is still an extremely high burden of preventable conditions (Commission on Macroeconomics and Health 2001, 40). A significant reason for this is the lack of resources of those living in poverty, and their governments, to ensure access to health-related services.

In recent decades, high-income countries have expressed increasing commitment to improving health in low-income countries, both as a goal in its own right and as an integral element of development and poverty-reduction initiatives (Swedish International Development Cooperation Agency 2002, 7; U.K. Department for International Development 2007c, 3). This is reflected in the Millennium Declaration, which was adopted in 2000 by the largest gathering of heads of state and government in history, and which gave rise to a set of development objectives, now commonly known as the Millennium Development Goals (MDGs). Health is a prominent theme among the eight goals, which also include a commitment to a global partnership for development (goal 8).

The MDGs and various other international political commitments include agreements by states to increase funds for development, including health, in low-income countries, and create a supportive international policy environment with this objective in mind. However, these good intentions have not—on the whole—been followed by the required injection of funds.[1] Furthermore, particular policies of some high-income states, including certain trade policies, create a difficult environment for the improvement of health in some low-income countries (Oxfam 2006).

Under several international human rights treaties, including the UN International Covenant on Economic, Social, and Cultural Rights (1966), states have a human rights responsibility of international assistance and cooperation in health. This means that states have a legal responsibility to ensure that their laws, policies, and activities support, and do not obstruct, the enjoyment of the right to health in other countries. Given the impact of high-income states on the right to health in low-income states, this responsibility has particular relevance in the context of the relationship between these countries.

The human rights responsibility of international assistance and cooperation in health has only recently attracted significant attention from international human rights mechanisms, civil society, and states. This chapter focuses on the contribution of Paul Hunt, the first UN special rapporteur on the right to the highest attainable standard of health,[2] to elaborate the meaning and scope of this responsibility. The special rapporteur's analysis builds on the conceptual framework on economic, social, and cultural rights, including international assistance and cooperation, developed by the Committee on Economic, Social, and Cultural Rights, and others. The special rapporteur has applied this analysis in the context of the right to the highest attainable standard of health, including particular right to health issues such as sexual and reproductive rights, mental health, access to medicines, and water and sanitation. He has also applied this analysis to specific interactions between high- and low-income states, including multilateral and bilateral trade agreements, development assistance, and the activities of international organizations.

The Global Health Crisis

Progress in improving health in many low-income countries has stagnated. Health inequalities are widening between high- and low-income countries, as well as within countries (Gwatkin et al. 2004).

The main causes of mortality in low-income countries are HIV/AIDS, malaria, tuberculosis, maternal and perinatal conditions, and childhood infectious diseases—precisely those health conditions addressed in the MDGs. These conditions pose a significantly lower threat in the majority of high-income countries. Compare, for example, the under-five mortality rates in Sierra Leone and Singapore, respectively 260 and 3 deaths per 1,000 live births in 2006 (UNICEF 2007, 113). Or take the example of maternal mortality. In 2005, while Ireland had a maternal mortality ratio (MMR) of 1 maternal death per 100,000 live births, Sierra Leone had a MMR of 2,100, and 13 other developing countries, mainly in sub-Saharan Africa, had MMRs of over 1,000 (WHO et al. 2007, 1). In sub-Saharan Africa, there were 22.5 million adults and children living with HIV/AIDS and 1.6 million deaths from AIDS in 2007. In western and central Europe, there were an estimated 760,000 people living with HIV/AIDS in the same year, and 12,000 deaths (UNAIDS and WHO 2007, 7). Malaria is rarely transmitted in the developed world. However, it is endemic to tropical and sub-tropical regions, causing more than 300 million illnesses and at least a million deaths annually, predominantly in the world's poorest countries.

As these disparities indicate, these deaths are almost all preventable. However, the required interventions often fail to reach the world's poor. Some of the reasons for this include corruption, mismanagement, and a weak public sector. However, a more fundamental problem is that the poor in low-income countries lack the resources to access these services, while their governments often lack the resources to provide them (Commission on Macroeconomics and Health 2001, 4).

In 2001, the Commission on Macroeconomics and Health estimated that by 2010, eight million lives could be saved by providing essential interventions against infectious diseases and nutritional deficiencies. These interventions—most of which address the health issues encompassed by the MDGs—would cost thirty-four dollars per capita per annum in 2007 and thirty-eight dollars per capita per annum in 2015. In addition to some resources raised at the national level in low-income countries, this would require additional assistance amounting to an additional 0.1 percent of donor GNP.

In addition to these main causes of mortality, other health problems continue to affect low-income countries. Many of these conditions receive comparatively little attention. Neglected diseases, such as lymphatic filariasis (elephantiasis), onchocerciasis (river blindness), leprosy, and human African trypanosomiasis (sleeping sickness), affect almost exclusively poor and powerless people living in rural parts of these countries. The diseases have led to severe and permanent disabilities and deformities in nearly one billion people worldwide (Kindhauser 2003). While effective treatment strategies have been developed for some neglected diseases, for others, such as African trypanosomiasis, there is no safe and effective treatment stratagem. Other health issues, such as mental health problems and sexual and reproductive ill-health, also continue to receive little attention in low-income countries (and often in high-income countries) and particularly affect marginalized groups, such as women, adolescents, and those with psychosocial disabilities.

The International Response

The international community of states has made numerous commitments to improving health in low-income countries. The outcome documents of the International Conference on Primary Health Care (1978), the World Conference on Human Rights (1993), the International Conference on Population and Development (1994), the Fourth World Conference on Women (1995), the Millennium Summit (2000), the UN General Assembly Special Sessions on HIV/AIDS and Children (2001 and 2002 respectively), the World Summit on Sustainable Development (2002), and the World Summit (2005) all recognize that in addition to national efforts by all states, developed states have a key role to play in supporting health in developing countries.

The MDGs, which arose from the Millennium Declaration, are of particular importance since they constitute the most prominent contemporary international development agenda and have come to define policies of low-income states, international organizations, and donors. Goal 8 is a commitment to a global partnership for development and includes a set of targets for developing further an open, rule-based, predictable, non-discriminatory trading and financial system; addressing the needs of the least developed countries, including bilateral debt cancellation; and more generous development assistance for countries committed to poverty reduction. This commitment has the potential to significantly benefit health in developing countries.

Despite these commitments, high-income states have often failed to deliver on their promises. For example, goal 8 of the MDGs includes a target for donors of the Development Assistance Committee (DAC) of the Organisation for Economic Co-operation and Development (OECD) to devote more to official development assistance, yet only five of the twenty-two member states of the DAC have met the UN target of 0.7 percent of gross domestic product. At the Gleneagles G8 summit in 2005, states agreed to raise development assistance from $80 billion in 2004 to $130 billion in 2010. By 2008, states had only programmed an extra $11 billion into planned development assistance, making it unlikely that targets will be achieved (Organisation for Economic Co-operation and

Development 2008a). Notably, international funding for health has increased in recent years, but neither at the rate required nor promised (Lancet 2006, 259; UN Millennium Project 2005, 14).

Some of the arrangements that have been put in place to deliver health in low-income countries have been problematic. To take one example, there are twenty global and regional health funds and ninety global health initiatives, working with, and alongside, forty bilateral donors and twenty-six UN agencies (Maxwell 2007). Many of the funds and international programs have been delivered through vertical, condition-specific, interventions. While vertical interventions may have a role, particularly in emergencies, in some cases they result in duplication and fragmentation, placing a heavy administrative burden on low-income countries and undermining the development of a comprehensive and integrated health system (Hunt 2008, par. 56; UN Millennium Project 2005, 39). A second problem is that development assistance in health has sometimes included policies that do little for, or even obstruct, the realization of the right to the highest attainable standard of health. For example, the U.S. "Global Gag Rule," reinstated by President George W. Bush in 2001, restricted foreign organizations that receive family planning funds from the U.S. Agency for International Development from using their own non-U.S. funds to provide legal abortion, to provide counseling or referrals for abortion, and to lobby for the legalization of abortion in their own countries. This policy, which was repealed by President Barack Obama in 2009, had reduced funding for vital reproductive health-care providers in developing countries during the years of the presidency of George W. Bush (Center for Reproductive Rights 2000, 13). A third problem is that development programs and international organizations have sometimes funded programs and projects that are extremely questionable, such as the refurbishment of outmoded and inappropriate psychiatric facilities that segregate persons with psychosocial disabilities from society (Rosenthal and Szeli 2002, 19). A fourth problem is the conditions attached to some development initiatives, which may hinder the improvement of health. For example, the Medium-Term Expenditure Frameworks, included in many Poverty Reduction Strategy Papers developed under the Heavily Indebted Poor Country Initiative (HIPC) of the World Bank and the International Monetary Fund, set out spending targets for health that have come to function in some countries as expenditure ceilings, at least temporarily (Ooms and Schrecker 2005, 1821–23).

Other international policies and agreements, as well as national policies in many high-income countries, also negatively affect the right to health in low-income countries. This effect gives rise to questions about whether international political commitment to health in low-income countries is in practice much more than rhetoric and good intentions. For example, while high-income countries are providing resources to support health in low-income countries, their public national health services, or private providers of care based within these countries, are actively recruiting thousands of health workers from low-income countries. This has led to severe shortages of health workers, particularly in sub-Saharan Africa (Bueno de Mesquita and Gordon 2005, 24). To take another example, trade agreements between high- and low-income states have included stringent protections of intellectual property rights, which go beyond flexibilities included in the Agreement on Trade-Related Aspects of Intellectual Property Rights (TRIPS), and which pose a threat to access to medicines in low-income countries (Hunt 2004, par. 67).

These obstacles to health are already the focus of international attention, and some are already attracting action. For example, in relation to the fragmentation and duplication of aid initiatives, many states as well as international organizations have signed on to the Paris Declaration on Aid Effectiveness (2005), which aims to simplify aid arrangements and make donors more accountable. Likewise, there are a range of new initiatives designed to support health systems, such as the International Health Partnership, convened in 2007 to support the realization of the health MDGs.

The right to the highest attainable standard of health provides a legal grounding and conceptual framework that can help address the health crisis in many low-income countries. It can help to enhance accountability, reinforce equitable policies and practices, and provide a framework for assessing and revising policies that do not work. For its part, the human rights responsibility of international assistance and cooperation in health provides a framework for assessing, in particular, the conduct of high-income countries in relation to low-income countries.

The International Legal Foundations of the Human Rights Responsibility of International Assistance and Cooperation in Health

The right to the highest attainable standard of health is recognized in five of the core international human rights treaties—the International Covenant on Economic, Social, and Cultural Rights (ICESCR), the International Convention on the Elimination of All Forms of Racial Discrimination, (ICERD), the Convention on the Elimination of All Forms of Discrimination against Women (CEDAW), the Convention on the Rights of the Child (CRC), and the Convention on the Rights of Persons with Disabilities (CRPD). The right is also recognized in regional treaties in the Americas, Europe, and Africa. Around two-thirds of national constitutions worldwide recognize a duty of the state to guarantee health or health care (Kinney and Clark 2004).

Three international treaties recognizing the right to health—the ICESCR, the CRC, and the CRPD—include a responsibility of international assistance and cooperation in health. In relation to each right recognized in the ICESCR, including the right to health, the treaty requires states parties to "take steps, individually and through international assistance and cooperation, especially economic and technical, to the maximum of its available resources, with a view to achieving progressively the full realization of the rights" (art. 2.1). Likewise, the CRC recognizes that measures taken for the realization of economic, social, and cultural rights should be undertaken "where needed, within the framework of international co-operation" (art. 4). Additionally, the CRC makes specific reference to the importance of international cooperation for the realization of the right to health, requiring states parties to "undertake to promote and encourage international co-operation with a view to achieving progressively the full realization of the right [to health]. . . . In this regard, particular account shall be taken of the needs of developing countries" (art. 24). According to the CRPD, states parties "recognize the importance of international cooperation and its promotion, in support of national efforts for the realization of the purpose and objectives of the present Convention, and will undertake appropriate and effective measures in this regard" (art. 31).

These treaty obligations, which are the main focus of our analysis, are supported by important references to international cooperation in a range of other international treaties and declarations. Articles 55 and 56 of the United Nations Charter establish a responsibility on states to engage in international cooperation for the achievement of human rights. The Universal Declaration on Human Rights recognizes the entitlement of each individual to the realization of his economic, social, and cultural rights "through national effort and international cooperation" (art. 22).

The right to the highest attainable standard of health has an intrinsic relationship to the right to development. The Declaration on the Right to Development (1986) establishes that the right to development is a right to a process of development in which all human rights—including the highest attainable standard of health—can be fully realized. The declaration variously recognizes that states have an individual and collective duty to formulate international development policies with a view to fully realizing the right to development; as a complement to efforts by developing countries, international cooperation is essential to provide these countries with appropriate means and facilities to foster their comprehensive development; and states have a duty to cooperate with each other in ensuring development and eliminating obstacles to development. This declaration does not impose binding treaty obligations, although the right to development is recognized in the binding African Charter on Human and Peoples' Rights.

The human rights responsibility of international assistance and cooperation in health reinforces the political commitments of high-income countries to improve health in low-income countries. This includes political commitments made at international conferences, such as the International Conference on Population and Development (1994), the Fourth World Conference on Women (1995), the Millennium Summit (2000), the UN General Assembly Special Session on HIV/AIDS (2001) and the World Summit (2005) in relation to, among others, sexual and reproductive health rights, and particular health issues such as reducing maternal and infant mortality and addressing the HIV/AIDS pandemic.

The Scope of the Human Rights Responsibility of International Assistance and Cooperation in Health

In the past five years, transboundary human rights obligations have been given increasing attention by academics, civil society organizations, and the international community. One area of focus has been economic, social, and cultural rights (Coomans 2004; Sepúlveda 2006). Like many elements of human rights, the parameters of international assistance and cooperation in economic, social, and cultural rights are not yet settled (Coomans 2004).

The Committee on Economic, Social, and Cultural Rights, which was established in 1985 to monitor progress made by states parties in implementing obligations deriving from their ratification of the ICESCR, reviews reports by states on the measures that they have taken to implement the covenant, and addresses its concerns and recommendations to the state party in the form of "concluding observations." The committee also adopts "general comments," which set out its interpretation of the provisions of the covenant, providing jurisprudential insights. The general comments are non-binding but have significant legal weight (Craven 1995, 91). In recent years, the committee and others have developed a way of analyzing or "unpacking" economic, social, and cultural rights, including the right to health, with a view to making these rights easier to understand and apply. This analytical approach, set out in general comments and concluding observations, includes international assistance and cooperation. The committee has yet to draft a general comment devoted to international assistance and cooperation. However, several general comments and concluding observations address the subject to some extent. In relation to health, the committee's *General Comment 14* on the right to the highest attainable standard of health, adopted in 2000, is of particular interest.[3]

In 2002, the Commission on Human Rights decided to establish a special rapporteur on the right to the highest attainable standard of health (resolution 2002/31; see UN Commission on Human Rights 2002). Under the mandate, the special rapporteur is asked to, among others, discuss areas of cooperation with all relevant actors; report on laws, policies, and practices most beneficial to the right to health, as well as domestic and international obstacles to their implementation; and make recommendations on appropriate measures to promote and protect the realization of the right to health.

Given the impact of the policies and activities of high-income countries on health in low-income countries, the first special rapporteur gave significant attention to the human rights responsibility of both sets of states in relation to international assistance and cooperation in health. The following paragraphs on the nature and scope of this human rights responsibility draw primarily on the special rapporteur's reports and focus on the responsibility of high-income countries.[4]

A Binding Legal Obligation

There has been significant debate about whether or not the human rights responsibility of international assistance and cooperation places binding legal obligations on states. The CESCR has argued that international cooperation for development is a binding obligation under the ICESCR (Committee on Economic, Social and Cultural Rights, par. 14). In our experience, many developing states agree with this position. However, developed states have refuted this claim (de Albuquerque 2005, 2006; O'Neill et al. 2007).

Deploying the legal arguments signaled earlier in this chapter, the special rapporteur on the right to health has, like CESCR, argued that the human rights responsibility of international assistance and cooperation is legally binding. Moreover, he has observed, "If there is no legal obligation underpinning the human rights responsibility of international assistance and cooperation, inescapably all international assistance and cooperation fundamentally rests upon charity. While such a position might have been tenable in years gone by, it is unacceptable in the twenty-first century" (Hunt 2008, par. 133).

A Supplementary Responsibility

A state's human rights responsibility of international assistance and cooperation in health does not qualify, limit, or condition the obligation of a partner state to do all it can to realize the right to the highest attainable standard of health at the domestic level within its available resources and consistent with its other human rights responsibilities. Along these lines, in its General Comment 8 on the relationship between economic sanctions and respect for economic, social and cultural rights, CESCR made the point that "the imposition of sanctions does not in any way nullify or diminish the relevant obligations [of the affected state]" (Committee on Economic, Social and Cultural Rights 1997, par. 10).

Responsibilities to Seek and Provide Assistance

International assistance and cooperation include a responsibility on states to seek appropriate assistance and cooperation, and a responsibility on states in a position to assist to provide appropriate assistance and cooperation. For example, they should request development cooperation where domestic resources are inadequate for the realization of the right to health. It also includes a responsibility on states and others in a position to assist to provide appropriate assistance and cooperation, including for health (Committee on Economic, Social and Cultural Rights, par. 45)

Resource Availability

States are required to take targeted steps to progressively realize the right to health, subject to "the maximum of its available resources" (International Covenant on Economic, Social and Cultural Rights, art. 2.1). This includes resources available from the international community. Hence the responsibility of a developing state to seek appropriate international assistance and cooperation. Equally, however, the human rights responsibility to *provide* international assistance and cooperation is also subject to the resources available to a donor. This gives rise to difficult questions. For example, how much should a donor be expected to contribute in the light of its available resources? When addressing this question, it can be very instructive to consider the record of comparable donors. It is because international assistance and cooperation give rise to complex, sensitive, and important issues that they should be subject to appropriate mechanisms of accountability.

Financial Assistance

The human rights responsibility of international assistance and cooperation includes a duty on high-income states to urgently take deliberate, concrete, and progressive measures toward devoting a minimum of

0.7 percent of their gross national product (GNP) to official develop-ment assistance. This responsibility has been consistently highlighted by CESCR in its Concluding Observations. In relation to those states not already meeting this target, the Committee has recommended that such states increase their assistance to 0.7 percent GNP. In the report on his mission to Sweden, the special rapporteur, addressing the right to the highest attainable standard of health, commended Sweden for meeting this target and for its move at the time to commit 1 percent of GNP to ODA by 2006 (Hunt 2007, par. 101).

Non-financial Dimensions of Assistance and Cooperation

Crucially, international assistance and cooperation must not be narrowly understood as a duty to provide financial assistance. States must ensure that their various international policies do not obstruct but rather sup-port the realization of the right to the highest attainable standard of health in other countries. They have a responsibility to work actively to-ward an equitable multilateral trade, investment, and financial system conducive to the reduction of poverty and the realization of human rights, including the right to the highest attainable standard of health.

Key Right-to-Health Features That International Assistance and Cooperation Should Support

The right to the highest attainable standard of health is not a right to be healthy. It is a right to the enjoyment of a variety of facilities, goods, services, and conditions necessary for the realization of the highest at-tainable standard of health. Broadly speaking, the right to health can be understood as an entitlement to an effective and integrated health system, encompassing health care and the underlying determinants of health, which is responsive to national and local priorities, and acces-sible to all. As well as this general entitlement, the right to health also includes specific entitlements, such as sexual and reproductive health rights, and the right to mental health.

International assistance and cooperation should be directed to give effect to key features of the right to the highest attainable standard of health, including freedoms and entitlements; equality and non-discrimination; participation; and monitoring and accountability (Hunt 2008, par. 21–30).

Freedoms include the right to be free from discrimination. Entitlements encompass medical care and underlying determinants of health, such as safe drinking water and adequate sanitation. Guaranteeing such freedoms and entitlements should be central to states' development and other international policies. The Committee on Economic, Social, and Cultural Rights confirms that donors should give particular priority to helping low-income countries realize their "core obligations" arising from the right to health (Committee on Economic, Social, and Cultural Rights 2000, par. 45).

Equality and non-discrimination are integral to the right to the highest attainable standard of health. In their international policies, states should give particular attention to securing the right to health for disadvantaged individuals, communities, and populations, such as women, ethnic minorities, indigenous peoples, persons with disabilities, the elderly, children, persons living with HIV/AIDS, sexual minorities, and those living in poverty. States should ensure that their international policies do not support policies that reinforce discrimination and other right-to-health violations against vulnerable groups. For example, in relation to persons with psychosocial disabilities, states should support the development of appropriate models of care.

Those affected are entitled to participate in health-related policymaking and implementation. Thus, in the recipient country, international assistance and cooperation in health should promote such participation, especially by those who are disadvantaged. Also, donors' policies of international assistance and cooperation in health should themselves be designed and implemented with the participation of such groups.

Without monitoring and accountability, the right to health can be no more than window dressing. Accordingly, international assistance and cooperation in health should promote effective monitoring and accountability in recipient countries. Also, donors should themselves be held to account for the discharge of their human rights responsibility of international assistance and cooperation in health.

Core Obligations: An International Minimum Threshold

States have a core obligation to ensure the satisfaction of a minimum essential level of the right to health. When grouped together, the core obligations for economic, social, and cultural rights establish an international minimum threshold that all developmental policies should be designed to respect. It is particularly incumbent on states in a position to assist to provide international assistance and cooperation to enable developing countries to fulfill their core obligations and help them respect this international minimum threshold (Committee on Economic, Social, and Cultural Rights 2001b, par. 15–17).

Obligations to Respect, Protect, and Fulfill

The right to health gives rise to three layers of obligations on states: to *respect, protect,* and *fulfill.* In the context of international assistance and cooperation in health, states must ensure that their actions *respect* the right to health in other countries. They must also, so far as possible, *protect* against third parties undermining the right to health in other countries. Depending on resource availability, states' obligations to *fulfill* the right to health include responsibilities to facilitate access to essential health facilities and services in other countries (Committee on Economic, Social, and Cultural Rights 2000, par. 39).

Procedural Fairness

The requirements of procedural fairness extend to international assistance and cooperation. For example, donors have a responsibility not to withdraw critical right-to-health aid without first giving the recipient reasonable notice and opportunity to make alternative arrangements (Hunt 2006).

Coherence

The international right to health must be applied consistently and coherently across all relevant national and international policy-making processes. For example, a state must do all it reasonably can to ensure that the right to the highest attainable standard of health is consistently and coherently integrated into the policies and programs of international financial institutions to which it belongs. Also, this fundamental human right should be integrated into states' international development, trade, and other policies that bear upon health.

International Assistance and Cooperation in Health: Selected Practical Examples

The CESCR has issued recommendations related to international assistance and cooperation in its concluding observations on states parties' periodic reports. These have tended to focus on policies that have a bearing on a number of rights. For example, in its concluding observations on Belgium's third periodic report, it recommended that the state party "increase its official development assistance to 0.7 percent of its GDP, as recommended by the United Nations, and continue to strengthen its activities in the area of international cooperation" (Committee on Economic, Social and Cultural Rights, 2008a, par. 27). In its concluding observations on Finland, the committee urged the state party to "take into account the provisions of the Covenant in its bilateral project agreements with other countries" (Commitee on Economic, Social and Cultural Rights, 2008b, par. 21). The committee has also addressed the protection of economic, social, and cultural rights in the context of trade agreements. In its concluding observations on Canada, the committee recommended that the state party consider "ways in which the primacy of Covenant rights may be ensured in trade and investment agreements, and in particular in the adjudication of investor-State disputes under chapter XI of the North American Free Trade Agreement (NAFTA)" (Committee on Economic, Social and Cultural Rights, 2006a, par. 68).

Following the example of the committee, the first special rapporteur addressed the human rights responsibility of international assistance and cooperation in particular contexts. The following sections highlight some of the missions and other activities undertaken by the special rapporteur with a view to understanding states' operationalization of their human rights responsibility of international assistance and cooperation. Here, we focus on three separate types of issues: the development policies of high-income states, and the relationship between donors and aid recipients; trade relations between high- and low-income states; and states' responsibility in the context of their membership in international organizations.[5]

Human Rights in Sweden's International Development and Health Policies

In 2006, the special rapporteur undertook a mission to Sweden (Hunt 2007). Sweden is a state party to international treaties recognizing the human rights responsibilities of international assistance and cooperation in health, such as the ICESCR and the CRC. One objective of the mission was to consider how Sweden implements this obligation.

Sweden's foreign policy reflects the fundamental principle that national and international human rights law, including the right to health, should be consistently and coherently applied across all relevant national and international policy-making processes. In *Human Rights in Swedish Foreign Policy* (Government of Sweden 2003a), the government pledges to integrate human rights into all areas of foreign policy and to mainstream human rights into the work of global and regional organizations.

The country's policies in the field of international development and poverty reduction are particularly commendable from the perspective of the right to health: they deserve applause, support, and study. Sweden is one of the few states to have surpassed the commitment by developed states to devote 0.7 percent of GNP to official development assistance. Additionally, in *Shared Responsibility: Sweden's Policy for Global Development*

(Government of Sweden 2003b), the government confirmed that a human rights perspective would be mainstreamed across all areas of policy related to international development. Subsequently, human rights have been integrated into many of Sweden's international development and health-related policies. For example, human rights are one of four key strategies guiding Sweden's international health and development policy, *Health is Wealth* (Swedish International Development Cooperation Agency 2002). In 2006, the government adopted its *International Policy on Sexual and Reproductive Health and Rights*, an important and pioneering policy that will contribute to a more rational and human-rights-based approach to these extremely important issues.

In this context, the government's foreign policy gives rise to two major questions. First, to what degree has the human-rights-based approach actually been brought to bear upon all aspects of Sweden's foreign policy? For example, while human rights have clearly been given consideration by the Swedish International Development Cooperation Agency (Sida), have they also been given due attention in relation to Sweden's policies regarding the World Bank, the International Monetary Fund (IMF), and international trade? Second, to what degree has the policy actually been operationalized? Has the Sida, for example, managed to operationalize a human-rights-based approach—and its commendable development policies—in its operations in developing countries?

During the special rapporteur's visit to Sweden in 2006, it became clear that these questions should not only be put to public officials in Stockholm, but also to some of those working overseas. Later in 2006, the government of Sweden agreed that the special rapporteur could visit the Swedish embassy and meet Sweden's development partners in Uganda, and that he could also meet the executive directors who represent Sweden in the World Bank and the International Monetary Fund in Washington, D.C.

The Sida's Program in Uganda

The special rapporteur visited Uganda in February 2007 (Hunt 2008). The visit provided an opportunity to consider how Sweden implements, in practice, its human rights responsibilities of international assistance and cooperation in health. The visit provided an opportunity to consider key issues, such as whether Sweden's development assistance strategy and programs integrate the right to health and support policies and projects that are consistent with this fundamental human right; the availability of resources; and coordination between the Sida, the government of Uganda, and other donors.

Sweden's *Country Strategy for Development Cooperation, Uganda: 2001–*

2005 remained the basis of Sweden's development assistance in 2007. Key elements of the strategy include support to social sectors, including health, and to democratic development and the promotion of fundamental human rights. The strategy places particular emphasis on strengthening the rights of women and children. Despite its commendable focus on health and human rights, the strategy does not explicitly recognize the right to health. In contrast to Sweden's international policy documents, human rights are not mainstreamed consistently throughout Sweden's development cooperation in Uganda, including in the Sida's support to the health sector. Thus, the Sida should take steps to mainstream human rights, including the right to health, in its country strategy for Uganda. Key features of the right to health will help Sweden realize its human rights responsibility of international assistance and cooperation in health.

The Sida's staff in Kampala is committed to integrating a human-rights-based approach into Sweden's forthcoming *Uganda Country Strategy.* An adequate understanding of human rights, including the right to health, by the Sida staff in country offices such as Uganda is vital if the organization is to operationalize its excellent policies on health, human rights, and development in Uganda and elsewhere. Accordingly, in his report the special rapporteur recommended that the Sida enhance its provision of training, resources, and advice on health and human rights that is available to its staff in country offices, including in Uganda. As far as possible, the Sida should also extend training and capacity building on human rights to Ugandan health policymakers and other health development partners in Uganda.

Funds for health are inadequate in Uganda. While African heads of state and government have set a target of devoting at least 15 percent of their budgets to health (Organisation of African Unity 2001, par. 26), the government of Uganda currently devotes only 9 percent. Without more funds, many of Uganda's impressive health policies will not be operationalized. In terms of volume of aid for health, the Sida is one of the largest donors working in Uganda. In 2006, the Sida provided U.S.$55 million development assistance to Uganda, including U.S.$13 million for health and U.S.$13 million for humanitarian assistance, which encompassed health. Consistent with its human rights responsibility of international assistance and cooperation in health, the Sida should continue to provide generous support to health in Uganda and work together with the government and other donors to ensure that they provide adequate funding to the health sector.

Four main agreements form the basis of Sweden's health development assistance to the government of Uganda, none of which refers to the right to health. Only the Memorandum of Understanding between the government of Sweden and the government of Uganda on Development Cooperation (2001–3) refers to human rights. The special rapporteur recommended that the right to the highest attainable standard of health, and other human rights, should be explicitly and consistently integrated into the Sida's development cooperation agreements with Uganda.

The health-related development cooperation agreements between the government and the Sida emphasize that the Sida's support to the government will be primarily provided by way of health sector support and direct budget support. In 2006, the Sida delivered approximately one-third of its development assistance by way of direct budget support, and one-third by way of sectoral support to the health sector. This arrangement is part of a range of initiatives promoted by the government of Uganda and its partners with a view to minimizing duplication and fragmentation of donor initiatives, which can undermine the health system.

The provision of development assistance by way of sector or budget support means that much of the Sida's development assistance to the government is aligned to the priorities identified in Uganda's national health-related policies. In order to understand how the Sida supports the right to health in Uganda, it is therefore important to understand how the right to health is promoted and protected in the context of Uganda's national health-related policies.

The Health Sector Strategic Plan II for 2005/6–2009/10 (HSSPII) is the key health policy document in Uganda. The HSSPII includes some references to human rights, particularly sexual and reproductive health rights, and the rights of persons with psychosocial disabilities. Although the right to health is not explicitly mainstreamed throughout the HSSPII, the document nevertheless includes commitments to some important right-to-health issues, including strengthening of the health system. However, other sensitive issues appear neglected, such as the high rate of unsafe abortion, and the right to health of men who have sex with men.

The HSSPII includes commitments to other key elements of the right to health, including non-discrimination, participation and monitoring, and accountability. However, from the point of view of the right to health, some elements could be strengthened. For example, indicators are not consistently disaggregated, making it difficult to monitor the human rights principles of equality and non-discrimination. The Sida should support the government of Uganda in its endeavors to mainstream the right to health in the HSSPII and other health-related policies, and to ensure that important right-to-health issues that are not fully captured in the government's policies, such as sexual and reproductive health rights, are given attention in its dialogue and agreements with the government and other actors.

The Sida provides support to a number of key intergovernmental organizations undertaking important work for the right to health in Uganda, such as WHO, UNFPA, UNAIDS, and UNICEF. Notably, since 2005, the Sida has provided funding for the appointment of a health and human rights officer in WHO Uganda, who played an important role in promoting awareness of health and human rights issues in Uganda and supported initial steps toward the integration of human rights in policy and development planning within the health sector.

The Uganda Human Rights Commission has recently established a right-to-health unit to monitor and hold to account national and international actors in the public and private health sectors. However, currently the unit has negligible funding. Accountability provided by national human rights institutions has an important role to play in holding duty bearers to account for the right to health. The special rapporteur recommended that the Sida and other development partners support this new initiative.

Civil society organizations are increasingly engaged in advocacy in Uganda. They have engaged with the government in formulating, implementing, and monitoring key health policies. Through their advocacy, they have enhanced awareness of human rights issues in the health sector. The Sida should continue to support the participation of these organizations in policy-making forums and monitoring mechanisms.

As well as promoting donor alignment with national policies, the government of Uganda promotes harmonization of development assistance between donors. This has led, for example, to a health-sector-wide approach in 2000, the *Partnership Principles between the Government of Uganda and Its Development Partners* (2003), and, most recently, the *Joint Assistance Strategy for the Republic of Uganda* (UJAS; see African Development Bank et al. 2005–9) prepared by seven donors, including the Sida. The UJAS will form a framework for the Sida's development cooperation with Uganda until 2009.

Alignment and harmonization have reportedly led to greater coordination between donors in the planning and delivery of aid, and have also lessened administrative burdens on the government of Uganda. From this point of view, harmonization is commendable. However, it is also important to ensure that the right to health informs harmonization and is not neglected in the search for common ground between donors.

As well as enhanced partnerships between donors in their support to governments, some donors, including the Sida, have discussed the establishment of a basket fund (that is, pooled funding) for health-focused civil society organizations (CSOs). Some CSOs were concerned that a basket-fund would jeopardize their funding. If or when a basket fund is established for health-related nongovernmental organizations (NGOs), this must not jeopardize the Sida's support for CSOs working on right-to-health issues, including those committed to sensitive initiatives, such as the provision of sexual and reproductive health information for adolescents.

Accountability is a vital feature of human rights, including the right to the highest attainable standard of health. In the development context, accountability has focused on recipient countries. Recipients have had to show that aid is spent as intended and with the desired outcomes. Such accountability is vitally important. However, the right to health (and other human rights) also demands the accountability of donors. Donors' accountability moves in two directions. First, they are accountable to their taxpayers, usually through Parliament. Second, they are accountable to recipients and the international community. These paragraphs focus on donors' accountability to recipients. For recipients the key question is this: has the donor honored its pledges and policies? In other words, has the donor discharged its human rights responsibility of international assistance and cooperation in health?

Commendably, Sweden and some other donors have produced Millennium Development Goal Reports highlighting how they are supporting the fulfillment of the Millennium Development Goals. The OECD Development Assistance Committee also has a peer review process that assesses the development policies and efforts of its members. The Paris Declaration on Aid Effectiveness enshrines a commitment to "mutual accountability," in other words, a commitment to mutual assessment by donors and partners regarding implementation of agreed undertakings.

A lack of information about donors' policies and programs, as well as a scarcity of accountability mechanisms, present significant obstacles to donors' accountability in Uganda. Accordingly, the Sida should prepare and distribute accessible information about its programs in Uganda and their implementation. Moreover, it should work with the government of Uganda and other development partners to enhance public access to information on national health policies and processes, such as HSSPII, since these initiatives are vital vehicles for donors' international assistance and cooperation in health. Also, the Sida, and others, should actively seek practical, realistic ways to enhance accountability to the Ugandan government, Parliament, and the public. For example, the Sida could submit reports to a Committee of the Ugandan Parliament, as well as to the National Health Assembly. The Uganda Human Rights Commission could monitor the Sida's health-related initiatives. These and other possibilities should be actively explored in close consultation with the government of Uganda.

Sweden's Role in the World Bank and the International Monetary Fund

The policies and programs of the World Bank and the IMF have sometimes had a significant impact on the right to the highest attainable standard of health, in particular in low-income countries (Hammonds and Ooms 2004). In 2001, the Committee on Economic, Social, and Cultural Rights encouraged Sweden, as a member of international financial institutions, in particular the World Bank and the IMF, to "do all it can to ensure that the policies and decisions of those Organizations are in conformity with the obligations of States parties to the Covenant, in particular the obligations contained in articles 2.1, 22 and 23 concerning international assistance and cooperation" (Committee on Economic, Social and Cultural Rights 2001a, par. 24). In October 2006, the special rapporteur met with the executive directors representing Sweden in the World Bank and the IMF, providing him with an opportunity to discuss how Sweden is operationalizing this recommendation in relation to the right to the highest attainable standard of health.

The highest decision-making bodies of the World Bank and the IMF are their boards of governors, which are composed of representatives from each shareholder's government. Sweden's representatives on the boards of governors should ensure that their votes and other activities are informed by Sweden's international human rights obligations, including its human rights responsibilities of international assistance and cooperation in health.

The governors delegate responsibility for overseeing the day-to-day business of the institutions to their designated representatives on the executive boards of the World Bank and the IMF. Sweden shares its representation on the executive boards of the World Bank and the IMF with seven other countries, all of which have ratified the ICESCR and the CRC: Denmark, Estonia, Finland, Iceland, Latvia, Lithuania, and Norway. The joint voting share of these countries is 3.34 percent and 3.45 percent of the total votes on the executive boards of the World Bank and the IMF, respectively. Executive directors representing more than one country cast a single bloc vote. The human rights responsibility of international assistance and cooperation requires the government of Sweden to do all in its power to ensure that the positions taken by the Nordic-Baltic executive directors promote policies and decisions that are in conformity with the right to the highest attainable standard of health.

Since the decisions of the boards are based on consensus, and the positions of individual executive directors and the countries that they represent are normally undisclosed, it is difficult to assess Sweden's impact on the overall decisions made by the boards. Sweden should make publicly available the views and positions taken by its executive directors in discussions on the executive boards.

Sweden should also use its influence on the governing and executive boards of the World Bank and the IMF to ensure that these institutions respect human rights in borrowing countries, and that the institutions integrate human rights within their policies and programs. The Swedish government should support initiatives that facilitate this objective. For example, in order to overcome the lack of human rights training opportunities for executive directors and staff at the international financial institutions, Sweden should provide its executive directors and other staff in the Nordic and Baltic office with human rights training, resources, and advice. The government of Sweden and Sweden's executive directors should support the provision of human rights training for other World Bank and IMF executive directors and the staff in their respective offices, and staff working in the World Bank and the IMF. Underrepresentation of developing countries on the executive boards of the World Bank and the IMF could be seen as one of the reasons for the failure of policies and programs of these institutions to take into account realities and priorities in these countries. Thus, Sweden should support the development of more democratic decision-making structures on the executive boards of the World Bank and the IMF.

World Trade Organization Agreements and the Right to the Highest Attainable Standard of Health

In 2003, the special rapporteur undertook a mission to the World Trade Organization to consider the impact on the right to the highest attainable standard of health of trade agreements, notably the Agreement on Trade-related Aspects of Intellectual Property Rights (TRIPS), and the General Agreement on Trade in Services (GATS). These agreements, which both entered into force in 1995, affect the right to the highest attainable standard of health in numerous ways (Hunt 2004).

The TRIPS agreement is the most comprehensive multilateral agreement setting detailed minimum standards for the protection and enforcement of intellectual property rights. The forms of intellectual property protection covered by the TRIPS agreement most relevant to the enjoyment of the right to health include patent protection, for example over new medical processes and products such as pharmaceuticals; trademarks, covering signs distinguishing medical goods and services as coming from a particular trader; and the protection of undisclosed data, in particular test data. For example, patent protection of a pharmaceutical allows the holder of the intellectual property right to exclude competitors from certain acts, including reproducing and selling the drug for a minimum period of twenty years. This period of exclusion theoretically allows the right holder to recoup the costs involved in medical research.

Apart from establishing minimum standards for various forms of intellectual property protection, the agreement also allows the member states of the WTO to adopt measures to protect public health and nutrition, and to protect against the abuse of intellectual property rights in certain cases. The agreement makes disputes between members concerning respect for the minimum standards subject to the WTO's dispute settlement procedures.

Intellectual property protection can affect the enjoyment of the right to health, and related human rights, in a number of ways. Importantly, intellectual property protection can affect medical research and this can bear upon access to medicines. For example, patent protection can promote medical research by helping the pharmaceutical industry shoulder the costs of testing, developing, and approving drugs. However, the commercial motivation of intellectual property rights encourages research, first and foremost, toward "profitable" diseases, while diseases that predominantly affect people in poor countries—such as river blindness and other neglected diseases (also known as tropical or poverty-related diseases)—remain underresearched. Further, intellectual property rights may affect the use of traditional medicines, such as those of indigenous peoples. While existing intellectual property protection can promote the health innovations of indigenous and local communities, the particular nature of this knowledge, and the knowledge holders, might require significant amendment to be made to intellectual legislation for protection to be comprehensive. Some traditional medicines have been appropriated, adapted, and patented with little or no compensation to the original knowledge holders and without their prior consent, which raises questions for both the right to health and cultural rights.

The exclusion of competitors as a result of the grant of a patent can also be used by patent holders as a tool to set excessively high prices for pharmaceuticals. High prices can exclude some sections of the population, particularly poor people, from accessing medicines. Given that the right to health includes an obligation on states to provide affordable essential medicines according to the WHO's essential drugs list, intellectual property protection can lead to negative effects on the enjoyment of the right to health. In other words, in some cases intellectual property protection can reduce the economic accessibility of essential medicines.

The TRIPS agreement includes some flexibility in some circumstances by permitting members of the WTO to authorize third parties to work a patent (that is, manufacture and sell pharmaceuticals at a lower price) without the authorization of the patent holder, subject to certain limitations, including payment of a reasonable fee. Nonetheless, such flexibilities are, in reality, only available to those members of the WTO that have a domestic pharmaceutical manufacturing capacity. The TRIPS agreement allows unauthorized working of the patent where sale is dominant locally. Thus, poorer countries without adequate manufacturing capacity might not be able to benefit from these flexibilities. The decision on Implementation of Paragraph 6 of the Doha Declaration on the TRIPS Agreement and Public Health (August 2003) allows countries producing generic copies of patented drugs under compulsory license to export drugs to countries with no or little drug manufacturing capacity. The protracted negotiations that led to this decision should have been informed by the rich states' human rights responsibility of international assistance and cooperation in health.

Regarding GATS, trade in services can occur through a number of recognized supply "modes": cross-border supply; consumption abroad; commercial presence; and presence of natural persons. Each of these supply "modes" is relevant to the delivery of health and health-related services, and thus to the right to the highest attainable standard of health. The liberalization of trade in services across each of these supply "modes" opens the health sector to higher levels of international competition. The effect of this liberalization will depend on the specific nature of a country's national health system, the regulatory environment, the government's policies, and the level of development and infrastructure of the country. While accepting that increased trade in health services could increase available resources and improve the state of health care in some cases, it could also lead to regression in the enjoyment of the right to health. For example, it might also gear health provision toward wealthy local and foreign patients, leading to a two-tier health system that caters to the healthy and wealthy rather than the sick and poor. A two-tier system could lead to specialized surgery responding to profitable areas (for example, elective surgery); "cream skimming," where services are provided to those who can pay more but need less; the "skills drain," with health-care professionals moving toward the higher-paying private sector focused on patients who can pay, and possibly diverting resources from rural and primary health care toward specialized centers (Hunt 2005a, par. 63). Thus, while increased trade in services might lead to an improvement in health services for some, it could also generate increased discrimination in the provision of health services—particularly discrimination on the basis of social status—and a withdrawal of resources from the poor toward the wealthy.

The right to the highest attainable standard of health requires that health facilities, goods, and services be accessible and of good quality. If increased trade in services were to lead to a reduction in rural primary health care, or reduced access for the poor because of user fees, prima facie this would be inconsistent with the right to health. Equally, if increased trade in services were to lead to substandard health facilities, goods, and services, this too would prima facie be inconsistent with the right to health.

The special rapporteur's report included several recommendations. When formulating their trade policies, all states must take into account their national and international human rights obligations, including those relating to the right to health. Developed states must take into account their human rights responsibility of international assistance and cooperation. These include a responsibility on states to conduct right-to-health impact assessments if a state chooses to engage in trade liberalization in those areas that affect the right to health, with a view to selecting the form, pacing, and sequencing of liberalization. They also include a responsibility on high-income states not to pressure a developing country to implement "TRIPS plus" legislation, unless reliable evidence confirms that such legislation will enhance enjoyment of the right to health in the developing country.

The Peru-U.S. Free Trade Agreement

The governments of Peru and the United States have negotiated a bilateral free trade agreement. The agreement, which strengthens patent protection beyond the twenty years required by TRIPS, has significant implications for access to essential medicines in Peru. The special rapporteur issued a press release on the agreement between Peru and the United States at the time of its drafting, calling for, among other items, safeguards in the agreement recognizing the right and duty of countries to adopt measures to protect human life and health and the right to health. The press release also called for the United States not to apply any pressure on Peru to enter into commitments that are inconsistent with Peru's constitutional and international human rights obligations. The press release also highlighted Peru's own domestic human rights obligations in this respect (United Nations 2005).

The U.K. Department for International Development in Peru

Donors have played an important role in realizing the right to health in Peru, through the provision of funding to the government and civil society organizations. Consistent with the United Kingdom's human rights responsibility of international assistance and cooperation in health, the Department for International Development (DFID) developed a pioneering program in Peru called "Improving the Health of the Poor:

A Human Rights Approach." Working with the Ministry of Health, the human rights ombudsperson, and civil society, this program and a series of more modest initiatives have sought to strengthen research and dialogue about poverty, health, and human rights.

In 2003, the United Kingdom announced its closure of the DFID bilateral program in Peru. This closure partly arose from the reallocation of resources to reconstruction in Iraq. The DFID continued to provide support for Peru via other regional and multilateral programs. Nonetheless, the DFID anticipated closing its commendable bilateral health and human rights program.

In 2004, the special rapporteur undertook a mission to Peru (Hunt 2005b). The mission primarily focused on the domestic obligations of the Peruvian government to give effect to the right to health. However, it also included a focus on the roles and responsibilities of international actors, including the DFID. In the report on his mission, the special rapporteur expressed his regrets that British policy toward Iraq is seriously jeopardizing such a valuable health and human rights initiative in Latin America. He urged the United Kingdom to find additional resources as a matter of urgency so that its health and human rights work in Peru could continue. Subsequently, resources were found by the DFID to continue to support some important health and human rights projects.

Conclusion

The human rights responsibility of international assistance and cooperation is a legally binding obligation on states parties to the ICESCR, as well as other relevant human rights treaties. This legal responsibility reinforces numerous international and other developmental commitments, including Millennium Development Goal 8 and the "flexibilities" in the TRIPS agreement designed to protect public health. For a country with a commendable record in international development, such as Sweden, recognition of this legal obligation will not herald a significant departure from its existing international policies and programs.

The human rights responsibility of international assistance and cooperation have only recently begun to attract the attention they richly deserve. Their precise parameters are not yet clearly defined. In our view, the way forward is to look at this human rights responsibility in relation to specific sectors, issues, and rights. For this reason, we have focused on the human rights responsibility of international assistance and cooperation in health. Moreover, we have looked at health in specific countries and contexts, such as Sweden's policies in Uganda, the World Bank, and the IMF. We suggest that such operational specificity makes these important issues easier to grasp. In the context of the human rights responsibility of international assistance and cooperation, the devil is *not* in the detail, but in sweeping generalizations of an entirely abstract nature.

A key priority is to develop mechanisms of monitoring and accountability in relation to the human rights responsibility of international assistance and cooperation. Existing international mechanisms, such as the UN Committee on Economic, Social, and Cultural Rights, as well as UN special rapporteurs, have a vital contribution to make, but it is unreasonable to expect them to carry this heavy burden by themselves. New monitoring and accountability initiatives are needed—and among the most promising are national mechanisms, in both donor and recipient countries, in relation to the human rights responsibility of international assistance and cooperation (Hunt 2005b, par. 86–88).

Chapter 6
The World Food Crisis and the Right to Adequate Food

Michael Windfuhr

The current world food crisis has highlighted a fact that might seem trivial but is essential when addressing the issue of extraterritorial obligations related to the right to adequate food. Even when food is eaten where it is produced,[1] it is at the same time a global market product, and price trends at the international level influence local prices all over the world—which has a direct bearing on the accessibility of food for hungry people. Thus, the current crisis, which has manifested itself in rising food prices, increased levels of hunger and malnutrition, and rioting and civil unrest spawned by these conditions, serves as a perfect backdrop to recognize the interplay of national and international factors in the realization of the right to adequate food.

The chapter will begin with a short overview of the right to adequate food and how this right has been interpreted over the past few years. It will then look into some cases of violations of extraterritorial obligations.[2] These case illustrations will be used to introduce typologies developed by civil society organizations for the classification of extraterritorial obligations related to the right to food. The results will be used in the last part of the chapter to discuss practical and theoretical problems related to the use of extraterritorial obligations and ways to overcome or deal with them.

International Factors and the Right to Food

Perhaps more than any other human right, the right to adequate food is greatly influenced by international factors. These factors create framework conditions for governments when they design policies to implement progressively the right to adequate food. Food is a private good traded on markets, and increasingly on open, international markets. Global price trends and changes in the input sector or in the food-processing industry are therefore important factors that influence the market signals for food products. However, these factors do not eliminate, limit, or reduce the obligations of governments to implement the right to food, but they do influence the strategies for the realization of this right.

The current situation has been characterized by intergovernmental organizations as a "world food crisis." In response to this, the UN secretary-general convened the High-Level Task Force in Bern in April 2008.[3] Robert Zoellick, the director of the World Bank, Jacques Diouf, the director of the UN Food and Agriculture Organization (FAO), and the heads of other intergovernmental organizations (IGOs) such as the International Fund for Agricultural Development (IFAD) and the World Food Programme (WFP), demanded a substantive increase in bilateral and multilateral aid to cope with the urgency of the situation. With this, they were already referring to one of the extraterritorial obligations under the right to food, namely, the obligations of international cooperation and assistance that are contained in article 2 of the International Covenant on Economic, Social, and Cultural Rights (ICESCR) as well as its article 11(2), which deals specifically with the right to be free from hunger:

> The States Parties to the present Covenant, recognizing the fundamental right of everyone to be free from hunger, shall take, individually and through international cooperation, the measures, including specific programmes, which are needed: (a) to improve the methods of production, conservation and distribution of food by making full use of technical and scientific knowledge, by disseminating knowledge of the principles of nutrition and by developing or reforming agrarian systems in such a way as to achieve the most efficient development and utilization of natural resources; (b) Taking into account the problems of both food-importing and food-exporting countries, to ensure an equitable distribution of world food supplies in relation to need.

As is clear, the ICESCR recognizes the importance of international cooperation as well as the relevance of trade for low-income food-deficit countries. Unfortunately, none of the IGO heads made any mention of article 11(2) or extraterritorial state obligations more generally during these talks, although this changed with the High-Level Task Force on the Global Food Crisis. Its Comprehensive Framework for Action makes several references to the right to adequate food. This nexus was also made by the resolution adopted on 22 May 2008 by the UN Human Rights Council, which considering the right to adequate food held its first special session devoted to one of the economic, social, and cultural rights. The resolution recognized that States have a primary obligation to make their best efforts to meet the vital food needs of their own populations, especially of the vulnerable groups and households, such as through enhancing programmes to combat mother-child malnutrition, and to increase local production for this purpose, while the international community should provide, through a coordinated response and upon request, support to national and regional efforts by providing the necessary assistance for increasing food production, particularly through transfer of technology, as well as food crop rehabilitation assistance and food aid. (UN Human Rights Council 2008, par. 4)

While recognizing the primary obligation of national governments to do their utmost to address this situation, the UN Human Rights Council also sees a major responsibility of the international community to respond to the situation. In this same session, the new UN special rapporteur on the right to food, Olivier de Schutter, advocated for a broad reading of the "international cooperation" clause. He defines areas of international cooperation such as trade, food aid, agrofuels, and policies that relate to climate change.

The international community must ensure that an enabling environment is created, allowing such national strategies to flourish, and providing financial and technical assistance where needed. This, indeed, constitutes another, and richer, meaning of the obligation of international cooperation. The required interaction between national strategies and the establishment of an enabling international environment should guide us both in our immediate responses to the current crisis, and in our mid- and long-term strategies. (de Schutter 2008)

The international dimension is therefore of utmost importance for the long-term guarantee of the right to adequate food. The main duty bearers are each of the state parties to the ICESCR, but they can only implement fully the right to adequate food when international framework conditions are conducive and not detrimental to this. The debate about extraterritorial obligations is a debate about addressing the responsible actors for these framework conditions because otherwise human rights protection for individuals remains incomplete. In a globalized world, human rights must be able to address *all* relevant actors in order to guarantee a universal protection of these rights.

World Food Crisis

The current situation is often described as a "world food crisis," although there are strong indications that there is nothing temporary about the present situation (Technical Centre for Agriculture and Rural Co-Operation 2008). Most notably, a joint study by the Organisation for Economic Co-operation and Development (OECD) and the FAO (2008) highlighted that while prices should decline from their peak in early 2008, they will remain substantially above the average of the past decade. The real trend has followed this forecast. Comparing the period of 1998–2007 to the projected price levels for 2008–17, it is estimated that beef and pork will be approximately 20 percent higher; raw and white sugar 30 percent; wheat, maize, and skimmed-milk powder 40–60 percent; butter and oilseed more than 60 percent; and vegetable oil more than 80 percent.

Listed below are some of the major reasons for the present (and future) world food crisis:

- The production of staple food will compete with other forms of using agricultural produce, such as fuels or energy resources, but also in the long run as a general replacement for oil.
- Demand for cereals will increase, to a large extent due to the changes in the patterns of food consumption in the rapidly expanding economies. In countries such as China and India, the demand for meat products is increasing rapidly. If cereal consumption worldwide approaches the average European consumption level, the world would need to harvest more than six billion tons of cereals, while the current production is slightly above two billion.
- Global food markets will also be confronted with a shrinking surplus production in the United States and the European Union, partially because of the World Trade Organization's commitments to end export subsidies, and partially because more agricultural produce will be used as agrofuels in these countries as well.
- Loss in fertile production areas through competing land use will continue to be an influencing factor. Urbanization will lead to a rapid growth of cities, particularly the mega-cities in the global south. The majority of the fast-rising mega-cities are located in fertile coastal areas. The size of living areas and those used for industrial purposes will increase, but so will traffic infrastructures, as can be seen in the fertile coastal areas of China. The mega-cities will also consume huge quantities of water, which will invariably lead to rural-urban conflicts, particularly if water is no longer available for irrigation purposes.
- The increase in world population will continue. It should stabilize in the second half of the century to slightly above nine billion people.
- Another factor is the anticipated escalation of the degradation of agricultural lands, grazing lands, and fishery resources. Degradation can be caused by the loss of fertile soils through soil erosion, salinization, contamination, and so on. The availability of irrigation water will decrease, fishing grounds will remain overexploited, and graz-

ing land will remain vulnerable to desertification. In addition, the expected negative impact of climate change must also be taken into consideration (UN Food and Agriculture Organization 2003).

- Some traditional surplus and exporting regions (for example, the southwestern United States, Australia, and southern Europe) might lose their potential for surplus production because weather conditions will become dryer and water availability is shrinking. While there are some areas in the northern hemisphere that will benefit from increasing temperatures, they will hardly offset what is lost in these traditional surplus regions.

All of these factors are contributing to a long-term scenario where an increasing demand for food goes hand in hand with limits in food-producing resources. While this scenario does not necessarily lead to scarcity of food in the coming years, it is an indication that prices for agricultural produce will not go down again to levels that prevailed during the last two to three decades. Fertilizer prices continue to rise, and energy costs serve as a major input factor for farmers. Therefore, the trends show that prices will stabilize at a higher level and that governments will have to deal with this challenge when designing policies to implement the right to adequate food.

Price trends are not only relevant for the rural or urban consumers who have to buy their staple food at local markets; they are also important for producers. In fact, half of all people who are currently hungry are smallholder farmers. The European Commission recently published an analysis of the food crisis and came to the conclusion that the rising prices affected net food-importing countries in Africa most severely. According to the commission's findings, the higher food prices have translated into greater poverty and malnutrition, and increased vulnerability to further external shocks for the world's poorest (European Commission 2008).

While the commission's report expressed hope that higher prices might present new income-generating opportunities for farmers in developing countries in the medium and long term, allowing them to better deal with the consequences of climate change, the OECD (Organisation for Economic Co-operation and Development 2008b) has been skeptical about that. According to the OECD, high prices will primarily benefit commercial producers but not necessarily the bulk of producers in developing countries where many farmers are not linked to markets. Prices are expected to become more volatile in the coming period, in part due to speculation and in part due to the increase in weather extremes. This will require a long-term policy response by governments in supporting those farmers who are not linked to markets and to poor rural and urban consumers.

Influencing Factors

As can be seen from this short summary, the realization of the right to adequate food is more reliant and more influenced by international factors than other economic, social, and cultural rights such as the right to education or the right to housing. In addition, there are a host of different variables at work. Thus far, we have looked at the issue of supply and demand. We now turn to three other factors—trade policies, policy advice, and models of production—that will play important roles in the area of the right to adequate food.

Trade Policies

Trade policies were historically developed by national governments, primarily as a means of protecting national producers from competition from abroad. Since the beginning of the 1980s, the World Bank and the International Monetary Fund (IMF) repeatedly stressed open markets in their policy advice to highly indebted developing countries. This policy of open markets promoted in the context of structural adjustment policies was later taken up in the Uruguay Round of trade negotiations, which resulted in the establishment of the World Trade Organization (WTO) in 1994. While some producers benefited, many farmers in developing countries were hard hit by rapid market liberalization, while at the same time developed countries were using huge export subsidies to place their agricultural overproduction on global markets. This dominant trend for more than two decades made it difficult for producers in developing countries to compete with these arbitrarily cheap imports. This situation has been widely documented by any number of development-oriented nongovernmental organizations (NGOs) and it has become one of the key conflict issues in global trade negotiations. In the meantime, an agreement was reached so that these export subsidies should be phased out by 2013. While export subsidies have become less of a factor, the effects of trade liberalization on local markets in many developing countries remain a major problem. It is noteworthy that imports are oftentimes no longer coming from the European Union but from competitive global producers, such as rice from countries like Thailand and Vietnam. The markets of most developing countries are open and many countries would like to regain the right to protect certain products or product lines with higher tariffs in order to protect national producers' incomes. The protection of "special products" and "sensitive products" are key negotiation issues of the Doha Development Round (DDR).

While the DDR is currently interrupted, many developed countries have started to include their own demands for open markets in developing countries through bilateral trade and investment agreements. For example, the European Union is currently negotiating economic partnership agreements (EPAs) with the countries previously entering into the so-called ACP agreements (Africa, Pacific, and Caribbean) and least developed countries. If the proposals of the European Union come through, all EPA countries will have to open up their markets even further. Agricultural trade policies are therefore a key factor influencing and limiting the abilities of national states to implement the right to adequate food. Countries that would like to support small-holder farmers need to protect them to a certain degree, particularly if they are not competitive in open global markets. Even the local markets to which they normally supply are dominated by imports (see case example below).

Policy Advice

Policy advice has become one of the main sources of international influence. The main policy advice comes from intergovernmental organizations, particularly the World Bank and the IMF, in the context of debt renegotiations and the conditions linked to new credits. Most developing countries have been advised to focus their agricultural development on those producers and those products that are competitive in international markets, and then to import the rest of their foodstuffs.[4] Due to four decades of artificially low prices for food products, most countries changed support policies to agriculture following that advice. Food production is rarely subsidized or supported in these states. Most producers of foodstuffs are small-holder farmers, many of whom are women. The policy advice led to a concentration of national agricultural policies on larger units based on the production of export crops, and not on small-holder agriculture. Therefore, policy decisions at the international level are exerting a tremendous influence on "national" policymaking with respect to which groups should receive government support. Unfortunately, in this process, marginalized groups are oftentimes ignored.

Models of Production

As a background to all of this is a larger debate about the models of production and the role of technology that should be used in an attempt to best combat hunger and malnutrition. There has been increased support for a new green revolution for Africa, from IGOs, some African countries, and private business such as Yara International, the large fertilizer company from Norway, and the Bill and Melinda Gates Foundation (BMGF). The objective is to improve the input supply for African agriculture. The BMGF is willing to provide a continent-wide seed-selling infrastructure in order to improve farmers' access to modern seeds.

While these groups highlight the low input side of African agriculture, other policymakers have argued that there is a more fundamental problem, namely, the long-term neglect of African governments to foster rural development and to support small-holder farmers. The High-Level Task Force, referred to earlier, has concluded that the yields in Africa could be at least tripled if small-holder farmers in low potential areas were supported better. It concluded that agricultural research has focused for too long on the high potential areas, and not taken enough care of farmers at more marginal sites.

This technical debate is rapidly being transformed into a subject of policy analysis. Under the slogan "food sovereignty," farmers' organizations worldwide, such as Via Campesina, have demanded that more attention be given to keeping people in rural areas. They argue that agrarian reform measures will increase the access to productive resources for those who are marginal producers. At the other side of the spectrum is the approach of the World Bank, reflected in the *World Development Report* on agricultural development (World Bank 2007). The bank differentiates three different sectors in rural areas. The first are farmers who are competitive in national and international markets and who are to receive the most support. The second consists of subsistence farmers who have enough potential to be stabilized as farmers. According to the bank, the income of this group might be supported by safety nets as a means of helping them to remain in rural areas. The third consists of marginal producers who are viewed as being unable to survive in the long term as small-holder producers, and who are expected to leave rural areas and migrate to cities and metropolitan areas.

The importance of small-holder agriculture for the long-term supply of food has been highlighted recently by a new institution, the International Assessment of Agricultural Science and Technology for Development (IAASTD), which is a group of experts set up after the Johannesburg environmental summit in a similar form to the International Panel on Climate Change. The IAASTD published its final report in April 2008, the product of three years of research and consultations involving four hundred experts. Perhaps its most important finding relates to the increase in food production of small holders in agriculture when these producers have access to certain input factors and productive resources.

Given the fact that more than half of those who are currently suffering from food deprivation are small-holder farmers, the issue of how to support them best is one of the key issues for combating hunger and realizing the right to adequate food. There is a consensus that support to rural development has to increase, but the debate is about the best way to support production and about which producers to support. Discussions on models of production, on the content of the policy advice, and on the best trade policies to pursue are undoubtedly complex. However, they can and should be analyzed from the perspective of a right to food, looking first at the effects on the most vulnerable groups. The analysis should be grounded in a substantive interpretation of the right to adequate food and the effects of certain policy choices that can be shown compared to other available options. At the same time, the discussion over models should not distract attention from the fact that the distributional effects of different national agricultural policy decisions can be compared at a specific country level. Policy choices are not neutral and can and must therefore be analyzed from a right-to-food perspective.

The Right to Adequate Food

The right to food was officially recognized as a universal human right by the United Nations in its Universal Declaration of Human Rights of 1948. Nearly two decades later, the ICESCR, which has been ratified by 159 states as of July 2008, made the right to food binding international law for those countries that become states parties to it.

The World Food Summit (WFS) of 1996 placed the right to food on a much higher level than before, and attention and analysis were given to what governments could do to end hunger and malnutrition. The WFS Plan of Action called for the clarification of the content and ways of implementing the right to adequate food as contained in international law. The UN Committee on Economic, Social, and Cultural Rights (CESCR) was asked to develop an interpretative text in the form of a general comment on the right to adequate food. The normative clarification was then largely achieved with *General Comment 12*, adopted by the CESCR in 1999. The content of this document was, and still is, highly important for understanding the right to adequate food as part of the right to an adequate standard of living. Following its adoption, civil society organizations and some governments started to ask for an additional tool to guide the practical implementation of the right to adequate food. At the World Food Summit in June 2002, states decided to develop voluntary guidelines to support the progressive realization of the right to adequate food in the context of national food security. The Intergovernmental Working Group (IGWG) for this purpose was established by the FAO Council and after twenty months of intensive negotiations it reported its results to the FAO Committee on World Food Security (CFS). The voluntary guidelines were adopted unanimously by the 127th Session of the FAO Council in November 2004.

While most states had already recognized the right to food and made commitments to its implementation, the voluntary guidelines constitute further normative development in that this is the first time states have agreed on the form of description of state obligations, which the CESCR has chosen to apply for all economic, social, and cultural rights. The CESCR differentiates three levels of obligations, the obligations to respect, protect, and fulfill the right to food.

Content of the Right to Adequate Food

In *General Comment 12*, the CESCR has given its interpretation of the right to adequate food: "The right to adequate food is realized when every man, woman and child, alone or in community with others, has physical and economic access at all times to adequate food or means for its procurement" (UN Committee on Economic, Social, and Cultural Rights 1999, par. 6). The right to adequate food implies the availability of food in quantity and quality sufficient to satisfy the dietary needs of individuals. The food has to be free from adverse substances and acceptable within a given culture. Furthermore, the food has to be accessible in ways that are sustainable, and this implies that the access and the availability need to be given over the long term.

Several components of this definition are of particular importance to understanding properly the content of the right to adequate food. Food must by physically available. Availability implies either a possibility of feeding oneself from productive land or on income from wage labor or the existence of a well-functioning food distribution system that guarantees that food is always there. Availability in a region or a village alone does not mean that a person or a household has access to food. In addition, food accessibly also means that people are not hindered in getting it due to the fact that they belong to a minority group that is discriminated against. Food must also be economically accessible. That is, people need to have the means to buy it. Accessibility of food is only sufficiently guaranteed when individuals or households do not have to sacrifice the fulfillment of other essential basic needs in order to get food. Any form of food procurement is therefore only viable when other economic, social, and cultural rights are not thereby breached. The term "dietary needs" refers to more than pure nutrients for physical needs. It refers to those dietary needs that are necessary for physical and mental growth and activity.

Another important component is access to adequate health care and control of disease. Many children who die from malnutrition do have access to food but cannot adequately utilize it because diseases are hindering them. For children, particularly small children and babies, it is also necessary that somebody gives adequate care so that they will be fed well and regularly.

General Comment 12 refers to a core content of the right to adequate food—the freedom from hunger. This refers to the immediate obligations of governments to guarantee that nobody dies from acute hunger due to man-made or natural catastrophes and emergencies. While the content of "freedom from hunger" has not been well elaborated so far, it reflects the intention of the drafters of the ICESCR to make sure that nobody dies from immediate hunger. The full realization of the right to adequate food can only be achieved progressively and will take time, even if many government obligations can be implemented immediately.

Obligations of Nation-States

Human rights set minimum standards for state behavior and these are to be adhered to when states negotiate and sign international agreements. States have to implement human rights norms on the national level. Basically, the state assumes obligations on three different levels. In terms of the right to food, the state first has to *respect* the existing access to food that people have, that is, it should ensure that the right to food is not violated by the state's policy measures. People should not be resettled through infrastructural measures without receiving adequate compensation, and they should not lose the basis of their livelihoods due to agricultural policy measures without adequate compensation. Second, the state should *protect* existing access to food that people have, that is, it should ensure that third parties—often economically powerful players—do not deny access to food, for instance by displacement of farmers. Third, the state has an obligation to *fulfill* the right to food for all people who currently cannot feed themselves. The state can, for example, redistribute idle-lying land or create jobs by providing an adequate regulatory framework in agricultural policy. The CESCR has subsumed two different kinds of policy measures as subcategories of the fulfillment obligation. Governments should *facilitate* the enjoyment of the right to adequate food by enabling people to have access to productive resources (land, water, seeds, credits, and so forth) and to grow their food on their own, or to have jobs that guarantee an adequate income. Facilitation is a key to a long-term strategy to implement the right to food fully. But there will be groups within a society that cannot make use of productive resources, perhaps because they are too old, too young, handicapped, or temporarily ill. For these groups, it is also necessary that states *provide* food and guarantee the enjoyment of that right directly.

The implementation of economic, social, and cultural human rights does not demand impossible efforts from states, as is often suggested by skeptics, but involves feasible objectives. The obligation to respect and protect rights can be fulfilled without recourse to extensive financial means. The obligation to fulfill human rights requires the investment of resources. However, article 2 of the ICESCR sets realistic standards. The article does not demand that all rights be immediately implemented for everybody; rather, states have to implement the rights progressively and use the maximum of resources available. This obligation can also be fulfilled by poorer states, as the article only requires the investment of resources available. The use of these resources should, however, focus on and prioritize the poor and sectors of the population that suffer from discrimination. Other requirements have been described in the literature and are becoming standard interpretations of the application of the obligation to fulfill. Governments have to show that they have taken specific steps vis-à-vis all vulnerable groups. The realization of the rights should be progressive and should be fostered "as expeditiously as possible."[5]

This typology of state obligations was first developed by the Norwegian scholar Asbjörn Eide and later adopted by the CESCR and it provides a useful characterization of what is expected of governments in order to avoid violations of the right to adequate food. Under the obligation to respect, the government has to try to end violations through direct policy acts and through de jure and de facto discrimination in national policies. The violations through direct policy acts are often linked to forced evictions of people from land on which they could gain a living through agricultural production. Such forms of forced resettlement, often implemented without proper compensation and rehabilitation policies, are often planned or initiated in the name of larger "development projects." The construction of large dams, other infrastructure facilities, the enlargement of cities, and so on, are typical forms of such projects. While some of these projects could have been developed in a different way by more carefully considering alternatives, which would minimize or avoid the damage that has been caused, some projects requiring forms of resettlements will be difficult to avoid. However, what has to be guaranteed is that affected people do not lose their sources of livelihood. Many of these projects are financed or co-financed by international actors. It is therefore easy to see that while the affected state has the primary obligation to respect, all other international actors also have an obligation to do no harm.

The control of third parties, which is the role for government policies under the obligation to protect, requires activities that are very similar for civil and political rights as well as for economic, social, and cultural rights. The government needs to establish regulations in order to control private actors that contribute to violations of the right to adequate food. While the legislative part of that endeavor should not be too complicated, the difficulties often begin with the implementation of land laws, workers' legislation, and so on. Powerful economic actors have a number of options available to them that help to hide violations, or at least the responsibility for such violations. For one thing, they can simply create new legal entities. They can also employ legal proceedings to start lengthy and costly procedures in courts, or even bribe policymakers and judges. Implementing the obligation to protect, therefore, often requires reforms at many governmental levels. In essence, the obligation oftentimes rests on good governance and the establishment of the rule of law. The implementation of the obligation to protect is also politically difficult because the responsible actors are often powerful entities, be it national or international, and very difficult to control, particularly when it comes to foreign direct investment. Every regulation taken by a government is then in competition with regulations (or the absence thereof) of other governments. Thus, it is difficult for governments to insist on certain levels of standards if other countries in a similar position do not follow these same standards.

The obligation to protect also requires from governments a fair and transparent management of processes that affect people, and the guarantee of functioning complaint mechanisms. People have the right to be heard in decision-making processes that affect them. They should have the ability to file a complaint and have access to effective recourse mechanisms if their rights are thought to be violated. Many of the powerful private actors are transnational corporations. Therefore, there are also obligations of the country of origin of these corporations to make sure that they do not bribe or contribute to human rights violations in other lands.

The obligation to fulfill applies to government action directed at improving the situation of persons or groups that are hungry and malnourished. This covers three different forms of activities. Governments must (1) be prepared for normal and regular forms of disasters, such as regular droughts; (2) design policies for vulnerable groups, and such policies must be directed to enable people in the long run to overcome hunger and malnutrition on their own; and (3) establish policy measures to help all those who need direct forms of help when they cannot earn a living from their own fieldwork or wage labor. This is especially the case for the elderly, the chronically sick, and the very young.

One of the great problems with the obligation to fulfill is placing government policy under scrutiny. Such analysis has to try to establish whether the policies chosen are adequate in protecting vulnerable groups, and whether the government is really using the maximum of available resources in order to supply those suffering from acute hunger.[6] What is also difficult to determine is whether the government is making effective use of its resources in order to address hunger and malnutrition. Answers to these questions are fundamental in the current debate on the right to adequate food. The voluntary guidelines have been formulated to help address these issues. Some of these problems will be further taken up below, but a general working principle is that the governments must shoulder the burden of proof. This is important for any functioning accountability mechanism. Civil society groups often do not have the capacity to discuss difficult policy choices; however, above all else, the government has to explain why hunger and malnutrition still exist.

The CESCR's *General Comment 12* contains one additional recommendation for the implementation of the right to adequate food: Governments shall develop a "national strategy" for the realization of the right to adequate food that must (1) assess the situation carefully and identify all vulnerable groups; (2) ensure that there is no discrimination under the law that is responsible for causing such vulnerability; (3) analyze whether the policy prescriptions seeking to protect vulnerable groups are adequate or not; (4) monitor the outcome of the policy choices that have been undertaken; and (5) guarantee effective recourse mechanisms for victim groups. This recommendation was taken up and reconfirmed by the Voluntary Guidelines of the FAO.

Extraterritorial Obligations: Case-Based Experiences

Taking up the international dimension of the right to adequate food adds another level of complexity to the recognition and protection of this right. To be clear, the home state has the primary obligation to make its own best effort to realize the right to adequate food within its own territorial boundaries. However, the extraterritorial dimension is relevant when a state is not able to protect this right of its citizens on its own, or else when outside states and actors pursue policies that affect the protection of the right to adequate food in another state. All of the case studies presented below, which come from the joint work of Bread for the World, FoodFirst Information and Action Network (FIAN), and the Evangelischer Entwickliungsdienst (eed), make reference to both national and extraterritorial obligations.

Bilateral Investment Treaty between Paraguay and Germany

Germany and Paraguay entered into a bilateral investment agreement (BIT) in 1993. For present purposes, what is important about this BIT is that it contains a provision that has prevented Paraguay from expropriating land owned by German nationals.

The background of these cases is the general situation related to access to land in Paraguay. As in many Latin American countries the land distribution is quite unequal, with 1 percent of the landholders owning 77 percent of the country's arable land, and at the other end of the income spectrum, 40 percent of small-holder farmers only owning around 1 percent of the arable land. The largest 351 property owners own 9.7 million hectares, which comes out to approximately 27,600 hectares per person. Due to this situation, Paraguay, like many other Latin American countries, has instituted an agrarian reform law that gives the government the possible option of expropriating land that has not been used for some period of years and by paying compensation to the owner. The land can then be used to resettle formerly landless families. These agrarian reform laws are consonant with the obligation to fulfill the right to adequate food in that they help to increase the access of poor landless families to productive resources.

As noted above, Paraguay's expropriation policy has an extraterritorial dimension by virtue of the BIT. A joint study financed by FIAN, Bread for the World, eed, and Misereor has shown that for the period 1994–2007, all attempts to expropriate land owned by German nationals was halted under the provisions of the German-Paraguayan BIT. What is also noteworthy is that while Paraguay has 28 BITs, only the one with Germany and the one with South Korea have been used to hinder the implementation of the agrarian reform law.

One case involves the community of Palmital in the district of Carlos Antonio Lopez, in the Department of Itapúa. About a decade ago the land, which had not been used for a long time, was occupied by 120 families with approximately 8 hectares per family (the whole area is 1003 hectares). These family farmers applied to the National Institute for the Development of the Land (Instituto Nacional de Desarrollo Rural de la Tierra, or INDERT) and the institute confirmed that the land fulfilled all the criteria for expropriation. However, the effort to expropriate was halted by reference to the BIT with Germany. In fact, these families were forcibly evicted, and their belongings and the houses they had constructed were destroyed. In addition, the farmer leaders were prosecuted. The situation is still not resolved as of this writing.

Another case involves the indigenous community of Sawhoyamaxa, which consists of 407 persons from 83 families. For a long period, the community had been scattered in different parts of the Chaco. Since 1997, they have come together and started to claim their ancestral land, which consists of 14,404 hectares. The traditional land of indigenous communities is strongly protected in the Paraguayan Constitution in chapter V. Additionally, the law 904/84 and the law 234/93 guarantee recognized indigenous communities' access to their traditional lands.[7] Responsibility for making such determinations rests with the National

Institute for Indigenous Development (Instituto Nacional del Desarrollo Indígena, or INDI). The Sawhoyamaxa community applied for the land and the INDI confirmed that it was in fact the traditional land of the community. However, the INDI also informed the community that the land was owned by a German and that it would be protected by the BIT. The community presented its case to the Inter-American Commission of Human Rights (IACHR) in May 2001 with the support of Terra Viva, an NGO from Paraguay. In February 2005, the IACHR took the case before the Inter-American Court. A final court decision was issued in March 2006 (*Sawhoyamaxa v. Paraguay*) in favor of the community, and the government was given three years to expropriate this land and hand it over to the indigenous community. The government was also told to finance a fund for the development of the community of Sawhoyamaxa. To date, the court decision has not been implemented.

These cases show the direct impact of German policies on the right to adequate food in another country. These cases are intended to begin a dialogue with the Foreign Affairs Ministry and the Ministry of Economics to encourage the German government to take its human rights obligations seriously, and to send a letter of clarification to the government of Paraguay in which Germany confirms that the BIT shall not serve as an obstacle to agrarian reform in Paraguay.[8] Thus far, dialogue with the German government has not been easy. In principle, the German government has accepted that it has extraterritorial obligations and that the decision of the Inter-American Court cannot be ignored. But at the time of this writing, the German government still has not sent a letter of clarification, ostensibly on the grounds that Paraguay has not paid adequate compensation in a reasonable period of time.

EU Chicken Exports to Cameroon

Sixty-five percent of the people in Cameroon make their living from agriculture. Around 20 percent of the population in Cameroon is malnourished. As in most other countries in Africa, the reason for this is not a general lack of food or food production potential. Only twenty years ago, Cameroon was producing 90 percent of its food needs inside the country, including chicken meat, which has been a traditional food, particularly at special events such as weddings and funerals. Raising and selling chicken has been a source of income for thousands of people in Cameroon, particularly women. The production of one ton of chicken meat in Cameroon represents income for three livelihoods in agriculture for producing and raising the chickens as well as for growing the corn to feed them, and two livelihoods in the urban area for plucking and selling them.

The situation of chicken producers in Cameroon has changed dramatically since cheap chicken parts from the European Union have begun to be sold in Cameroon after domestic markets were opened. Chicken parts from Europe (whose export is not subsidized) have become much less expensive due to the fact that consumers in the European Union increasingly prefer only selected parts of the chicken (in particular, the tender meat of the chicken breast or upper parts of the leg). For the rest of the chicken (legs, wings, and gizzards) there is no market in Europe. Thus, selling these parts in West Africa is more profitable for European traders than selling them for alternative use in Europe. Over the past decade, the European Union has increased its exports of frozen chicken parts to West Africa (in particular Cameroon, Ghana, and Senegal) from 48,000 tons in 1996 to 200,000 tons in 2004. Cameroon imported 978 tons in 1996—but 24,000 tons in 2004. Approximately three-quarters of these imports come from the European Union, mainly from France, Belgium, the Netherlands, and Spain. Until 1996, Cameroon was basically self-sufficient in the poultry market.

The total annual demand for poultry in Cameroon is estimated at about 35,000 tons. In 2002, 21,000 tons were produced domestically. However, a year later, this production had already dropped by 8,000 tons. This resulted in the loss of approximately 40,000 livelihoods of vulnerable people in Cameroon in just one year. Cameroon law limits imports to 7,000 tons per year. The Ministry for Animal Breeding determines import volumes, but the country lacks inspectors. Bribery is rampant. For the importers, frozen chicken parts are good business: They buy one kilogram for 0.80 € and sell it for 1.50 €. Local producers can only survive with a price of 1.80 € per kilogram.

Exporting European frozen meat to a tropical country like Cameroon, which does not have proper cooling chains or refrigeration, also creates a health risk for the consumer population. After being unloaded, it might take hours for chicken imports to reach markets in the countryside. In addition, chicken is often sold in open stands without cooling. The Centre Pasteur in Yaunde classified 83.5 percent of the frozen chicken parts on the Cameroon markets as "unsuitable for human consumption" (FIAN, Brot für die Welt, eed, 2006 18). Food poisoning increasingly occurred after weddings or funerals where EU chicken parts were consumed. The incidence of the respective disease patterns in the hospitals of Cameroon was found to be statistically correlated with the increasing imports of frozen chicken. The import of frozen chicken without proper cooling chains means a health risk for the population. Cameroon is a state party to the ICESCR and, therefore, duty-bound to protect the population's "highest attainable standard of physical and mental health" (art. 12.1) against destruction by third parties. By not intervening against the distribution of food that is a health risk, the government of Cameroon has violated the ICESCR. The import of frozen chicken at rates far below the production cost of local producers has destroyed local chicken production. Given the lack of state social security provisions, the loss of income opportunities through self-employment as a farmer can easily turn into the loss of livelihood—and a deprivation under article 11 of the ICESCR (the right to an adequate standard of living). One of the measures of the implementation of the obligations under article 11 covers the guarantee of access to productive resources and the possibility to gain an income from that access. The sharp increase of imports is violating that possibility of gaining an income from productive resources. Therefore, the ICESCR would demand that Cameroon take effective protective measures for the vulnerable local chicken producers, which it has not undertaken.

With respect to European states, a food-exporting country has extraterritorial obligations under the human right to health to take measures individually within its control and in cooperation with the importing country to protect the right to health of persons, in so far as the consumption of the exported food is concerned. To date, the European Union has not taken effective measures to meet its members' commitments under the ICESCR. The export of chicken not only has enormous implications for the right to health and the right to adequate food, but for the right to earn an income through self-employment or other work. The larger point is that just because Cameroon has not adequately protected its consumers and its producers, this does not exonerate the European Union's member states from complying with their own extraterritorial human rights obligations.

Ghana: Newmont Ahafo South Gold Mining Project

On 31 January 2006, the international board of directors of the International Finance Corporation (IFC) (established by and as part of the World Bank Group) approved a loan of U.S.$125 million to the U.S. mining company Newmont to support its Ahafo South gold mining project in Ghana, 300 kilometers northwest of the capital city of Accra. The total mine area of the Ahafo South project is 2,992 hectares. According to the Resettlement Action Plan, approximately 9,500 individuals are directly affected by the project, which means that they have lost their major source of livelihood—their land. About 5,000 individuals (823 households) also lost their homes to the project and are either relocated in one of the two resettlement villages or they have moved out of the area. Ninety-seven percent of the families depend on small-scale agriculture. When farmers lost their property, they did not receive replacement land, nor were they compensated for the land in cash. They only received very meager compensation for crops lost and they were effectively impoverished by the project. This constitutes a violation of their right to food and an adequate standard of living. In addition, the right to water and the right to health have been severely affected by the project: the company dammed the river Subri and is pumping from the river Tano to ensure water supply for the mine. As a result, communities living next to the mine have lost access to safe drinking water, and residents report an increase in malaria because of the stagnant water.

State institutions have the obligation to protect people's rights from violations by the company. In the case of the Ahafo South project, the state institutions have failed to adequately protect the right to food of affected people in the negotiating processes when it comes to the level of compensation, access to land, and restoration of livelihoods. *General Comment 15* of the CESCR on the right to water defines the "failure to enact or enforce laws to prevent the contamination and inequitable extraction of water" as a violation of the obligation to protect the right to water (UN Committee on Economic, Social, and Cultural Rights 2002b, par. 44). The diversion of the river Subri constitutes an "inequitable extraction of water," especially as it seriously influences people's access to water. To protect the right to water effectively, binding environmental regulation would have to be enacted and enforced, and monitoring capacities increased. The major issue was that the 9,500 people affected by the project—97 percent of whom are peasants—had lost their land without being provided with replacement property. Non-compliance with World Bank Operational Directive 4.30 (on involuntary resettlements) was confirmed by an independent expert during a visit to the project area in December 2005 (Giovannetti 2005).

However, management claimed that the independent expert had merely described priority activities that needed to be addressed during the first quarter of 2006, and disagreed that the project was not in compliance with Operational Directive 4.30 when it was approved in January 2006. In response to the monitoring report, and in order to positively influence the board decision on the project, Newmont released a progress update on the issues raised by the independent resettlement expert and committed to present a land action plan, among other measures (Giovannetti 2005). In early May 2006, the independent resettlement monitor again visited the Ahafo South project, but his report was only disclosed to the public in July 2006. During project approval, the IFC board had asked management to report back on outstanding issues by the end of June 2006. In this report, management admitted that the land access program, as prepared by Newmont, was inadequate to ensure long-term access to land, but no timeline was given in the report on how to develop a revised land access program in consultation with the affected farmers.

In November 2005, FIAN informed the German government about the human rights violations in the context of the Ahafo South project and urged the government not to support the project until major issues had been resolved in line with Germany's extraterritorial obligations. The government took an active role and finally decided to vote against the project. In fact, the German executive director of the IFC was the only executive director who voted against the project—in line with Germany's extraterritorial human rights obligations. Three other executive directors (representing the United States, Belgium, and the Netherlands) abstained. These executive directors cannot be made responsible for the voting behavior of the majority of the board. However, they are still in the position to influence the human rights situation of the project and should, therefore, attempt to carry out the obligation to protect the rights of those affected by the Ahafo South project. The question remains how to achieve a better and more efficient way that would provide some form of recourse for the victims. And as this case has shown, working only through one country (Germany) might be quite limiting.

Trade Liberalization and the Right to Adequate Food:
The Example of the Rice Market in Ghana

The Ecumenical Advocacy Alliance undertook a study on the impact of rice market liberalization on the right to adequate food. The study looked into the three country cases: Ghana, Honduras, and Indonesia (Paasch et al. 2007). The example of Ghana is chosen here to show the complexity of factors influencing the living situation in the northern village of Dalun, which had been selected as the site for the study in that country. Whereas rice has long been a niche product for the urban elite in Ghana, demand in all segments of the population has grown remarkably over the last ten years. This development could have opened a window of opportunity for growth in domestic rice production and an increased well-being for the estimated eight hundred thousand Ghanaian rice producers. However, the opposite has been the case. Domestic rice production has diminished in terms of volume and planted area. The reasons for the rice production crisis are manifold. One of the major reasons has been the increase in rice imports during the 1990s and the surge in imports from the United States, Vietnam, and Thailand between 1998 and 2003 (UN Food and Agriculture Organization 2006). As a result, local rice has been displaced from urban markets. "In Ghana rice farmers in the poorest northern part of the country have seen markets squeezed by cheap US-imports" (UN Development Programme 2005, 132).

The peasant families of Dalun have faced increased hardship over the last few years compared to the 1990s. This is particularly true in the "hungry months"—the time between when one harvest has been consumed and next harvest arrives—when families are forced to reduce their meals in quality and sometimes even in quantity. The first victims are children, followed shortly by women. In addition, peasants have increasingly been forced into debt in an attempt to purchase food. Peasants have also become more and more vulnerable to unexpected shocks, such as bad yields caused by droughts or pests.

The study pointed to three factors that contributed to the boost of rice imports, which in turn has had a devastating effect on the livelihoods of local producers. The first factor is the removal of import controls and the introduction of a low applied tariff on rice imports of 20 percent in 1992, which was followed by import increases over the 1990s. The second factor is the high incidents of rice dumping, particularly rice imported from the United States, Vietnam, and Thailand. Dumping is an important reason why imported rice is often cheaper than Ghanaian rice. The third factor is the progressive removal of support to the Ghanaian rice sector between 1983 and the late 1990s. This removal was the result of a poor national infrastructure in terms of the production, processing, and marketing of rice, leading to serious supply constraints on the domestic rice sector in terms of quantity and quality. In Dalun, the removal of state support resulted in an increase in the share of production costs to be shouldered by the farmers, resulting in reduced incomes. There is a good deal of evidence that these policies have significantly increased malnutrition and food insecurity, and thus have resulted in violations of the human right to adequate food.

Three states (or groups of states) are responsible for these policies and for the breach of the right to food: Ghana, the member states of the IMF, and the origin states of imported rice, particularly the United States. Ghana reduced import protection in 1992 by dismantling quantitative restrictions and introducing an applied tariff of 20 percent, thus allowing an unlimited quantity of imports to enter the market regardless of the threat of dumping and the displacement of domestic rice producers from the market. Furthermore, Ghana progressively reduced its support to rice peasants from 1983 until the late 1990s. This support had previously facilitated access to credits, seeds, fertilizers, and the use of machinery at favorable conditions. Ghana thereby increased the costs of production of the rice peasants in Dalun, reduced the net incomes of farmers, and caused food insecurity among them.

The IMF has played a very active and crucial role in convincing and pressuring the respective Ghanaian governments to remove market protection and support to producers, policies that resulted in violations of the right to food among rice peasants in Dalun and elsewhere in Ghana. By imposing various Structural Adjustment Programs starting in 1983, the IMF pressured Ghana to progressively remove import protection, finally decreasing tariffs to only 20 percent in 1992. In 2003, when the Ghanaian parliament passed ACT 641, which increased tariffs for rice once again, the IMF played a crucial role in pressuring the government to suspend the law only four days after the law had been implemented. According to one commentator:

The sequence of events arouses serious suspicion that IMF even used funds as an instrument of pressuring or "convincing" the government to follow its advice. On *May 8* of 2003, the Customs, Excise and Preventive Services (CEPS) started implementation of the ACT 641. On *May 9*, the Executive Board of the IMF concluded a consultation on the Ghana Poverty Reduction Strategy (GPRS) and approved a three-year arrangement under the Poverty Reduction and Growth Facility (PRGF) amounting to SDR 185.5 million. And on *May 12*, just three days after the approval of IMF fund, the suspension of the implementation of Act 641 was issued. Thus it is very probable, that the same "consultations" which lead to the approval of the fund, also "convinced" the Ghanaian government to cut the tariffs to the old level again. While approving funds for poverty alleviation, the IMF thus obstructed necessary steps to protect the right to food of rice peasants, one of the well known groups vulnerable to poverty and food insecurity. (Paasch et al. 2007, 44)

Finally, it is also necessary to look at the actions of the states that were responsible for dumping rice in Ghana. According to the WTO definition, the comparison of the export price with the home market price is just one method of measuring dumping. Another way is to compare export prices with production costs. Taking this approach, the margins of dumping would be much higher for the United States than for the other two main exporters. Between 2000 and 2003, growing and milling of one megaton of white U.S. rice cost U.S.$415. However, it was exported at an average of U.S.$274 only, thus at a price 34 percent below its true costs of production (Oxfam 2005, 35). This margin of dumping is much higher than in the case of Vietnam and Thailand, as production costs for rough rice in these countries are much lower. Even though the prices of imported rice in Ghana are not necessary lower than for domestic rice, it is evident that dumping is a decisive factor making the imported rice competitive and available for Ghanaian consumers in terms of price. Hence, subsidies such as "export credits, the misuse of food aid, which lead to dumping, have contributed to the displacement of domestic rice from the markets of the cities like Tamale and to the losses of income of the rice peasants in Dalun. Through these dumping practices, the exporting countries, especially the U.S., have breached their extraterritorial obligation to respect the right to food of rice peasant families in Dalun and elsewhere" (Oxfam 2005, 35).

State Obligations and the Right to Adequate Food

The tripartite classification of state obligations at the national level that has been presented above can and should also be applied to extraterritorial obligations. In its *General Comment 12* on the right to food, the CESCR provided that states parties should "respect the enjoyment of the right to food in other countries, to protect that right, to facilitate access to food and to provide the necessary aid when required (UN Committee on Economic, Social, and Cultural Rights 1999, par. 36). Similarly, Jean Ziegler, the former UN special rapporteur on the right to food, discussed states' extraterritorial obligations in this fashion in his report of 2005 to the UN Commission for Human Rights:

> The obligation to respect is a minimum obligation which requires States to ensure that their policies and practices do not lead to violations of the right to food in other countries. The obligation to protect requires States to ensure that their own citizens and companies, as well as other third parties subject to their jurisdiction, including trans-national corporations, do not violate the right to food in other countries. The obligation to support the fulfilment of the right to food requires States, depending on the availability of resources, to facilitate the realization of the right to food in other countries and to provide the necessary aid when required. (Ziegler 2005, par. 48)

Beyond this, a number of civil society organizations and international law experts (some of whom are represented in this volume) have also begun to push the notion that states' human rights obligations are not simply and merely restricted to the domestic realm, but that they can also extend outside those borders. Yet, it would be a mistake to see extraterritorial obligations as differing substantially from those obligations that states have domestically. The obligation to respect is essentially the same for states whether they are acting at home or abroad: do no harm. The obligation to protect is also similar in the national and extraterritorial context: control third parties.

The major difference between national and extraterritorial obligations comes at the fulfillment level. Civil society has generally promoted the idea of an "obligation to support fulfillment" for the simple reason that a full application of the obligation to fulfill would bound the citizens of one country to use the maximum of all available resources to help other states implementing their obligations to fulfill. Such an interpretation would be too far reaching but also unrealistic, particularly in terms of obtaining popular support. At the same time, the "obligation to support fulfillment" is not a totally new concept and it is already recognized in many international law instruments. Perhaps the single most important example is the broad consensus that developed countries will provide, at a minimum, 0.7 percent of their GDP for development aid.

Beyond merely recognizing the existence of extraterritorial obligations, what also needs to be done is to contextualize and operationalize these principles. For example, although states' extraterritorial obligation to respect is straightforward enough, also needed are mechanisms for implementing human rights impact assessments. Regarding the extraterritorial obligation to protect and fulfill, the national obligations of the victims' state and the actions that state has taken (or not taken) must also be taken into account. However, it should be kept in mind that extraterritorial obligations are obligations toward people and not toward states, and that these obligations exist regardless of the role of the victims' state in a particular situation.

What also has to be said is that compliance with extraterritorial obligations will not only require bilateral and multilateral cooperation, but unilateral action as well. These three levels are closely interwoven. Unilateral action is most obviously required regarding the obligation to respect economic, social, and cultural rights. However, the state might also take unilateral action regarding its obligation to protect by imposing and enforcing internationally recognized human rights standards on transnational corporations that are headquartered within its jurisdiction. Bilateral agreements or policies are normally easier to change than multilateral ones because they refer to contracts or policies that can be changed by the two states involved. In the case of multilateral aid, the situation is more complicated as countries operate in a community with other states and it is not always possible for one state to convince the others to vote in a certain way (as seen in the gold-mining case from Ghana). In bilateral agreements (see, the example, the bilateral investment agreement with Paraguay), a government must ensure that the ability of the other state to protect and fulfill rights will not be undermined. Thus, investment agreements might well include human rights clauses as a contribution to the protection of economic, social, and cultural rights of workers or communities affected by foreign direct investments.

The multilateral context is the level that has received the most attention in the human rights debate on globalization during the last few years. The negative effects on economic, social, and cultural rights of agreements negotiated in the World Trade Organization and of conditionalities imposed by the IMF and the World Bank have been at the center of this debate. Much of the focus has been on documenting the effects of the policies promoted by the WTO, the IMF and the World Bank, as well as establishing direct legal obligations and the human rights accountability of these international organizations. In this context it is important to note that during the last few years, the CESCR has encouraged most states parties that belong to the international donor community to ensure that the policies and decisions of those organizations are in conformity with the obligations of states parties to the ICESCR. In addition, the CESCR in several of its general comments has addressed the national and extraterritorial obligations of states when acting in international organizations. For example, in its *General Comment 18* on the right to work, the CESCR stated:

In negotiations with international financial institutions, States parties should ensure protection of the right to work of their population. States parties that are members of international financial institutions, in particular the International Monetary Fund, the World Bank and regional development banks, should pay greater attention to the protection of the right to work in influencing the lending policies, credit agreements, structural adjustment programmes and international measures of these institutions. The strategies, programmes and policies adopted by States parties under structural adjustment programmes should not interfere with their core obligations in relation to the right to work and impact negatively on the right to work of women, young persons and the disadvantaged and marginalised individuals and groups. (UN Committee on Economic, Social, and Cultural Rights 2005, par. 30)

Member states of the WTO, the IMF, and the World Bank should be held accountable for human rights violations that have been facilitated by these organizations. If all states parties to the ICESCR acted according to their obligations when taking decisions on the board of the World Bank, this would constitute a majority of 83 percent (77 percent in terms of voting power). Limited influence and a lack of effective control should, therefore, not be an argument against holding states accountable for their decisions in international fora. In its *General Comment 15* on the right to water, the CESCR has made it clear that it is the action of the state party that has to be scrutinized and that each of the states parties was to ensure that its actions as members of international organizations took due account of the right to water (UN Committee on Economic, Social, and Cultural Rights 2002b).

Difficulties and Challenges Ahead

One of the problems in recognizing and determining states' extraterritorial obligations is establishing the casual link between policy decisions at the level of trade, economic, or agricultural policies on the one hand, and violations of economic, social, and cultural rights on the other. It is, of course, necessary to do the same thing at the national level, but even more difficult in the context of extraterritorial obligations. For example, the economic situation of farmers is influenced by many factors (national and international alike), and it is not always easy to show that a particular economic policy decision has led directly to a certain income or economic results. At the same time, as the case descriptions have shown, it is quite possible to make such connections, even under complex economic situations.

Another difficulty relates to the specific impact of policy measures. Governments often are aware that policy measures might have negative short-term consequences, but hope that these policy measures will lead to a positive effect in the long run. A human rights analysis must therefore be very policy specific and examine all details. Which groups are negatively affected, and what are the provisions chosen by a government to compensate those who do lose? Are people starving and are policy measures apparently causing gross or severe violations of human rights? Only when these questions are analyzed thoroughly is it possible to render a more definitive judgment on whether policy measures are acceptable and properly implemented—or whether they have led to human rights violations instead. This complexity is only heightened in the international context, whether it be through the actions or advice of the WTO, the World Bank, and the IMF.

In terms of extraterritorial obligations, the question of human rights accountability is twofold: (1) How can states with voting power ensure that international organizations are accountable to human rights norms; and (2) How is it possible that intergovernmental organizations become accountable to the states in which they are operating through policy advice or through the funding of development projects? In that vein, in its *Concluding Observations* on Germany's report, the CESCR encouraged Germany "as a member of international financial institutions, in particular the International Monetary Fund and the World Bank, to do all it can to ensure that the policies and decisions of those organizations are in conformity with the obligations of States parties to the Covenant, in particular the obligations contained in articles 2(1), 11, 15, 22 and 23 concerning international assistance and cooperation" (UN Committee on Economic, Social, and Cultural Rights 2001, par. 31)

Conclusion

The realization of economic, social, and cultural rights will be influenced by a number of factors. Some relate to the situation of a person's household, such as the loss of a job or the death of a working spouse. Others relate to governmental policies, such as the regulation of tenancy rules, or the impact of budgetary decisions for certain groups, or the availability of safety nets. In an increasingly globalized world, it has become increasingly evident that many of the factors that affect the realization of economic, social, and cultural originate outside a person's own national borders, whether it is through international trade rules, bilateral investment agreements, policy advice tendered by intergovernmental organizations, the actions of transnational companies, and so on.

An adequate analysis of economic, social, and cultural rights must begin to consider these factors. Judicial bodies at the national level and quasi-judicial procedures at the international level must also heed these various factors. Methodological problems exist. They are complex and need to be taken seriously, but the case examples show that they can be overcome. Universal human rights need to be protected universally. The universality principle is reflected in the fact that the realization and the protection of economic, social, and cultural rights—including the right to adequate food—should not be limited to the territorial boundaries of each state party alone. Cooperation is not a goal in itself but an instrument to achieve the progressive realization of these rights. The current debate concerning extraterritorial obligations is, therefore, both a timely and necessary step.

Chapter 7
Labor Standards and Extraterritoriality: Cambodian Textile Exports and the International Labour Organization

Virginia A. Leary

This chapter describes a unique program of obligations accepted by Cambodia in order to gain increased access to foreign markets for its textiles. It focuses on the central role in the program of the International Labour Organization (ILO), a UN agency. The Better Factories Cambodia (BFC) project is an example of extraterritorial or transnational human rights obligations willingly accepted rather than imposed. Under the terms of the program, adopted in 1999, Cambodia agreed to guarantee labor rights within its garment industry; in return, the United States agreed to grant favorable import treatment to garments produced in Cambodia. And, after some hesitation, the ILO, based in Geneva, agreed to monitor working conditions in Cambodia.

Unlike projects that threaten withdrawal of benefits, the program between the United States and Cambodia has used a carrot rather than a stick approach by providing increased access to the U.S. market if labor rights are guaranteed. The program, in which an international organization has played a central role, is credited with having a positive effect on improving labor conditions in Cambodia.

Recent Controversies

The agreement of the ILO, at the request of the United States, to monitor labor conditions in Cambodia, was an essential element in the U.S. grant of preferential treatment for Cambodian textiles. Political developments since 1999 have led to the decrease in U.S. interest in the Cambodian project and the increasing role of the ILO, now the major actor in promoting good labor practices in Cambodia. Credited with accomplishments in improving working conditions, it has been criticized by the Cambodian government and industry exporters for making Cambodian garments more expensive on the international market.

In January 2007, the Cambodian prime minister, Hun Sen, made an unusual public criticism of the ILO. At a meeting with clothing industry employers, he accused the organization of false reporting about working conditions and suggested that high labor standards could negatively affect exports by increasing costs. "The ILO is a good organization," he said, "but there could be some bad people working for it. Sometimes, some of its staffers may even try to extort money from factory owners, like 'if you give me money, I will write a good report about you'" (Associated Press 2007, 1).

This public criticism of the ILO's role in the program was new. Cambodia had originally favored the program since it granted increased access to the U.S. market. In September 2007, shortly after Hun Sen's comments, the Better Factories Cambodia program, in collaboration with the International Finance Corporation (IFC), the UN Development for Women, and other organizations, convened an International Buyers' Forum in Phnom Penh. Buyers from seventeen international garment brands, represented by forty-three retailers, including Adidas, Gap, H&M, Wal-Mart, Levi Strauss and Co., and the Walt Disney Company, agreed that they would continue to source their garments from Cambodia for the coming year, but complained about the repeated social audits to which they were subjected.

The buyers' announcement was welcome news for Cambodia's garment industry, which employed more than 340,000 people in 300 factories.

The industry had been fearful of losing market share in 2008 if the US decided to remove quotas on Chinese imports. This would threaten Cambodia's 2006 position as the fifth-largest supplier to the US, with a total global export value at $2.6 billion. At the same time, buyers underlined that the existence of the Better Factories program and its emphasis on working conditions and productivity were major reasons behind them choosing to work with Cambodia. They affirmed the need for strong support for BFC as it goes through the transition period towards sustainability as an independent entity in the near future. (International Labour Organization 2008, 1–2)

Since the ILO's activist role in the Cambodian garment industry is well known today, it may be forgotten that, in 1999, the suggested role was an innovation for the organization and the subject of considerable debate.

The History of the ILO's Involvement in Cambodia

In 1991, the Paris Peace Agreement ended Cambodia's two decades of war and civil strife. Millions were pledged by foreign nations to assist the country to recuperate. Despite the substantial international help provided then and later, Cambodia has remained a developing country with many problems. The incredibly brutal reign of Pol Pot from 1975 to 1979 with forced labor and the execution of some two million Cambodians—in particular, the well educated—led in 1978 to the invasion of troops from Vietnam. The new government of Hun Sen became the effective ruler of the country. But the effects of Pol Pot's regime continue to date, with many children crippled by leftover land mines. At the moment of writing, criminal trials under international and Cambodian auspices are being held for the surviving members of Pol Pot's government. The trials are facing numerous obstacles, including the declining health of the few remaining members of that regime.

The development of the textile industry was one bright spot during the early years following the Pol Pot period. Firms from Taiwan, China, and other East Asian countries invested heavily in Cambodian textile industries, leading the United States to call for quotas on the importation of textiles from Cambodia, but eventually leading to the U.S. adoption of incentives for Cambodian imports if the ILO could guarantee that workers' rights were protected. "The apparel industry requires relatively low levels of investment and limited skills on the part of workers and is often the first step in the process of industrialization. . . . The infant apparel industry grew rapidly. From virtually no apparel exports in 1994, exports had grown to almost half a billion dollars in value by 1998" (Polaski 2006, 3).

The ILO has not often been praised, or criticized, for its effectiveness, despite its innovative approach to labor supervision, the participation of workers' organizations as full members, and a generally competent staff. Member states and employers' organizations comprise the majority of its members and have frequently appeared more interested in damage control than in improving labor rights. The participation of workers' organizations as full members has not always been sufficient to offset the majority membership of states and employers' organizations.

When the United States first approached the ILO for collaboration in the Cambodian program in 1999, the ILO was reluctant. "The request from the US and Cambodia to take up a new role evoked a cautious response from the Director-General of the Organization, Juan Somavia, and provoked debate within the ILO bureaucracy and governing body. After a deliberative process, Somavia decided that the ILO should support a project that was seen to have value by the member states involved and that had the backing of both employers and labor unions in the target country" (Polaski 2006, 4).

The establishment of the ILO in 1919 predates the creation of the United Nations. The Treaty of Versailles, which ended World War I, established the League of Nations and the ILO. In 1919, the Bolshevik regime in Russia was gaining international support for its protection of workers, and agitation over labor conditions was increasing in western European states. The European states responded by setting up of the ILO, an organization whose purpose was the protection of workers through the adoption of labor conventions. It became the only agency of the League of Nations to survive World War II. After a move to Montreal during the war, it returned to Geneva and became a specialized agency of the newly established United Nations.

The main activity of the ILO in the early years was the drafting and adoption of conventions on labor conditions to be ratified by states. It was thought that countries that adopted the conventions would see to their enforcement. But it soon became evident that an external agency was required to promote national enforcement of the conventions. The ILO Committee of Experts on the Application of Conventions and Recommendations was established in 1928 to supervise the application of conventions and it continues its important activity to date.

In recent years, the ILO has taken on a number of new activities beyond its traditional role of supervision of labor conventions and recommendations. Juan Somavia, the director-general of the ILO, has pointed out that "in the last two decades . . . the traditional cornerstones of the ILO's activities have changed, shifted by the transformation of the economic and social environment brought about by the emerging global economy" (www.ilo.org). The ILO's participation in the Cambodian project in 1999 was one of the major new projects.

Overview of ILO's Project in Cambodia

A number of U.S. trade agreements that both preceded and followed the ILO's project in Cambodia include references to the promotion of labor rights. But, as Don Wells has pointed out, these agreements were largely aspirational, lacking enforceable provisions. The Cambodia Textile Agreement (UCTA) differed by providing the positive incentive of increased Cambodian imports into the U.S. market. "The UCTA contributed importantly to the promotion and protection of labor rights and standards in Cambodia's garment industry and is the best example of links between enhanced trade and improvements in labor standards in the global South" (Wells 2006, 360). Rewards would prevail over punishment and the ILO would supervise the conformity with labor rights.

The Cambodian project had the following objectives:

- to develop and maintain an independent system to monitor working conditions in garment factories;
- to help draft new laws and regulations for improving working conditions and to make labor laws more effective;
- to increase worker and employer awareness of core international labor standards and of their rights under Cambodian labor law;
- to increase worker, employer, and government capacities to improve working conditions, and to comply with national and international labor standards.

The ILO was responsible for inspecting factories to check on conformance with the program's objectives. It issued public reports on the general labor situation and confidential reports on each factory. Since it was impossible to inspect all factories each year, the inspections were based on the monitoring of 30 percent or fewer of the factories and were used by the United States to continue the grant of quotas to Cambodia. Cambodia, in turn, agreed to certain tariff and non-tariff restrictions on imports. In 2000 and 2001, the United States awarded a 9 percent increase in quotas for Cambodia textiles and bonuses of 9 percent, 12 percent, and 18 percent from 2002 through 2004.

The textile agreement has benefited Cambodian workers with employment in the industry, which has grown from 97,000 employees when the agreement began to approximately 270,000 in 2004. From 1995 to 2005 apparel exports quintupled. "With about $2 billion in annual exports, Cambodia's garment industry provides over 80% of its annual exports and over 12% of its GDP. Under the UCTA Cambodia became perhaps the most dependent country in the world on this highly competitive industry with its high rate of bankruptcies and rapidly changing consumer markets. The United States alone accounts for 71% of Cambodia's garment exports. In sum, the UCTA reflects and reinforces a highly asymmetrical power relationship between a small, poor country in the South and a large rich country in the North" (Wells 2006, 366).

Monitoring by the ILO has been a factor in continuing foreign investment in the garment industry. Nike had left Cambodia in 1999 after complaints of the use of child labor in one of its factories, but it returned after the ILO began its monitoring function. The World Bank has estimated that in 2005 the livelihoods of a quarter of Cambodia's population depended on the garment industry.

Chris Watson of the U.S. Labor Department has pointed out that "perhaps one of the most significant unintended consequences of labor activism in Cambodia's garment industry has been political. Cambodia's adolescent union movement has recently moved forward towards greater democratization. In 2006, three labor unions federations, representing more than 120,000 garment, shoe and rubber workers and teachers, democratically elected new leaders. The Independent Cambodian Coalition of Apparel Workers Democratic Union (CCAWDU), one of the country's largest and most active garment sector unions with 36,000 members, was praised for running a largely transparent election. The union movement is fast becoming the most democratic and independent group in the country" (Watson 2007, 2).

In the early days of the ILO's involvement, the ILO concentrated on developing an inspection system of working conditions by a team of independent observers. They then began training sessions to assist the factories and professional organizations of employers to improve the situations within the factories. The Better Factories Cambodia project consisted of three levels: (1) it observed and reported on working conditions within export industries; (2) it assisted enterprises to improve productivity by creating better working conditions; and (3) it collaborated with the government, employer's organizations, and labor unions (Vargha 2008, 2).

The project's evaluators make unannounced visits to the factories to observe working conditions, salaries, freedom of labor unions, and the work of children. The evaluations are based on replies to five hundred questions concerning working conditions. The project combines independent monitoring with finding solutions, through suggestions to management, training, advice, and information (International Labour Organization 2006, 1).

The ILO publishes a detailed report on the Better Factories project each year. The Synthesis Report of 2006 lists the names and number of factories registered with the project (305) and the number of workers (317,142) in the registered factories. During the period covered by the report of 2006, 212 factories were monitored, some having had multiple visits during previous years. In order to understand the statistics contained in the report, it is necessary to read carefully the explanatory information.

The report acknowledges that some of its analysis can be misleading. For example, a factory that terminates workers when they join a union has no real freedom of association. However, because a number of items are monitored in connection with freedom of association, that factory could still have a high average compliance rate using an average compliance calculation. It is noted that there is a high level of compliance among the factories examined for minimum wages, but a lower percentage of compliance for payments for maternity and sick leave as well as involuntary overtime.

The difficulties in monitoring labor rights in Cambodia are spelled out in a section of the report concerned with detecting the number of underage workers in the factories. The lack of a universal birth registration system in Cambodia, as well as falsification of documents, impedes detection of age. The report also states that the ILO is "aware of credible allegations of corruption in Cambodian garment factories between some managers and unions. Such arrangements adversely affect genuine workers freedom of association. This is very difficult to independently verify" (International Labour Organization 2006, 7). This admission gives credence to Hun Sen's remarks, reported earlier in this chapter, regarding corruption in the supervision of working conditions in Cambodia.

Recent Developments: Phasing Out of the ILO's Role

The original agreement of 1999 between the United States and Cambodia evolved over the years into the Better Factories Cambodia project, with a lesser degree of U.S. involvement and an increased role of the ILO. In 2007, another new development began with the collaboration in the program of the International Finance Corporation (IFC), the private sector financing arm of the World Bank. The World Bank had recently proposed labor standards for its investment clients. In an address to the ILO's governing body in Geneva in March 2008, Robert Zoellick, the president of the World Bank, stated that the ILO had helped to improve labor practices and competitiveness in the global supply chain. He cited a number of areas of joint concern to the World Bank and the ILO, including the development of skills and expanding efforts on gender issues.

Beginning in 2009, the joint program of the ILO and the IFC will develop three new pilot country projects in Vietnam, Jordan, and Lesotho, while taking a lesser role in the Cambodian textile market. Concern had been expressed that Vietnam's joining of the World Trade Organization (WTO) might result in garment factories moving to that country, which has lower labor standards (Associated Press 2007, 1). The ILO reported that country projects in the new countries would be adapted and developed for sectors other than textiles, such as agribusiness, construction, and electronics. The aim of the country projects was to build sustainable independent organizations that would survive outside funding and become self-sufficient within five years.

The ILO also announced that "an interdisciplinary team from Tufts University is designing a framework for Better Work to measure impact at the factory, industry, country and global level. In addition, the Tufts team will be conducting a controlled experiment with factories in Vietnam that will show the causal relationship between Better Work interventions at the factory level and the economic, social and human development outcomes" (International Labour Organization 2007b, 2).

The role of the ILO in the Cambodian project is scheduled to end in 2010 when an autonomous Cambodian organization will take over the direct governance of the project, financed 40 percent by the Cambodian government, 30 percent by Cambodian employers, and 30 percent by international buyers. In 2008, the program was financed by the U.S. Labor Department, USAID, the French development agency, the World Bank, and the GAP Foundation. However, USAID has recently made deep cuts in its funding for labor projects in Cambodia. There was also the threat of the possible closure of the office of the AFL-CIO's American Center for International Labor Solidarity (Watson 2007, 2). The decreasing interest of the U.S. government in the Cambodian project for which it was the initial founder may be one of the factors in the discontinuance of the Cambodian project, although the ILO appears convinced that the project can continue adequately under the new auspices described above.

Conclusion

Has the ILO's innovative program in Cambodia, originally promoted by the United States through import incentives, been successful? At the date of writing, it appears so. Since the program began, labor unions have been established where there were few before; the main international garment manufacturers have pledged to remain in Cambodia so long as the improved labor conditions continue; and fundamental labor rights now exist in the garment industry where they did not exist before.

As Watson has reported, however, the labor situation in Cambodia is not without problems: "Negotiations between management and workers are often unwieldy. Labor disputes often occur over vague wage issues. Garment manufacturers fear that the unions will demand higher wages when the industry has to keep costs under control. Factory owners also complain that unions jeopardize the industry with wildcat strikes. In contrast, garment buyers not only complain about corrupt and illegal union behavior and factory-instigated violence but remain concerned about anti-union discrimination, an inept Ministry of Labor, and poor enforcement of labor law" (Watson 2007, 2).

According to one commentator, "a further element of the experiment that was largely unanticipated but has proven critical to its ongoing success is the use of the ILO reports by private retail apparel firms that buy from Cambodian producers. These buyers, conscious of their brand reputations, use the reports to determine whether their supplier firms comply with labor standards, to encourage remediation of problems, and to shift orders in some cases" (Polaski 2006, 2).

But if the program appears successful in 2008, how sustainable will it be in the future when the ILO is less involved and the fear of competition may make the Cambodian government less favorable to the program? Is the contemplated withdrawal of the ILO from the program in 2010 a result of its success—or a realization of the difficulty of sustaining the program given increased competition from countries that have not adopted the labor standards in Cambodia? Is the extension of a similar program to Vietnam, Syria, and Lesotho a measure of the success of the Cambodian program—or a recognition that a program in one country only is fragile, subject to competitive inferior working rights elsewhere?

One surprising omission from the extensive literature on the ILO's program is the failure of commentators to draw attention to the fact that it has primarily benefited women. Wells has noted that "since 85–90% of the workers in the garment industry are young women, the contribution these jobs make to greater gender equality in Cambodia's highly patriarchal society are particularly significant" (Wells 2006, 368). The ILO's report of 2006 has a section on the effects of the industry on child labor, but it does not mention the extensive number of women in the garment industry who are positively affected by the program. Earlier reports may have contained such information. It is to the credit of the Better Factories Cambodia project that it has substantially improved the working conditions primarily of women.

Labor rights are human rights and the Cambodia Better Factories project is an example of the effect on human rights of international governmental organizations and private entities, as well as on states. The description of the project of which this chapter is a part, points out that what human rights has almost totally ignored is that in an increasingly interdependent world, it is not sufficient to simply assess what domestic governments are doing in terms of human rights, but it is equally important to assess the effect of other actors as well. The "other actors" in the Cambodian project include the ILO, an intergovernmental international organization, labor unions, manufacturing and export firms based in Europe, America, and Asia, workers in the export industry, and the U.S. and Cambodian governments.

The Cambodian project, based on a "carrot and not a stick approach," appears to be a relative success. But what about the future? Was it an experiment that depended on exceptional circumstances that cannot be duplicated? Or is it a forerunner of a new role for the ILO and the international community in other countries? Only time will tell.

Chapter 8
A Sort of Homecoming: The Right to Housing

Malcolm Langford

Housing issues are regularly caught in the cross-hairs of extraterritorial human rights claims. Forced eviction is the most visible manifestation. An array of foreign actors—states, international and regional development banks, multinational corporations, paramilitaries, and so on— have been involved in activities that have led to forcible displacement of individuals and communities, without any effective remedy for the dispossessed. Extraterritorial activities also contribute to other forms of displacement such as traditional market-based displacement, where development policies encourage liberalization of land holdings, or newer phenomena in the form of forced climate displacement with rising sea levels and changing rainfall patterns (Leckie 2008) and even removal from forests as part of some preventative climate change policies and practices. Beyond eviction and displacement, the level of international development aid for the low-income housing sector (even if water and sanitation services are included) is pitifully low, and it is even questionable whether most of this aid would conform to the strictures of the right to housing.

As far back as 1990, the UN Committee on Economic, Social, and Cultural Rights (CESCR) warned that "international agencies should scrupulously avoid involvement in projects which . . . involve large-scale evictions or displacement of persons without the provision of all appropriate protection and compensation" (UN Committee on Economic, Social, and Cultural Rights 1990a, par. 17). The following year, in a general comment on the right to housing, the CESCR issued a clear statement on the extraterritorial obligations of states toward the right:

Traditionally, less than 5 per cent of all international assistance has been directed towards housing or human settlements, and often the manner by which such funding is provided does little to address the housing needs of disadvantaged groups. States parties, both recipients and providers, should ensure that a substantial proportion of financing is devoted to creating conditions leading to a higher number of persons being adequately housed. International financial institutions promoting measures of structural adjustment should ensure that such measures do not compromise the enjoyment of the right to adequate housing. (UN Committee on Economic, Social, and Cultural Rights 1991, par. 19)

This directive notwithstanding, many questions on the extent of extraterritorial obligations remain to be investigated—while both remedial possibilities, as well as limitations, have become more apparent.

Over the last decade, the legal literature on the subject of extraterritorial obligations has exhibited a strong tendency to try and categorically pin down obligations. One school of thought has focused on the "obligations" part of extraterritorial obligations by attempting to map both state and non-state obligations across the taxonomy of duties to respect, protect, and fulfill, with some experts concluding that the former are more relevant and binding than the latter (Skogly 2001 and 2003a; Sepúlveda 2006; Darrow 2003b). However, these analyses have in large part ignored some of the emerging critiques of this approach (Koch 2005; Craven 2005; Langford and King 2008). The categorical taxonomy is useful in mapping out potential spaces for obligations in a simple and understandable framework as well as grouping emerging jurisprudence. However, putting aside the internal contradictions of trying to draw neat lines between the three duties in theory and practice, it remains a rather imprecise tool for capturing legal obligations. Indeed, two international bodies that use versions of this taxonomy have either given it much deeper substance from the outset (for example, the Inter-American Court of Human Rights speaks of a range of more precise protective duties) or added other extraterritorial obligations outside the taxonomy (for example, the UN Committee on Economic, Social, and Cultural Rights, especially in its *General Comments 8* [1997b] and *15* [2002b]).

What is particularly worrisome is that this categorical approach can lead to quick and "hare"-like conclusions. For example, the use of the categorical approach has arguably led some commentators such as Skogly (2001) to only accept the duty to respect when it comes to international financial institutions. It thus excludes the possibility of other obligations and principles which might emerge from a more "tortoise"-like deductive and contextualized analysis of different actors (for example, the International Olympic Committee, as will be discussed further), along with different rights and different contexts, such as has been recently emerging in the context of state's domestic obligations (Langford 2008).

A second school of thought tends to be more focused on the "territory" in extraterritorial obligations. How far can the obligations extend offshore, how much "effective control" is needed, and so on? The danger with these sorts of debates is that many key international legal standards use the word "jurisdiction," not "territory," and jurisdiction is often endogenous in both law and fact. Given the ever increasing globalization of activity and concern the factual scope of a state's jurisdiction is a continuous work in progress, potentially stretched out in many new directions.

This chapter will therefore take as its point of departure the right to housing in the context of human rights violations and corresponding case law and policy debate without necessarily adopting an overarching normative framework. In order to keep things manageable, the focus will be principally on the field of international cooperation, particularly the field of development. The impact of international and internal armed conflict and international environmental cooperation on the right to adequate housing will only be mentioned in passing, although in some instances they are intertwined. Moreover, the human rights discourse does not exist in a vacuum and discussions on extraterritorial obligations have a tendency to be dominated by the legal fraternity. There is a need to engage with other discourses that both drive extraterritorial housing rights violations and propose solutions, and some will be considered briefly. For example, are the Millennium Development Goals with their target 7D on slum upgrading and Goal 8 on global partnership part of the solution—or part of the problem?

After an examination of the extraterritorial dimensions of the right to housing in international and regional human rights treaties and instruments, a number of which have not been examined before, the chapter proceeds to examine the case of forced evictions and urban upgrading in international development. The question of whether these housing rights obligations attach themselves to non-state actors, such as international financial institutions and multinational corporations, will be addressed in two case studies.

The Right to Housing, Extraterritorial Obligations, and International Law

The Right to Self-determination

It is customary in the legally oriented literature in this field to begin with an analysis of the potential extraterritorial obligations in the respective and differing versions of article 2 in the UN International Covenant on Civil and Political Rights (ICCPR) and the UN International Covenant on Economic, Social, and Cultural Rights (ICESCR) (Skogly 2006; Coomans and Kamminga 2004; Vandenhole 2007a). However, it is unfortunate that the identically worded article 1 in both treaties is almost universally ignored.[1] If the right of all peoples to self-determination is not exclusively reduced to the domain of postcolonial nations, then we are able to discern a number of obligations that are quite relevant to our present discussion on housing and related land rights. For one thing, it is abundantly clear from the text that these rights are against the world and, for good measure, article 1(3) expressly sets out the extraterritorial obligations of all states parties to the two covenants to both "respect" and "promote" the right to self-determination. A number of the rights or elements listed in article 1 are pertinent to housing and land rights, including the right of peoples to freely pursue economic, social, and cultural development (art. 1[1]) and not be deprived of their own means of subsistence (art. 1[2]).

The extent to which sub-state groupings, particularly indigenous peoples and minorities, have the right to self-determination is obviously controversial. While customary international law is conservative on the question of the rights of these groups to secede, the right to internal self-determination has received limited recognition (Cassese 1999, 102–8). However, the UN General Assembly's recent Declaration on the Rights of Indigenous Peoples (2007) has essentially removed such doubt. It affirms their general right to self-determination, their specific right to autonomy or self-government in matters relating to their internal and local affairs, and their right to maintain and strengthen their distinct political, legal, economic, social, and cultural institutions (art. 3–5).

The Declaration on the Rights of Indigenous Peoples is structured much like a treaty and includes rights to ancestral lands, improvement of housing conditions, and protection from forcible eviction and population transfer. If one compares the various preambular paragraphs, the declaration is ambiguous on whether the obligations are extraterritorial. However, it must be said that there is no limiting territorial clause, and agreements between states and indigenous peoples are given quasi-public international law status, which allows for the possibility of diagonal relationships. Article 39 is particularly noteworthy and provides that "indigenous peoples have the right to have access to financial and technical assistance from States and through international cooperation, for the enjoyment of rights contained in this Declaration." This article seems to implicitly encourage direct bilateral forms of cooperation between donors and indigenous peoples, and possibly represents an exception to the current emphasis on "national ownership" and national budget support in development aid as captured in the Paris Declaration on Aid Effectiveness (2005). The declaration provides for

- the right to just and fair conflict resolution procedures with states or other parties (art. 40);

- the duty of UN agencies and other intergovernmental organizations to contribute to the realization of the rights and mobilize financial cooperation and technical assistance (art. 41); and
- the need for states to "promote respect for and full application of the provisions of this Declaration and follow the effectiveness of this Declaration" (art. 42).

Whether the right to self determination carries extraterritorial obligations or not, it has to be said that the remedial consequences for violations are few. The UN Human Rights Committee has held that complaints based on part I are inadmissible since the optional protocol to the ICCPR is confined to communications from individuals (*Bernard Ominayak v. Canada* 1990). However, the recently adopted optional protocol to the ICESCR reopens this question. In the draft protocol presented to the UN Human Rights Council in May 2008, the rights available for complaints were restricted to part II (that is, self-determination was excluded). Protests from Algeria and Pakistan led to a compromise text that permits complaints on all economic, social, and cultural rights in the covenant, which was then adopted by the UN General Assembly on 10 December 2008 and will be open for ratification 10 September 2009 (see Langford 2009a; Mahon 2008). This wording conceivably brings the internal and socio-economic dimensions of right to self-determination under the remit of the procedure. However, the possibility that the CESCR would allow this is somewhat remote given the legal interpretation by the Human Rights Committee in *Ominayak v. Canada*. However, the optional protocol to ICESCR also contains an inquiry procedure which can be triggered when "the Committee receives reliable information indicating grave or systematic violations by a State Party of any of the economic, social and cultural rights set forth in the Covenant" (art 11(2), OP to ICESCR (see general discussion in Courtis and Sepúlveda 2009). It is notable that there is no bar to this procedure being applied to Article 1, but it is only applicable to a state if they make a seperate declaration accepting the inquiry procedure upon ratification of the protocol (Article 11(1) of the OP to ICESCR).

Scheinin (2008) argues that article 1 of ICCPR is also relevant in the state reporting procedure and covenant interpretation. He points to the following language from the Human Rights Committee's conclusion in its report on Canada, which also directly raises issues of land rights:

The Committee emphasizes that the right to self-determination requires, inter alia, that all peoples must be able to freely dispose of their natural wealth and resources and that they may not be deprived of their own means of subsistence (art. 1, para. 2). The Committee recommends that decisive and urgent action be taken towards the full implementation of the [Royal Commission on Aboriginal

Peoples] recommendations on land and resource allocation. The Committee also recommends that the practice of extinguishing inherent aboriginal rights be abandoned as incompatible with article 1 of the Covenant. (UN Human Rights Committee 1999a, par. 8)

Cassesse notes that the United Kingdom agreed to discuss questions relating to Northern Ireland under article 1, although Turkey refused to discuss the Kurds in a similar fashion (Cassese 1999, 107–8). In *Apirana Mahuika and Others v. New Zealand* and *Marie-Hélène Gillot and Others v. France*, the UN Human Rights Committee stated that article 1 may have interpretive effect in cases adjudicated under other provisions of the ICCPR through the Optional Protocol. Under the ICESCR, the Committee on Economic, Social, and Cultural Rights has also been interrogating states on autonomy and land rights issues of indigenous peoples during its sessions, but it tends not to always specify the article to which it is referring in its concluding observations.

In sum, therefore, the common language of article 1 of both covenants not only provides a relevant locus for examining extraterritorial obligations of states with regard to indigenous and other peoples in other states; it also provides a semi-accountable space in the form of the state periodic reporting procedures in which these issues can be aired. Since many international infrastructure and development projects are affecting indigenous communities (see the section titled "Forced Evictions" below), the scope for applying article 1 in emerging legal, policy, and accountability frameworks is considerable. The Declaration on Indigenous Peoples also opens up the possibility for more direct forms of development cooperation in the field of land and housing between donor states and indigenous peoples.

The Right to Adequate Housing

As noted by a number of authors in this volume, article 2 of the ICESCR contains no territorial, or even jurisdictional, limitation. It is instead explicitly imbued with extraterritorial applicability: all states parties must "take steps, individually and through international assistance and co-operation . . . with a view to achieving progressively the full realization of the rights recognized in the present Covenant." This is supplemented by article 22, which empowers the Economic and Social Council to make recommendations to specialized agencies (see the broad interpretation in *General Comment* 2 [UN Committee on Economic, Social, and Cultural Rights 1990a]), and article 23, in which states parties agree that international action is needed to achieve realization of the rights set forth in the covenant.

While these obligations apply to all of the rights in the covenant, the extraterritorial dimension is given extra weight in article 11(1): "The States Parties to the present Covenant recognize the right of everyone to an adequate standard of living for himself and his family, including adequate food, clothing and housing, and to the continuous improvement of living conditions. The States Parties will take appropriate steps to ensure the realization of this right, recognizing to this effect the essential importance of *international co-operation* based on free consent" (emphasis added).

Skogly (2003a) points out that this stress was intentional and survived a debate in the UN Third Committee. She notes that the Third Committee's conclusion that "a reference to international cooperation in the article which dealt with the question of standard of living was deemed particularly essential since some countries, especially those which were under-developed, would not be able to provide their people with adequate food, clothing and shelter without international assistance" (Third Committee 1957, par. 142).

The right to housing was the subject of *General Comment 4* (UN Committee on Economic, Social, and Cultural Rights 1991). It was issued before the committee succumbed to its sometimes inflexible three-fold taxonomy for the normative content of rights and provides a rich, contextualized, and grounded understanding of the right. In the comment, the committee notes that the "right to housing should not be interpreted in a narrow or restrictive sense which equates it with, for example, the shelter provided by merely having a roof over one's head or views shelter exclusively as a commodity" (par. 7). Rather it should be interpreted as a "right to live somewhere in security, peace and dignity" (par. 7), which entails seven essential elements: (a) legal security of tenure; (b) an availability of services, materials, facilities, and infrastructure; (c) affordable housing costs; (d) habitability in terms of space and protection from the weather and hazards; (e) accessibility for marginalized and disadvantaged groups; (f) a location sufficiently close to place of employment and services and a safe distance from health-affecting pollutants; and (g) cultural adequacy.

The committee's headlining of security of tenure was prescient as it not only undergirds the other elements, but is frequently the first demand of marginalized groups, whether those living informally or in rental housing or facing discrimination and poverty. The committee adopted a broad interpretation of security of tenure, emphasizing its universal applicability:

Tenure takes a variety of forms, including rental (public and private) accommodation, cooperative housing, lease, owner-occupation, emergency housing and informal settlements, including occupation of land or property. Notwithstanding the type of tenure, all persons should possess a degree of security of tenure which guarantees legal protection against forced eviction, harassment and other threats. States parties should consequently take immediate measures aimed at conferring legal security of tenure upon those persons and households currently lacking such protection, in genuine consultation with affected persons and groups. (ibid., par. 8a)

General Comment 4 provides very detailed instructions on the substantive and procedural protections concerning forced evictions, which relate to the duties to respect and protect. Furthermore, the dimensions regarding fulfillment are captured in the discussion of the duty of the state to develop and implement effective housing policies with full participation. The committee closes *General Comment 4* with an analysis of the extraterritorial obligations of states that tends to focus on the categorical obligation both to *fulfill* (the amount and nature of international assistance) and to *protect* (participation in multilateral institutions).

General Comment 7 on forced evictions (UN Committee on Economic, Social, and Cultural Rights 1997a) was seminal in providing clarity on the precise duties of states in cases of evictions. It noted that substantive justification must be given for any eviction and that a range of procedures must be followed, including consultation on alternatives to evictions, due process and provision of alternative accommodation and/or land to a level compatible with the state's resources. The comment also addresses the issue of forced evictions in the context of extraterritoriality:

17. The Committee is aware that various development projects financed by international agencies within the territories of State parties have resulted in forced evictions. In this regard, the Committee recalls its General Comment No. 2 (1990) which states, *inter alia*, that "international agencies should scrupulously avoid involvement in projects which, for example, . . . promote or reinforce discrimination against individuals or groups contrary to the provisions of the Covenant, or involve large-scale evictions or displacement of persons without the provision of all appropriate protection and compensation. Every effort should be made, at each phase of a development project, to ensure that the rights contained in the Covenant are duly taken into account."

18. Some institutions, such as the World Bank and the Organisation for Economic Cooperation and Development (OECD) have adopted guidelines on relocation and/or resettlement with a view to limiting the scale of and human suffering associated with forced evictions. Such practices often accompany large-scale development projects, such as dam-building and other major energy projects. Full respect for such guidelines, insofar as they reflect the obligations contained in the Covenant, is essential on the part of both the agencies themselves and States parties to the Covenant.

In the process of receiving international financial cooperation, the committee reminds states parties they cannot project their own human rights responsibilities on to international actors. They, therefore, must "seek to indicate areas relevant to the right to adequate housing where external financing would have the most effect. Such requests should take full account of the needs and views of the affected groups" (UN Committee on Economic, Social, and Cultural Rights 1991, par. 9).

The adoption of the optional protocol to ICESCR now opens up additional remedies for the covenant, in particular an individual complaints procedure, inquiry procedure and state-to-state complaint procedure. While the substantive covenant includes no territorial or jurisdictional limitation, Courtis and Sepúlveda (2009) are highly critical of the inclusion of a jurisdictional limitation in the procedure for individual complaints (art. 2). However, complaints can still be made where a state can be shown to have jurisdiction in *fact* and a number of possible examples are discussed later in this paper. As discussed above, there is no extraterritorial jurisdictional restriction in relation to the inquiry procedure and the state-to-state procedure could also be used, although experience from other human rights treaties indicate this is unlikely. Moreover, during the "remedies" stage of an individual complaint, the committee is empowered to make recommendations to other parties who may have either a negative or positive, actual or potential, effect on a state's ability to realize the right of a complainant (see discussion in Langford 2009a). This opens up the possibility for the committee to make direct recommendations to bodies such as the World Bank and International Monetary Fund.

Housing Rights in International and Regional Human Rights Treaties

The right to housing, whether in full or in part, is also protected in a range of international and national instruments that possess some measure of extraterritorial applications. Articles 17 (protection of the home) and 27 (cultural rights of minorities) of the International Covenant on Civil and Political Rights (ICCPR) have been respectively interpreted by the Human Rights Committee to provide guarantees against forced eviction (UN Human Rights Committee 2005) and protection of land use by minorities (see *Länsman v. Finland*). The Human Rights Committee has commented that the right to freely choose one's residence "includes protection against all forms of forced internal displacement" (UN Human Rights Committee 1999b, par. 7). The territorial restriction in article 2 of the ICCPR obviously diminishes its extraterritorial applicability (McGoldrick 2004) but Scheinin persuasively argues that it is triggered when states have "factual control in respect of facts and events that allegedly constitute a violation of a human right" (Scheinin 2004, 76).

Other international human rights treaties that also protect housing rights include

- the UN International Convention on the Rights of the Child, which assists parents with realizing their children's right to adequate standard of living, including housing (art. 27);
- the UN Convention against Torture, in which forced eviction has been adjudged as cruel and degrading treatment in some circumstances;[2]
- the UN Convention on the Elimination of All Forms of Discrimination against Women, which supports equal access in rights to property and land reform and resettlement, and which stipulates that states have a duty to take steps to support rights of rural women to adequate housing (art. 14 and 16);
- the Convention on All Forms of Racial Discrimination, in which states must prohibit and eliminate racial discrimination in the enjoyment of the right to housing (art. 5);
- the International Convention on the Protection of the Rights of All Migrant Workers and Members of Their Families, which supports equal access to housing (art. 43); and
- the UN Convention on the Rights of Persons with Disabilities, which supports the right to adequate housing, the right to equal access to housing and public housing programs, and the right to own property (art. 9, 12, and 28).

The extraterritorial application of the first two mentioned treaties has been analyzed elsewhere. Skogly (2006) concludes that states have obligations of international cooperation and assistance under the Convention on the Rights of the Child with regard to economic and social rights, and potentially extraterritorial duties concerning civil and political rights where there is "effective control." Similarly, the "jurisdictional" and "territorial" limitations in the Convention against Torture should be construed narrowly given the text of the treaty (see the chapter by Manfred Nowak in this volume). This can be seen particularly in article 5, which obliges states to take necessary measures to prosecute any offenders on their territory if they do not extradite them to another jurisdiction for that purpose—an obligation that is quite relevant to our present discussion, particularly if the denial of a right to housing constitutes cruel, inhuman, or degrading treatment or punishment.

The lack of scholarly analysis of other international human rights treaties, such as the Convention on the Elimination of All Forms of Discrimination against Women, has been criticized by Darrow (2003a, 135), but curiously continues. A comprehensive analysis is beyond the scope of this chapter, but it is interesting to track the historical trend in other instruments. The Convention on the Elimination of All Forms of Racial Discrimination of 1966 contains no extraterritorial limitation except for a jurisdictional limitation on state obligations to eradicate apartheid, provide effective national remedies, and allow international complaints to the Committee on the Elimination of Racial Discrimination. The Convention on the Elimination of All Forms of Discrimination against Women likewise contains no limitations, with the only exception being individual complaints under the optional protocol.

Unsurprisingly, the Convention on the Protection of the Rights of All Migrant Workers is jurisdictionally and territorially focused since it is essentially concerned with the rights of non-nationals within a host state's jurisdiction, while questions of supporting greater migration remain significantly controversial. States have obligations "to all migrant workers and members of their families within their territory or subject to their jurisdiction" (art. 7). Nonetheless, the convention does set out a wide range of softer obligations of states parties to consult and cooperate with a view to promoting sound, equitable, and humane conditions in connection with international migration of workers and members of their families.

The recently concluded Convention on the Rights of Persons with Disabilities gives a possible indication on the direction of international law, especially the manner in which it resonates with the Declaration on the Rights of Indigenous Peoples. To begin, the convention lacks any territorial or jurisdictional limitation. Furthermore, article 32 not only recognizes the "importance" of international cooperation, but also requires states to "undertake appropriate and effective measures in this regard. . . ." Suggested measures include ensuring international cooperation and development that is "inclusive of, and accessible to, persons with disabilities," the facilitation and support of "capacity-building," and the provision of "technical and economic assistance." However, the complaints mechanism under the optional protocol to the treaty is explicitly limited to individuals subject to the "jurisdiction" of a state party.

At the regional level, the European Convention of Human Rights, the European Social Charter, the American Declaration of Human Rights, the American Convention on Human Rights, and the Africa Charter on Human Rights have all been deployed to protect various aspects of housing rights (Langford and Nolan 2006; Langford 2008). The extent to which each treaty has extraterritorial application is the subject of considerable discussion. The extraterritorial reach of the European Convention of Human Rights was firmly established in a housing rights case (Lawson 2004). In *Loizidou v. Turkey*, a case heard by the European Court of Human Rights, a Cypriot woman successfully challenged the interference by Turkish troops with her home and property, even though northern Cyprus was not part of Turkey. However, the court held that the "effective control" test established in *Loizidou v. Turkey* was not triggered in the controversial *Banković* case, also of the same court, where NATO members were found not to have "effective control" when their forces bombed a Serbian television station in 1999, killing or injuring thirty-two people. More recently, the European Court of Human Rights found in *Öcalan v. Turkey* that the arrest by Turkish officials of a Kurdish military leader in Kenya did pass the "effective control" test, suggesting that the *Banković* case may have been motivated by more political considerations, and that extraterritorial obligations could extend outside the actual "region."

The Inter-American Court has generally been more expansive on the topic (Cerna 2004), although a key challenge for the Inter-American Commission on Human Rights will be how it deals with its own "Banković"; the Centre on Housing Rights and Evictions (COHRE) has sued many states that are members of the Executive Board of the Inter-American Development Bank and the World Bank for executions and evictions during the construction of a dam in Guatemala (see further below). The African [Banjul] Charter on Human and Peoples' Rights contains no limitation and requires state parties "individually and collectively" to exercise the right to free disposal of their wealth and natural resources with a view to strengthening African unity and solidarity. In addition, the charter obligates state parties to "eliminate all forms of foreign economic exploitation" (art. 21[1]).

When considering forced evictions, it is also important to ask whether obligations extend much wider than circumstances where actors have direct or indirect effective control. For example, do mass forced evictions trigger a state obligation to take action to stop it or take remedial and prosecutorial action? For example, did the eviction of hundreds of thousands of urban residents in Zimbabwe (2005) and Nigeria (2006) require a state to prosecute those responsible in its own courts or to support international action, for example, through a referral of the matter by the Security Council to the International Criminal Court? This is obviously stretching the legal outer limits, and one may only be able to conclude that states have the *discretion* to take such action (Centre on Housing Rights and Evictions 2007), an issue that remains heavily contested. However, article 5 of the Convention against Torture provides that each "State Party shall likewise take such measures as may be necessary to establish its jurisdiction over such offences in cases where the alleged offender is present in any territory under its jurisdiction and it does not extradite him," and forced evictions have been adjudged by the Committee against Torture to constitute cruel and degrading treatment (see *Hijirizi v. Yugoslavia*). Legislation in a number of countries (Germany, Belgium, South Africa, and the Netherlands) allows for prosecution of perpetuators of crimes against humanity committed in other jurisdictions regardless of their nationality, and such crimes would cover human rights violations relating to housing, such as forced deportations and displacements (Amsterdam International Law Clinic 2007).

Forced Evictions

International Financial Institutions and Bilateral Development Agencies

Forced evictions from international development projects have been well documented over the past half century. Graham Hancock, one of the harshest critics of foreign aid generally, provides this assessment of some of the massive displacements brought about by internationally financed dams:

> Long after the experts and professionals from the United Nations or the EEC or USAID or World Bank have packed their bags and their cute souvenirs, boarded their aircraft and fled northwards, the ill-conceived development projects they have been responsible for continue to wreck the lives of the poor.
> During the past twenty years millions of rural people in Africa, in Asia and in Latin America have been forcibly removed from their homes to make space for the expanding reservoirs of giant hydroelectric dams; like ghosts not yet laid to rest, troubled but invisible, the dispossessed *still* wander from place to place in search of recompense. (Hancock 1989, 113)

One of the earliest international undertakings was the Akosombo Dam project on the Vlota River in Ghana, which commenced in the 1950s with financial support from the World Bank, the United States, and the United Kingdom. The project was completed in 1965. Gyau-Boakye (2001) concludes that the dam and the world's largest human-made lake led to the relocation of eighty thousand people as well as environmental damage and a massive loss of traditional livelihoods. In this case, resettlement was provided but Gyau-Boakye notes that such efforts were wholly inappropriate for large and polygamous families. Moreover, seven hundred traditional settlements of different ethnic groups were combined in fifty-two townships and the psychological trauma of the loss of traditional land and culture caused an accelerated death rate among the aged. There is also a large debate over whether dam lakes increase seismic risk (Chandler 1999), resulting in earthquakes or the breach of dam walls, which obviously pose significant threats to human settlement. In the case of the Akosombo Dam, three earthquakes have since been registered in the area. Furthermore, the economic and broader utilitarian benefits for the dam, which were used to justify this development project, are problematic (Okaampa-Ahoofe 2007). Furthermore, while the government of Ghana paid for more than half of the costs of the dam, upward of 80 percent of the energy generated is licensed to an American-owned aluminum plant, which imports aluminum from Louisiana for smelting.

The World Bank has attracted sustained criticism for its sponsorship of such projects which lead to displacement and ecological destruction. Even when it is a minor financial contributor, its concessional loans provide a stamp of creditworthiness that can be used by borrowing states to leverage other investment. In the main, bilateral donors generally prefer such multilateral financing for large-scale infrastructure projects, although separate or additional finance is often provided. In some instances, the backlash against these projects has affected the bank's involvement. One example is the Polonoreste project in Brazil, which led to massive deforestation and ecological destruction, along with the eviction of numerous indigenous communities. The agricultural returns for the project were also disappointing as the soil has not been found to be suitable for farming. Ultimately, an international campaign led to the suspension of loan activity in 1985 (Hancock 1989). This was followed shortly by the establishment of the Morse Commission, which was authorized by the World Bank to undertake an independent review of the Sardar Sarovar Dam project on the Narmada River in India. In its report of 1992, the commission concluded that staff of the World Bank had violated the bank's environmental and social policies and had failed to enforce loan covenants with the borrowing government. One of the results was the forced displacement of hundreds of thousands of local people, including *adivasi* (indigenous people) living in the flood zone (Clark 2008).

Drawing on the experience of the Morse Commission, civil society advocates and some member governments of the World Bank called for an independent accountability system. In 1993, the World Bank's Board of Executive Directors created the Inspection Panel and elevated some guidelines into official policy, such as the Operational Policy on Involuntary Resettlement. The panel commenced work the following year with a mandate to independently investigate breaches of operational policies upon a request for inspection. After a preliminary review and approval from the Board of Executive Directors to proceed, the panel collects information and makes its independent assessment and conclusions available to the board. The executive directors will consider the actions, if any, to be taken by the bank after receiving concurrent recommendations from the bank's management.

In terms of applicable standards regarding eviction, the bank's Operational Policy on Involuntary Resettlement (OP 4.12, revised April 2004) provides that "involuntary resettlement should be avoided where feasible, or minimized, exploring all viable alternative project designs" (par. 2[a]). It also notes that "bank experience has shown that resettlement of indigenous peoples with traditional land-based modes of production is particularly complex and may have significant adverse impacts on their identity and cultural survival" (par. 9). However, the panel has no explicit mandate to address human rights, and this particular Operational Policy on Involuntary Resettlement is barely consistent with a human rights approach. The guidelines essentially presume "expropriation" and relocation are necessary, and beyond the sentiment expressed in the quotation above, they pay almost no attention to the justification for the eviction or process for consultation and negotiation. The focus is mostly on compensation and relocation schemes, and revisions to the resettlement guidelines in 2001 also narrowed compensation to social and economic impacts, excluding psychological and cultural impacts. However, the decision in the Chad-Cameroon case reveals an evolving human rights approach within the panel.[3] In coming to their decision that operational policies had been violated, the panel criticized the bank management's narrow view on the application of human rights to the bank's work: "It is not within the Panel's mandate to assess the status of governance and human rights in Chad in general or in isolation, and the Panel acknowledges that there are several institutions (including UN bodies) specifically in charge of the subject. However, the Panel felt obliged to examine whether issues of proper governance or human rights violations in Chad were such as to impede the implementation of the Project in a manner compatible with the Bank's policies" (par. 215).

The World Bank's Indigenous Peoples' policy (OP 4.10 of July 2005) is more explicit, with a requirement of majority community support for resettlement. It seeks to protect indigenous peoples from negative impacts of projects, as well as ensure that they share in the development benefits associated with a project (Clark 2008). Projects go through a screening process if indigenous peoples are present in or have a collective attachment to the project area. A process of free, prior, informed consultation with affected indigenous peoples must be carried out at each stage of the project, and in the absence of broad community support, the World Bank will not proceed with a project. If the project proceeds and indigenous people are affected, the bank must require a borrower to prepare an Indigenous Peoples Plan.

However, this requirement is less than what the Colombian Constitutional Court, for example, has itself required in such cases. It has stated that "any authorisation to exploit natural resources in indigenous territory requires the participation of the indigenous community, which has a 'fundamental right to be consulted' when a project for resource exploitation is proposed in its territories" (Constitutional Court of Colombia SU-383/97). Sepúlveda notes that according to this court the mere physical participation of the indigenous community in consultations is not sufficient; rather, it is necessary to comply with a set of requirements, including that the community: (a) be informed of the overall project and of the procedures and activities for the implementation of the project; (b) be informed of the effects that the project might have on its way of life, economy and culture; (c) have the opportunity, freely and without any interference, to convene its members or representatives to evaluate the advantages and disadvantages of the project on the community and its members; and (d) have the opportunity to make itself heard in relation to its concerns and opinions on the feasibility of the project. In addition, the State authorities have an obligation to submit to the community alternatives for a settlement or an agreement. (Sepúlveda 2008, 158)

The most important question, of course, relates to the effectiveness of the Inspection Panel process. Unfortunately, the panel's findings are not enforceable vis-à-vis bank management, and most studies have found that resettlement programs sponsored by the World Bank have rarely provided adequate compensation or livelihoods (Clark 2002), although in some cases it has improved the coverage or quality of resettlement, as in the case of the Rihand power plant in India (Clark 2008).[4] Furthermore, the inability of the panel to supervise its recommendations (a resolution of 1999 explicitly prevented it from doing so), means it has little control over the remedying of violations. A former member of the panel believes the guidelines themselves are essentially the problem, with their focus on restoration and not improvement of livelihoods, especially since livelihoods after eviction almost always decline (Scudder 2005).

The panel has two other shortcomings. Requests can only be entertained during a restricted period (up to the point that 95 percent of the project funds have been disbursed) and the procedure is not retroactive. It is worth noting that the Asian Development Bank has partly rectified this in its own complaint procedure and extended the period to the issuance of a project completion report or one year after completion (Clark 2008). However, the problem with this approach is that many of the negative effects of a project are only visible much later in the process—for example, the quality and appropriateness of a resettlement scheme or the extent of damage to environment and livelihoods.

In the case of the Chixoy Dam in Guatemala, the issue of retroactivity has spurred a creative legal complaint to make the World Bank and the Inter-American Development Bank directly accountable for human rights violations. In the late 1970s, communities residing along the Rio Negro were forcibly and violently displaced for a hydroelectric dam that was principally financed by these two banks (Thiele and Gomez 2005). Despite the government's claim that the project would bring about an improvement in living conditions, the resettlement site has been described as having conditions "far worse than their existing conditions at

Rio Negro, with cramped, poorly constructed houses and infertile land" (Centre on Housing Rights and Evictions 2004, par. 26), and the agency that oversaw the entire resettlement process has now cut off water and electricity to the community after it was privatized. In order to secure the movement of residents, the state engaged in widespread violence and intimidation and between March and September 1982, 444 villagers, including 142 children, were murdered by state agents and militias.

However, throughout this period, the World Bank and the Inter-American Bank continued to disperse loans for the project. After failing to achieve justice in negotiations with the Guatemalan government and the financial institutions, the Geneva-based Centre on Housing Rights and Evictions filed a complaint on behalf of the Rio Negro community to the Inter-American Commission on Human Rights against the government. The respondents named in the claim included not only Guatemala but also the members of the executive boards of the World Bank and the Inter-American Development Bank. The latter named satisfied two criteria used by COHRE: they had (a) signed or ratified the American Convention on Human Rights or the American Declaration on Human Rights; and (b) held "disproportionate voting power" (more than 5 per cent) at the time of the alleged violations in one of the two banks. These criteria covered the United States, Brazil, Argentina, Mexico, and Venezuela. This approach cleverly limited the extent to which the petitioner had to file against all states in the Americas that were members of the two banks (a classic problem in trying to operationalize extraterritorial litigation involving multilateral responsibility), although it remains to be seen if the commission will be convinced of the "disproportionate voting power" test.

The complaint squarely and concretely raises the long-standing debate over whether international financial institutions are bound by international human rights law (Bradlow 1996; Skogly 2001; Darrow 2003b; Clapham 2006). Traditionally, the World Bank and the IMF have skirted the question by raising their Articles of Agreement, which prohibit them from taking into account political considerations in their activities and interfering in political affairs of member states (Shihata 1995). However, the legal opinion of 2006 by the World Bank's legal counsel takes a more instrumentalist approach by acknowledging that human rights are consistent with many of the bank's evolving objectives and do raise economic considerations (Dañino 2006).[5] However, the opinion stops short of accepting that the bank is effectively bound to abide by international human rights obligations, and the opinion calls for the bank only to "disengage" with a project when there are gross violations ("egregious situations") and, rather nebulously, the bank "can no longer achieve its purposes" (Dañino 2006, par. 22).

Scholars and UN human rights bodies have usually advanced two arguments as to the responsibility of international financial institutions for human rights violations. The first is that international organizations are bound by human rights law by virtue of being international organizations. Experts point to various sources of such law—for example, human rights contained in international customary law or the UN system—with the argument for the latter running that as a specialized agency of the United Nations the World Bank cannot defeat the purposes of the UN Charter, which expressly and implicitly includes human rights (Darrow 2003b).

Debate still lingers over whether the right to housing, like other economic and social rights, has achieved the status of customary law (Clapham 2006, 147–49). However, a strong argument could be made that this right, and particularly protection from forced eviction, has in fact achieved this status—especially with near universal ratification of treaties like the Convention on the Rights of the Child—and even the World Bank's legal counsel tilts in this direction (Dañino 2006, par. 16). Echoing the UN Human Rights Commission on forced eviction in 1993, the Declaration of International Law Scholars on Forced Relocations states that "forced relocation is a particularly egregious violation of international law because it implicates a variety of fundamental human rights including the right to liberty and security of the person, the right to be free from arbitrary detention or exile, the right to be free from arbitrary interference with one's privacy, family and home, the right to freedom of movement and residence, and the right to human dignity."[6] While this argument for direct responsibility provides an important space for influencing bank policy—for example, efforts by the governments of Norway and Sweden to impose human rights conditionalities on their support to the bank—there is a lack of remedial opportunity for victims of violations of actions outside the quasi-judicial mechanisms of the Inspection Panel and the IFC's ombudsperson.

The second arrow in the argument, and that used by the complainants in the Chixoy Dam case, is that member states carry their international human rights obligations into their membership of international organizations. In 2005, the International Law Commission provisionally adopted the first three Articles on the Responsibility of International Organizations (see United Nations), which affirmed that states carry international responsibility for acts or omissions that breach an international obligation and are attributable to an international organization under international law. Echoing Pierre Klein (1999), COHRE argues in its petition that the banks had a particular "responsibility to ensure that the Chixoy project was carried out in a responsible manner" (Centre on Housing Rights and Evictions 2005, par. 74), which is further clarified as a duty not to act with gross negligence or reckless disregard. COHRE derives this duty from the wording of the guidelines of each bank as well as human rights law and claims that it was breached since the bank failed to supervise the project adequately when acts of displacement and violence were occurring, and then subsequently failed to evaluate the project properly. COHRE claims that the causation test is satisfied on the basis that bank officials "knew or should have known" what was occurring. The Chixoy Dam case is now awaiting an admissibility determination and COHRE was asked to bifurcate the case into separate petitions against Guatemala and the banks if that would expedite the case against Guatemala given the greater likelihood of a friendly settlement being reached. The advocate in the case, Bret Thiele, takes the "fact that they have not declared the bank portion inadmissible . . . as a good sign" (author's personal communication with Thiele, 6 June 2008).

It is important to note that the World Bank is not the only actor accused of being responsible for forced evictions in development cooperation. Indeed, their greater sensitivity to human rights partly increases the likelihood that some states will seek concessional or other loans from bilateral donors and bilateral development banks. After a negative report by the Inspection Panel regarding the Mumbai Urban Transportation Project, the World Bank in 2006 temporarily suspended financial support on the road and resettlement components until issues concerning the affected persons were addressed (Clark 2008). A state official responded by saying that it was their oversight that they signed an agreement, which said those displaced can't be worse off and the state government's next preferred partner is Japan, along with some Indian financial institutions (Deshmukh 2006).

States are, of course, often directly involved in extraterritorial forced evictions—many infrastructure projects have had separate funding from bilateral development agencies or smaller groupings such as the Nordic Trust Fund. In the Chixoy Dam case, the United States was twice added as a respondent due to its direct and indirect support of military and paramilitary forces behind the massacres and displacement. However, many bilateral "donors" lack even the operational policies on resettlement that the World Bank has, and thus, there is no quasi-judicial complaint procedure such as the Inspection Panel, which facilitates local complaints supported by nongovernmental organizations (NGOs). Some "bilateral" cases have been resolved by regional human rights courts, although not in the development context. We have already noted the seminal European Court of Human Rights Case of *Loizidou v. Turkey* in which Turkey was found liable for preventing a Greek Cypriot from returning to her home on northern Cyprus. Other forced eviction cases have been challenged locally, but not against the foreign actor. In the case of a slum upgrading project financially sponsored by the German Development Corporation (GTZ), slum landlords challenged the violation of their property rights in a case against the Catholic Church, which was implementing the project. Tenants, who were overwhelmingly poor, entered as third parties as they stood to gain from the slum upgrading, but they differed with the church over the way in which the project was bring implemented (Centre on Housing Rights and Evictions 2006). What is apparent from the jurisprudence is that the actions against a state in its own domestic courts based on its own development activities has not yet been fully explored, certainly not as much as litigation against transnational corporations in their home jurisdictions. The extent to which a state may be involved and legally responsible for extraterritorial forced evictions is of course a matter of degree and debate. In the forced eviction of fifty thousand residents from the Mau Forest in Kenya, the U.K. Department for International Development paradoxically funded the environmental study that suggested that the state evict the residents—and then funded three human rights organizations that investigated and opposed the eviction.[7] While it may be difficult to attach liability to funding studies, direct financial contribution or proactive advice may trigger justiciable claims.

The International Olympic Committee

Other multilateral organizations may also be responsible for human rights violations in forced evictions. One such example is the International Olympic Committee (IOC) which, COHRE has argued, has been responsible (along with the host country) for forced evictions in preparation for various Olympics Games.[8]

In Seoul, 720,000 people were forcibly evicted from their homes in preparation for the Olympic Games in 1988. In Barcelona, housing became so unaffordable as a result of the Olympic Games that low income earners were forced to leave the city. In Atlanta 9,000 arrest citations were issued to homeless people (mostly African-Americans) as part of an Olympics-inspired campaign to "clean the streets[,] and approximately 30,000 people were displaced by Olympics-related gentrification and development." In Athens, hundreds of Roma were displaced under the pretext of Olympics-related preparations. In the lead up to the 2008 Olympic Games in Beijing, COHRE estimates that over 1.25 million people already have been displaced due to Olympics-related urban redevelopment, with at least another quarter of a million displacements expected in the year prior to the staging of the event. In London, housing for 1,000 people is already under threat of demolition, over five years before the Olympic Games are due to be held. (Centre on Housing Rights and Evictions 2007, 11)

The arguments are similar to those concerning the World Bank's human rights obligations discussed above. COHRE alleges that the IOC must not only respect the right to adequate housing but, in accordance with the opening lines of Universal Declaration of Human Rights, it must also *promote* respect for human rights on behalf of other actors. COHRE points to members of the Olympic movement under the IOC's direct authority (including, among others, the host city, the host state, the Organising Committee for the Olympic Games and Olympic sponsors) over which the IOC has considerable influence. The privileged position of the IOC in selecting host cities should be used responsibly, and COHRE has argued that cities should execute an Olympic project that respects the right to housing. It also points to some solutions that the IOC could ensure are adopted. In Sydney, for example, the government was pressured to establish a protocol to ensure that homeless people would not be targeted for removal during the Olympic Games. In some other cities, athletes' accommodations have been used as affordable housing after the games have been completed.

Multinational Corporations

Multinational corporations (MNCs) are frequently engaged in large-scale infrastructure and extractive projects, often as part of international development cooperation given the World Bank's mandate to promote private foreign investment. In a number of cases brought before regional human rights tribunals, oil and timber extraction by multinationals has been found to trigger state liability for failure to adequately protect local residents and indigenous peoples from violations of the right to housing, such as forced eviction (Joseph 2008).

However, direct liability of multinationals is still an emerging area of international and comparative law (Clapham 2006). The OECD's Guidelines on Multinational Enterprises of 1976 require OECD-based multinational corporations to respect the human rights of those affected by their activities consistent with the host government's international obligations and commitments. This would include those international human rights treaties affecting housing that were discussed in the preceding section. National Contact Points established under these OECD Guidelines on Multinational Enterprises in finance ministries in OECD states have heard some complaints against multinationals under the OECD's Guidelines on Multinational Enterprises but the procedure is weak and not transparent. Furthermore, at this point none of the cases appear to involve housing, although the OECD and the National Contact Points seem partly alive to the issue (Organisation for Economic Co-operation and Development 2007).

Transnational litigation has attempted to hold states responsible before their own domestic courts, such as Alien Tort Statute cases brought against U.S. multinational corporations in American courts (for example, *Doe v. Unocal*). While this case was dismissed, others such as *Wiwa v. Royal Dutch Petroleum Co.* remain pending, raising similar issues. However, as Joseph (2008) has pointed out, no merits decision has been delivered in a transnational human rights case against a company. Rather, many have been tied up in procedural objections by companies, while a few cases have been settled confidentially.

The Equator Principles initiative of 2003 seems to be more cognitive of housing-related issues than the OECD framework. The principles are more of a voluntary compact signed on to by forty multilateral and multinational financial institutions and updated in 2006. These principles are intended to serve as a common baseline and framework for the implementation by each financial institution of its own internal social and environmental policies in finance projects of more than $10 million. The principles for social and environmental assessments are to include "protection of human rights," "socio-economic impacts," "land acquisition and involuntary resettlement," "impacts on affected communities, and disadvantaged or vulnerable groups," "impacts on indigenous peoples," and "consultation and participation of affected parties in the design, review and implementation of the project." Some observers have heralded the strengthening of some rights in the new draft, but others still "decry the failure to implement adequate transparency, accountability, and governance mechanisms" (Baue 2006).

Urban Housing and International Development Cooperation

Housing has never featured prominently in international development cooperation. It receives slightly greater prominence in emergency relief and, while that topic won't be covered, the discussion of the complexities of housing interventions in this chapter is nonetheless relevant in emergency situations, particularly the lack of attention of international agencies and NGOs given to tenure issues. It was thus not until 1976 that a UN program for housing was created and only in 2002 was it given the status of a UN specialized agency. A measure of the international community's lack of interest in housing is glaringly shown in the Millennium Development Goals (MDGs). Target 7D calls for the improvement of the lives of one hundred million slum dwellers by 2020. However, as of 12 May 2009, the UN-Habitat estimates that there are 1.14 billion slum dwellers, with forecasts of upward of two billion by 2030 if no corrective action if taken. While targets for improvement in other development goals range between 50 and 100 percent by 2015 (and even these are criticized; see UN Office of the High Commissioner for Human Rights 2008), the effective target for improving the lives of slum dwellers is a miserly 11 percent and achievement is set at a later date.

The reason for such complacency is complex, but it is generally tied to a strong rural bias in international and national development, together with a naive assumption that rural-urban migration and urban growth could be halted. Harris and Arku (2007) also point out that until the 1980s, housing was largely viewed by economists as a social need and not important for economic growth, which resulted in it attracting little international development funding. In addition, they make the critical point that housing is a particularly difficult area to support in developing countries. Most of the need is located in the informal sector with high levels of informal and customary land tenure. In addition, developing countries mostly lack any autonomous building sector that can be supported, particularly in comparison to, say, health or education. This complexity means that most successful instances of development support have come about through long-term engagement in slum-upgrading processes, with the German Development Corporation (GTZ) serving as an example in some cases of the patience needed in most urban upgrading projects (Bassett 2007).

UN-Habitat paints a rosier picture and argues that "from 1997 to 2002, by which time half the world had become urban, UN-Habitat—guided by the Habitat Agenda and the Millennium Declaration—underwent a major revitalisation, using its experience to identify emerging priorities for sustainable urban development and to make needed course corrections" (UN-Habitat 2009). However, a review of the MDG reports by three donor countries that tend to have programs in urban areas (Sweden, Germany, and the United Kingdom) reveals no significant increase in funding to the area and in some cases most of the focus is on the environment as part of Goal 7. With the exception of Germany, all donors tend to channel most of their support for slum upgrading and non-emergency housing programs through multilateral organizations, particularly UN-Habitat and the World Bank, and there is little additional bilateral cooperation that tends to assist the housing or urban sectors. In 2000, the World Bank and UN-Habitat established the Cities Alliance to better finance both housing and urban sector governance, but its budget pales in comparison to other trust funds. In the last six years, the Global Aids Fund committed U.S.$10.7 billion in 136 countries, while the Cities Alliance has committed a mere U.S.$88 million in eight years.[9] While the Cities Alliance claims its contributions leverage other capital contributions, the Global Aids Fund often plays a similar role and its finances need to be set against both national and international contributions. Faced with these sorts of numbers, it is difficult to conclude that developed countries are using the maximum available resources for housing in development. The absence of substantive urban or housing departments in most development agencies is perhaps a key indicator of the problem.

Of equal concern has been the international housing development paradigm. In this field, there is no shortage of models that have been attempted with multifaceted cyclical faddishness for different approaches. Zanetta (2001) has tracked the evolution of the World Bank's urban lending over fifty years and found that the development of its approaches have been "slow and uneven." Until the 1970s, most of the World Bank's urban funding was directed at energy and transport, and it was only during the new poverty focus during the McNamara era in the 1970s that the World Bank begin to finance slum-upgrading projects and, importantly, "site and service delivery," where demarcated plots with basic amenities would be prepared in order to meet urban population growth and residents would be expected to develop their own housing. The World Bank deserves particular credit during this period for rallying against the slum clearance policies of many developing countries, which were demolishing more low-income housing than was being built (Centre on Housing Rights and Evictions 2006). However, many of these projects have come to be viewed as only isolated successes, although the reasons behind this are diverse, ranging from the lack of local institutional capacity and autonomy to sustain the projects to the wider economic crisis from the mid-1970s (Zanetta 2001).

In the 1980s, the World Bank moved in the opposite direction, focusing on city-wide institutional development across a range of sectors and mechanisms for financial intermediation. The result was a marked decline in funding for specific shelter and infrastructure projects and arguably a loss of focus. By the late 1980s and mid-1990s, this pattern was largely replaced by policies with a strong neoliberal bias, which included efforts to privatize local services such as water, sanitation, and energy, and they also put a greater emphasis on liberalizing land, such as removing rent controls. Beyond this direct opening to greater market-based displacement, it is arguable that accompanying cuts to education and health funding and macroeconomic decline spurred a greater increase in the numbers of informal settlements, as even the middle class could not find affordable housing options (Centre on Housing Rights and Evictions 2006). Beginning in the late 1990s, the World Bank has taken a step back from the neoliberal Washington consensus and has tended to support a greater array of approaches. This has meant a remarkable heterogeneity of approaches at the country level, which makes it difficult to assess their policy globally. The bank also appears to work more closely with UN-Habitat on a range of initiatives, such as Cities Alliance, as mentioned above. Mukhija (2005, 57–58) notes that within this alliance, the bank emphasizes urban governance and competitiveness while UN-Habitat stresses slum upgrading, an approach that could create synergies but also significant conflicts.

This brief history of urban housing and international development points to four key issues in the context of extraterritorial obligations. The first is that ideological shifts greatly affect the ability of international development cooperation to support the realization of the right to housing for the poor. The advocacy by the World Bank in the 1970s on forced eviction and its support of localized approaches such as slum upgrading and site and service schemes arguably made a significant contribution (even allowing for lack of sustainability and corruption concerns) compared to other periods of engagement. Indeed, with a gradual acknowledgment that urban growth cannot be halted, site and service schemes are starting to gain favor again. At the same time, it is difficult to argue that the period of structural adjustment contributed much to the realization of the right to adequate housing—indeed, probably the reverse is true. Indeed, one of the most outstanding human rights impunity questions is what responsibility the World Bank, the IMF, and their members share for their contribution to retrogression in socio-economic rights in the South from their structural adjustment policies—policies that many Northern governments expressly rejected for their own countries.

Second, supporting slum dwellers is complex in developing countries, as it was in developed countries in much of the twentieth century. The enduring and fundamental problem is that policymakers fail to understand informal land and housing markets and local cultural norms. They presume that informal economies and institutions can be immediately transformed into formal paradises without any cost. These top-down approaches, however, have a long history of failure. Witness this example from the 1930s in the United Kingdom where researchers at the time "found that the health of families who moved into new council housing actually deteriorated—a doubling of rents had compelled families to scrimp on food and other necessities" (Harris and Arku 2007, 2). Fast forward seventy years to Kenya, where a recent slum upgrading project in Dandora by the national housing corporation led to a rise in housing payments by 1,000 percent in a space of one month for the previous slum residents, followed by attempts to evict them forcibly for non-payment. It is often forgotten that successful slum-upgrading projects (such as those in Norway in the 1940s and 1950s) received generous subsidization and operated in an environment of relatively low corruption. Other projects have failed because they did not address cultural concerns of minorities, indigenous peoples, or religious groups, leading to the non-use or even destruction of the housing.

International housing agencies are not immune from making these mistakes and UN-Habitat's flagship slum-upgrading project for the MDGs has been strongly criticized by local residents and international human rights NGOs for its almost total lack of participation, and designs that appear unaffordable and could lead to forcible displacement and gentrification of the buildings (Centre on Housing Rights and Evictions 2007).

This naivety has been particularly revealed in the debates over Peruvian economist Hernando de Soto's proposals for legal empowerment of slum dwellers and his establishment of the UN Commission on Legal Empowerment for the Poor (for a critical overview of the process, see Langford 2007). De Soto's ability to view those living and working in the vast informal economy and settlements of the developing world as active economic contributors, and not criminal elements, is certainly welcome (Patel 2007). However, the simple prescription of formalization by de Soto can worsen the situation. By exposing the poor to market forces, people living in poverty may be more quickly deprived of their homes, assets, and livelihoods than under informal or customary arrangements (see generally, Payne et al. 2007; and Nyamu-Musembi 2006). Individual-based formalization such as freehold title or individual leases may not be the preference of all or many indigenous peoples, rural communities, or informal settlements. A lack of attention to human rights baseline standards such as protection from forced eviction, protection of women's rights, and adequate participation of those being "empowered" has thus led many formalization projects to fail to achieve their goals in practice. However, after significant civil society mobilization and lobbying of commissioners, the final work of the UN Commission on Legal Empowerment for the Poor (2008) attempts to straddle a more nuanced approach.

Third, the first-mentioned element of the right to housing, security of tenure, continues to be largely ignored in international development cooperation on slum upgrading. Providing basic security of tenure along with services allows the minimal space for slum dwellers to develop their own housing and thus complement other housing policies attempting to provide new low-income housing directly. The Millennium Development Goals provide no target on security of tenure and while they formed part of the indicators for slum upgrading, this aspect was removed in June 2007. It is arguable that provision of basic security tenure for all by 2015 would be more consistent with human rights, effective in addressing slum dwellers and arguably even more affordable than expensive slum-upgrading projects that are pursued by many agencies. The new Global Land Tool Network being developed by UN-Habitat may hopefully steer international development cooperation and national and local governments in a better direction by suggesting tools that support improvements in existing land tenure as opposed to attempts to shift immediately to freehold tenure.

Indeed, the poor wording of the target has allowed countries such as Vietnam to report what amounts to human rights violations, such as slum clearance, as part of their efforts in achieving the Millennium Development Goals (Government of Vietnam 2005, 12). Marie Hucherzermeyer (2008) argues that a provincial slum clearance law in South Africa and moves to replicate it country-wide are based on a "fundamentally flawed" interpretation of MDG Target 7D. While the slogan "Cities without Slums" accompanies this target, she notes that "improving the lives of 10% of slum dwellers by 2020 was conceptualised as a first step to eventually achieve cities without slums."

Last, the level of international accountability in all these aspects is depressingly low. For example, in the Kenyan slum-upgrading project being led by UN-Habitat and the government of Kenya, there is no effective official forum that residents can utilize to make the agency and government accountable. An election for a community committee was organized but was marred by corruption and intimidation by local officials. It has thus required long-term engagement by NGOs and community groups to get the government and agency to at least listen to the fundamental concerns. This holds true for most of the shifts in the World Bank's policy, where campaigning by civil society has helped shift the thinking of the World Bank from the 1960s (Zanetta 2001). The question is whether, given the many failures in this area, accountability should be left to international organizations—or is there a need to fundamentally reshape policymaking and project design to incorporate grassroots concerns and non-mainstream opinions?

Conclusion

This review of extraterritorial obligations and the right to housing reveals in poet Paul Celan's words, a sort of homecoming. Over the past two decades, international human rights law has gradually affirmed a range of extraterritorial obligations in the field of housing, some of which have been judicialized through litigation. Levels of accountability have partly improved, particularly in relation to international development banks, but less so for other forms of development cooperation and the activities of multinational corporations. There has also been some evolution in the development of policy approaches, with at least some recognition of the dangers of large infrastructure projects and neoliberal approaches. There are some instances of positive forms of self-regulation and advocacy, although not all of this is current—the World Bank has yet to return to its high level of engagement on urban forced evictions in the 1970s, for instance.

However, the strength of these developments is still offset by the failure to truly operationalize effective forms of accountability. This means not only accountability for direct involvement in housing rights violations such as forced eviction, but also accountability for "advice" and "policy," which can often lead to the same devastating consequences, for example, through market-based displacement. In addition, there has also been no accountability for failures to undertake participatory approaches. One sometimes wonders whether the "human rights approach to development" community has acquiesced in the international development community's understanding of participation without demanding minimum standards, equality norms, and accountability mechanisms for any participatory process. Last, the paltry focus on housing, slum dwellers, and urban areas in international development cooperation in both existing and potential funding and staff is not only short-sighted as the world's slum population grows exponentially larger, but is arguably a violation of their housing rights obligations as well.

However, the human rights paradigm is not the only game in town that is addressing extraterritorial questions. Engaging with international development cooperation requires familiarity with other solutions being proposed. This chapter has briefly analyzed the Millennium Development Goals, which have trumpeted global partnership and responsibility. The MDGs have helped increase the international focus on poverty and slum upgrading, and seemingly helped the World Bank shift toward a greater acceptance of human rights (Dañino 2006). However, the MDGs are fundamentally flawed from the perspective of housing rights due to their spectacular lack of ambition, failure to focus on security of tenure, and the likelihood that they will encourage expensive but inappropriate solutions for a few. Other discourses such as *global public goods* as promoted by Kaul and others at the United Nations Development Programme (UNDP) encourage states to draw up and address lists of the positive and negative externalities that they are responsible for in the world (Kaul et al. 2007). They see participation as being improved through a move away from state-driven approaches toward global participation where citizens, states, businesses, and civil society cooperatively develop solutions. Promoters of the *human security* discourse point to the greater acceptability of their non-rights-based but human-centered discourse, particularly in the Asian region, where it has been used to deal with some transnational development and human rights issues. While each of these approaches brings pragmatic and soothing language in environments often hostile to human rights, the compromise in language can often mask a failure to tackle the power and structural inequalities that drive the violations of human rights (see Langford 2009b). The case of housing demonstrates that a human rights approach is more than ever needed to tackle the failures and potential of global cooperation.

Chapter 9
Protecting Rights in the Face of Scarcity: The Right to Water

Amanda Cahill

The attention to water as a human right is relatively recent, as specific codification of the right was not included in the UN International Covenant on Economic, Social, and Cultural Rights (ICESCR). Nevertheless, the recent attention given to the study of the human right to water is imperative as water is necessary for human survival. As such, a discussion concerning obligations of the right to water is a necessary and important debate in international human rights law. In terms of extraterritorial obligations, the right to water may be seen as even more controversial than the general extraterritorial obligations due to the continued deliberation as to whether this right constitutes an independent human right in itself or whether it can only be deemed a derivative or constitutive right, that is, an element of related rights such as the rights to food, health, and an adequate standard of living (Cahill 2005; Bluemel 2004). The case for recognizing water as an independent right has been made both morally and legally, albeit that the legal codification requires further clarification (Cahill 2007, 320–39; Tully 2005). Therefore, the starting point for this discussion takes the position that water is a fully independent human right as provided for, inter alia, by articles 11 and 12 of the ICESCR, article 24.2(c) of the UN International Convention on the Rights of the Child (CRC), and article 14(h) of the UN Convention on the Elimination of All Forms of Discrimination against Women (CEDAW). The right to water must also be seen in relationship to international transboundary water law, where an extraterritorial aspect of obligations is already established.

Furthermore, the Millennium Development Goals (MDGs) were adopted at the outset of this new century in response to continuing global poverty, an element of which is a lack of access to clean and sufficient water and adequate sanitation (UN Committee on Economic, Social, and Cultural Rights 2002b, par. 1 [hereafter cited simply as *General Comment 15*]; WHO 2000, par. 1; WHO 2003, par. 7). Access to clean and sufficient water and adequate sanitation constitute a specific target within these internationally agreed MDGs (MDG 7, target 10). Unfortunately, in the report of 2006 on progress toward achieving these goals it was noted that "world targets for safe drinking water are in sight, but coverage remains spotty in rural areas and as half of developing country populations still lack basic sanitation, the world is unlikely to reach this target" (United Nations 2006, 18–19). As such, there is a clear need for a corresponding direct international legal obligation (in addition to this international policy) to realize adequate safe clean water for everyone. Alston and others have argued that many of the MDGs, including the water target of goal 7, constitute customary international law (Alston 2005b, 755–829; Nakani et al. 2005, 475–97). Furthermore, an important precedent may have been established in the *Nuclear Weapons Advisory Opinion* (1996, pars. 27–31) when the International Court of Justice (ICJ) held that the Stockholm Declaration (1972) and the Rio Declaration (1992) both provide a general legal obligation upon states to protect the natural environment from harm and damage despite their nature as declarations.

The concept of extraterritorial obligations can act as a framework for such an international legal duty. With this aim in mind, the first part of this chapter will examine the provisions for extraterritorial obligations concerning the human right to water by applying the widely accepted tripartite typology of obligations used as a basis for obligations correlative to all economic and social rights. The second part of the chapter will assess the United Kingdom's compliance with its extraterritorial obligations regarding the right to water through an examination of its current foreign policy regarding international development assistance, specifically, the role of the Department for International Development (DFID). These activities include unilateral, multilateral, and bilateral actions or omissions, that is, acting individually, with another state, or as a member of an international organization. Finally, in the concluding part I will highlight problematic areas in terms of the current law and policy and suggest improving and clarifying legal codification of the right and access to legal remedy, as well as elaborating on further steps to be taken by the government of the United Kingdom and other states in order to strengthen extraterritorial obligations regarding the right to water and to promote compliance with the obligations set forth in the ICESCR.

It should be noted that due to chapter constraints, I do not undertake an assessment of other parts of the United Kingdom's foreign policy, such as the actions of trade and industry, private companies, or security and military cooperation, although all these activities may also have implications for the enjoyment of the right to water in third states. Each of these forms of activity requires further research to assess as a whole a government's compliance with its extraterritorial obligations concerning the right to water.

The Extraterritorial Obligations Regarding the Right to Water

The legal basis for extraterritorial obligations regarding the human right to water is to be found in the general provision of article 2(1) of the ICESCR and under articles 11 and 12 of the ICESCR, which contain the implicit provision for a right to water. The extraterritorial obligations concerning water are explicitly detailed in *General Comment 15, The Right to Water*, adopted by the UN Committee on Economic, Social, and Cultural Rights (CESCR) in 2002. This was drafted as a response to continuing violations of the right as examined by the CESCR in its state-reporting system. The comprehensive guidelines set out in *General Comment 15* are intended to outline and clarify the normative content of the right as well as confirming its legal basis, and setting out the obligations of states parties to the ICESCR in realizing this right. General states parties' obligations to respect, protect, and fulfill are detailed within paragraphs 21–25 and include obligations to refrain from interference with the enjoyment of the right to water (par. 21, respect), to prevent third parties from interfering with the enjoyment of the right (par. 23, protect), and, finally, the obligation to fulfill:

The obligation to fulfil can be disaggregated into the obligations to facilitate[,] promote and provide. The obligation to facilitate requires the State to take positive measures to assist individuals and communities to enjoy the right. The obligation to promote obliges the State party to take steps to ensure that there is appropriate education concerning the hygienic use of water, protection of water sources and methods to minimize water wastage. States parties are also obliged to fulfil (provide) the right when individuals or a group are unable, for reasons beyond their control, to realize that right themselves by the means at their disposal. (*General Comment 15*, par. 25)

Further obligations to fulfill are elaborated in paragraphs 26–29 of *General Comment 15*, which include provisions for according sufficient recognition of the right within the national political and legal systems, preferably by way of legislative implementation; adopting a national water strategy and plan of action to realize the right; ensuring that water is affordable for everyone and facilitating improved and sustainable access to water, particularly in rural and deprived urban areas; ensuring that water is affordable; adopting comprehensive and integrated strategies and programs to ensure that there is sufficient and safe water for present and future generations; and progressively extending safe sanitation services.

General Comment 15 then expands upon these three levels of obligations to incorporate a specific extraterritorial aspect under the section
on international obligations. These paragraphs are comprehensive and
follow the framework for international provisions as set out in previous
general comments (for example, UN Committee on Economic, Social,
and Cultural Rights 2000, pars. 38–42). Moreover, the legal commitment
required by states parties to extraterritorial obligations is emphasized by
the explicit recognition of the extraterritorial element of states parties'
duties present in these detailed and strongly worded provisions (pars.
31–36).

In relation to the extraterritorial obligation to respect, paragraph 31
provides that states have a duty to respect the enjoyment of the right
to water in other countries by refraining "from actions that interfere,
directly or indirectly, with the enjoyment of the right to water in other
countries." Furthermore, "any activities undertaken within the State
party's jurisdiction should not deprive another country of the ability to
realize the right to water for persons in its jurisdiction." This provision
should be interpreted to include not only an obligation to refrain from
actual actions and activities that are detrimental to the enjoyment of the
right to water, but also encompass an obligation to refrain from formulating and implementing policies that "can be foreseen as having negative effects" upon the right to water (Zeigler 2005, par. 51).

This level of obligation is the least controversial in terms of its extraterritorial application (Coomans 2004, 193), as it is a negative obligation rather
than a positive one and also implies a continuing respect for state sovereignty (Skogly and Gibney 2002, 796–98). However, even at this minimal
level of obligation, one state can interfere with the enjoyment of the right
to water for people in another state. For example, the U.K. Department of
Trade's policy and practice concerning arms exports to Israel has affected
the existing enjoyment of the right to water in the Occupied Palestinian
Territories (see further discussion below). What is undisputed is that at a
minimum, states have a duty to respect economic and social rights in third
states (Vandenhole 2007b). However, with regard to the right to water this
may not be so clear-cut, as the status and content of the right is challenged
by states parties and international bodies alike.

The obligation to protect is also reiterated in the context of extraterritorial activities. *General Comment 15* provides that states parties must
take steps to "prevent their own citizens and companies from violating
the right to water of individuals and communities in other countries."
Moreover, it stresses that "where States parties can take steps to influence
other third parties to respect the right, through legal or political means,
such steps should be taken in accordance with the Charter of the United
Nations and applicable international law" (*General Comment 15*, par. 33).

This provision is significant in that many companies now have branches and operations outside the state of origin. Therefore, these entities need to be regulated to ensure that they do not violate the right to water of the citizens in third states through their indirect or direct policy or practice. Specific examples include the activities of mining companies, soft drinks companies, and damming and engineering companies, all of which can negatively affect the local population's right to water through pollution and/or lack of or insufficient access to water (FIAN/Brot fur die Welt 2006, 10–13; FIAN 2008a and 2008b; Shiva 2002; U.K. House of Commons International Development Committee [hereafter IDC] 2007a, 47–50).

The final level of obligation—the obligation to fulfill—is seen as the most controversial, as it could be interpreted as a positive obligation alone and an obligation to provide for a third state's population (Coomans 2004, 195; Skogly 2006, 71). Obviously, this interpretation is unrealistic and untenable and undermines the continuing obligation to fulfill held primarily by the domestic government in question. Therefore, it has been argued that the obligation to fulfill in its extraterritorial aspect must be limited to a duty to facilitate or to "support the fulfillment" of a right by the domestic state (Zeigler 2005, par. 47). Practically, this would seem appropriate, as a third state cannot interfere with domestic policy without cooperation from that state. Realistically, a state party cannot be expected to fulfill the right to water in a foreign state if the domestic government of that state is not taking action itself to fulfill its obligations.

Generally, the obligation to fulfill or support fulfillment is framed in terms of international assistance and cooperation and *General Comment 15* notes the general obligation of all states parties to international assistance. It requires that state parties recognize "the essential role of international co-operation and assistance and take joint and separate action to achieve the full realization of the right to water" (par. 30), reflecting the general provision in article 2 of the ICESCR. This approach of international cooperation with the aim of realizing access to safe and sufficient water is parallel to the approach taken under the UNECE *Water Convention Protocol on Water and Health* (Cahill 2007, 19). *General Comment 15* details how this obligation should be met particularly in relation to the right to water:

Depending on the availability of resources, States should facilitate realization of the right to water in other countries, for example, through provision of water resources, financial and technical assistance, and provide the necessary aid when required. In disaster relief and emergency assistance, including assistance to refugees and displaced persons, priority should be given to Covenant rights, including the provision of adequate water. International assistance should be provided in a manner that is consistent with the Covenant and other human rights standards, and sustainable and culturally appropriate. The economically developed States parties have a special responsibility and interest to assist the poorer developing States in this regard. (*General Comment 15*, par. 34)

Although states parties must provide necessary aid when required, the obligation to fulfill or to support fulfillment is dependent on the availability of resources. However, the provision in paragraph 34 is important as it acknowledges the particular responsibility of economically developed states parties in assisting the poorer developing states and states involved in emergency situations (Craven 1995, 150; Skogly 2006, 83–98; UN Committee on Economic, Social, and Cultural Rights 1990b, pars. 13–14). If richer, more developed states do not have an obligation to assist those poorer states in realizing their obligations, they may continue to thrive to the detriment of economic and social human rights in those poorer states. By holding the poorer state to be in violation, without examining the aspect of international assistance, what will likely become obscured is the fact that much of the responsibility for poverty and deprivation in the world lies with the developed states' approach to international trade and the economic order. Because of this, "responsibility should be placed upon the international community and not merely confined to the victim state" (Craven 1995, 144). As such, the application of extraterritorial obligations offers a framework in which the legal duties of states parties pertaining to international assistance and the right to water can be understood and complied with, thus allowing for implementation of the right to water without discrimination across national borders. The focus on extraterritorial obligations highlights the crucial importance of legal recognition of states parties' obligations pertaining to international assistance, rather than seeing international assistance as an additional goal or an optional practice.

In addition to the extraterritorial obligations of states parties to be carried out unilaterally and bilaterally, *General Comment 15* also considers the actions of states multilaterally as members of international or regional organizations. These provisions are crucial in today's international system as the majority of development assistance is undertaken on a multilateral basis, through partner governments and donor partnerships. Paragraph 35 relates to international and regional agreements and their impact upon the right to water, noting that the right to water should be given due attention in international agreements and that implementation of other international and regional agreements should not adversely affect the right to water. This is particularly interesting in terms of the effect the obligation may have on the implementation of regional or bilateral agreements, which may affect access to, or quality and sufficiency of, water. For example, member states of the European

Union have an obligation to ensure their actions as part of the European Union do not negatively affect the enjoyment of the right to water in a third state. This includes implementation of regional and bilateral agreements to which they are a party. Under the EU-Israel Association Agreement, which governs trade between the European Union and Israel, Israel exports fruit to the European Union. However, much of Israel's fruit produce is sourced from illegal Israeli settlements in the Occupied Palestinian Territories of the West Bank, although it has been classified as "made in Israel," thereby benefiting from the agreement (IDC 2007c, par. 39). These settlements and their agricultural production negatively affect the Palestinians' water supply and water quality. As such, the implementation of this agreement is having an adverse effect upon the right to water, which is contrary to obligations of states parties to the ICESCR, as detailed in paragraphs 35 and 36 of *General Comment 15*. The IDC now maintains that a new system of postcode labeling has been introduced that will eliminate harm to the Palestinian population (IDC 2007c, par. 39). However, the government of Israel compensates these settlers for this loss of preference. Therefore, this agreement requires further scrutiny and review to ascertain how the agreement can be amended to ensure compliance by EU member states with their extraterritorial obligations concerning the right to water.

It is notable that the same provision in *General Comment 15* singles out agreements concerning trade liberalization and states that they "should not curtail or inhibit a country's capacity to ensure the full realization of the right to water" (par. 35). Again, this is imperative as trade liberalization often entails multilateral action by the domestic home state in conjunction with international organizations such as the World Trade Organization (WTO).

Furthermore, the actions of states parties as members of international organizations is further considered in paragraph 36 where it is explicitly stated that states acting as members of international organizations, including members of international financial institutions, are required "to take into account the right to water in their lending policies, credit arrangements and other international measures." However, the wording here could be firmer to strengthen this aspect of extraterritorial obligations, requiring states parties as members of these organizations to refrain from actions that could be seen to have a negative impact upon enjoyment of the right to water in third states.

States parties also have extraterritorial obligations in relation to water and political, security, and military concerns. Paragraph 32 of *General Comment 15* emphatically states that water should never be used as an instrument of political and economic pressure and asserts that "states parties should refrain at all times from imposing embargoes or similar measures, that prevent the supply of water, as well as goods and services essential for securing the right to water.. . . In this regard, the Committee recalls its position, stated in its General Comment No. 8 (1997), on the relationship between economic sanctions and respect for economic, social and cultural rights."

This paragraph reiterates the provisions set out in the CESCR's *General Comment 8* (1997), in which the committee notes how economic sanctions can jeopardize the availability of clean drinking water and disrupt adequate sanitation (UN Committee on Economic, Social, and Cultural Rights 1997b, par. 3; hereafter cited simply as *General Comment 8*). Moreover, it notes that provision for repairs to infrastructure essential to provide clean water should be a humanitarian exemption under any sanctions regime (*General Comment 8*, pars. 4–5).

Importantly, this provision highlights the relevance of an extraterritorial aspect of states parties' obligations concerning the right to water as an issue to be considered within a state's foreign policy actions, not just as part of international development or assistance but also as an aspect of political, security, and military actions. As will be addressed below, recent examples of such policy with considerations for the right to water and sanctions can be seen in Iraq previous to the war that began in March 2003 and in the boycott of the Palestinian Authority since the election of Hamas in January 2006 (Dugard 2006, par. 70)

A further significant aspect of clarifying the existence of extraterritorial human rights obligations in general, as well as in relation to the right to water, concerns occupation. One example concerns the protection of economic and social rights of Palestinians living in the Occupied Palestinian Territories of the West Bank (Cahill 2007). In the significant advisory opinion on the *Legal Consequences of the Construction of a Wall in the Occupied Palestinian Territories* (2004, 107–9), the International Court of Justice considered the extraterritorial obligations of human rights treaties and concluded that the ICESCR was applicable to the territories, thereby confirming the stated position of the Committee on Economic, Social, and Cultural Rights (UN Committee on Economic, Social, and Cultural Rights 2003, pars. 15 and 31). The ICJ's advisory opinion observed that "although the treaty does not contain any provision on its scope of application, nevertheless, this cannot be interpreted as excluding areas where a state exercises extraterritorial jurisdiction" (par. 112). As such, the ICJ held that Israel was responsible for the implementation of these rights as a state party to the ICESCR and as the occupying power exercising effective control: "The territories occupied by Israel have for over 37 years been subject to its territorial jurisdiction as the occupying Power. In the exercise of the powers available to it on this basis, Israel is bound by the provisions of the International Covenant on Economic,

Social and Cultural Rights. Furthermore, it is under an obligation not to raise any obstacle to the exercise of such rights in those fields where competence has been transferred to Palestinian authorities" (par. 112).

Finally, extraterritorial obligations are particularly pertinent for the right to water as geographically water resources are often shared between states' territories, and the actions of a neighboring state or its citizens can have consequent effects upon individuals' right to water in another state. Under the norms of international water law, the concept of transboundary responsibility for actions is established and accepted (Stockholm Declaration 1972, principle 21; UN Convention on the Law of the Non-Navigational Uses of International Watercourses [CNNUIW], 1997; *Trail Smelter* case *(United States v. Canada)*, Ad Hoc International Arbitral Tribunal, 1941). However, many of the provisions relating to transboundary responsibility apply only to riparian states, that is, states that share a boundary with the water source. This is therefore different, as the extraterritorial obligation is not a shared responsibility among all states parties to an international treaty, such as the ICESCR. Notwithstanding this point, general principles such as the prohibition of causing significant harm can correspond to the extraterritorial human rights obligation to respect the right to water in other states. A similar point was presented at the recent *Consultation on Human Rights and Access to Safe Drinking Water and Sanitation* where a participant highlighted the fact that paragraph 31 of *General Comment 15* is in line with the principle of non-significant harm as recognized under transboundary water law (UN Office of the High Commissioner for Human Rights 2007, 9).

However, one of the concerns also raised at this particular consultation was whether regarding a human right to water may conflict with existing obligations under such international water law (ibid., 8). This is unlikely, though, as transboundary water law encompasses a rights-based approach within several of its key principles, most importantly, emphasizing the priority of water for basic needs (CNNUIW 1997, art. 10.2). If this primary principle were adhered to, there would be no conflict with obligations—both domestic and extraterritorial—regarding this human right.

Moreover, international transboundary water law also advocates equitable use of water, which can be seen as parallel to the obligation for non-discrimination under international human rights law. For example, the CNNUIW contains obligations of equitable and reasonable utilization of water, including taking into account the "social and economic needs of the watercourse States concerned" (art. 6b) and "the population dependent on the watercourse in each watercourse State" (art. 6c).

Similarly, one other substantive treaty governing the use of water is the UN Economic Commission for Europe's (UNECE) Convention on the

Protection and Use of Transboundary Watercourses and International Lakes (1992) and the Protocol on Water and Health (1999). The convention includes principles that could be expanded to constitute extraterritorial human rights obligations to respect and protect the right to water, such as prohibition of pollution and quality control. Thus the well-established area of international water law can be viewed as supporting the concept that the human right to water has extraterritorial obligations, which are practical and enforceable given the appropriate mechanisms for compliance.

The United Kingdom and Its Extraterritorial Obligations Concerning the Human Right to Water

In the case of the right to water, the United Kingdom has extraterritorial obligations resulting from its ratification of the ICESCR in 1976. To determine how these extraterritorial obligations work in practice, an assessment of the international development activities of the U.K. government in relation to the human right to water is offered. The focus of this research is based upon the policies and practice of the Department for International Development (DFID) and will address unilateral actions, bilateral actions with partner governments and nongovernmental organizations (NGOs), and multilateral actions as part of international donor organizations, for example, the World Bank and the United Nations.

On the face of it, the DFID has taken considerable action to improve its performance in meeting water and sanitation goals. For example, the DFID has increased its budget for water and sanitation projects in Africa from £95 million in 2007–8 to £200 million by 2010–11 (U.K. Department for International Development [hereafter DFID] 2007a, 4). Many seemingly worthwhile and focused projects are underway, with the new impetus for the DFID's water and sanitation policy being the realization of the Millennium Development Goals, in particular goal 7, target 10: to "halve, by 2015, the proportion of people without sustainable access to safe drinking water and basic sanitation." The DFID also notes that achieving this target is necessary if the majority of other targets and goals are to be fulfilled (IDC 2007, 6, pars. 1–2). With this in mind, in its proposed Global Action Plan (DFID 2006c), the DFID suggests three basic aims to improve effectiveness of aid and assistance in these sectors: (a) to increase global funding; (b) to ensure money is spent effectively, with longer-term coordinated funding; and (c) to develop capacity building at the local level and to put necessary infrastructures in place to make progress (DFID 2006c, 1).

All of this is promising policy, but where does it place the United Kingdom in terms of its extraterritorial obligations correlative to the right to water? There are two questions that need to be asked: First, does the U.K. government accept that the actions taken by the DFID are part of implementing legal obligations or does the government rather view them as foreign policy objectives? Second, do these projects actually realize the extraterritorial obligations of the United Kingdom in respect of the right to water?

Initially it is necessary to examine the United Kingdom's position on the legal existence and acceptance of the human right to water, especially as the ICESCR has no legal equivalent in U.K. domestic law. On 9 November 2006, the U.K. government recognized the existence of a human right to water as a part of its new Global Action Plan for Water (DFID 2006a). However, on closer inspection, it is clear that the rhetoric implored in the public relations is not backed up with comprehensive legal provision. The actual legal position of the U.K. government concerning the right is presented in the DFID's draft position paper, "The Human Right to Water" (DFID 2006c). This position paper provides the basis for any action taken by the DFID in regard to implementing the right to water as a part of its water and sanitation actions. In addition, it outlines the U.K. government's view of its extraterritorial human rights obligations in relation to water.

According to this document, it is evident that the government of the United Kingdom does not accept that the human right to water is an independent right to be realized or that it is even a derivative right (DFID 2006c, par. 4). The position stated within this paper, then, would seem to contradict its recognition of the right as it negates its existence as both an independent or a derivative right. The wording used in paragraphs 3 and 6, however, states that recognition of a right to water is an element of the general right to an adequate standard of living under article 11. Therefore, this is the basis for any obligations regarding water. Despite this, within paragraph 4 it is then stated that the right to water is not derived from other rights. Thus, the position regarding the legal status of the right, as stated by the DFID, is confusing and extremely unclear.

The document also omits any recognition of immediate core obligations in relation to economic and social rights generally, inclusive of the right to water, espousing that all rights under the ICESCR are to be achieved progressively (DFID 2006c, para. 4 and 14[i]), although it explicitly notes that the right is legally binding. This opinion contradicts the position taken by the CESCR and other human rights bodies and may have a consequential effect upon the United Kingdom's view of its extraterritorial obligations.

In terms of the provisions set out in *General Comment 15*, the U.K. government states categorically that *General Comment 15* contains some useful guidance for governments on how to meet their obligations. However, the United Kingdom "does not accept the General Comment in its entirety but we regard it as an important contribution to the debate about what having a right to water means" (DFID 2006c, par. 5).

In the first instance, then, it would seem that despite a proclamation of the right to water, the U.K. government's legal position on the existence of the said right is uncertain and in contradiction to much international legal opinion, including the opinion of the CESCR, which interprets the rights contained within the ICESCR to which the United Kingdom is a state party. As such, the United Kingdom may be in breach of its extraterritorial obligations under the ICESCR, as we do not know which provisions within the general comment the government does not accept. Furthermore, it is difficult to comply with the objective obligations of the treaty concerning the right to water when the very nature of the right (in legal terms) is questioned.

Despite these statements, the draft paper offers an explanation as to why the DFID supports developing countries in realizing the human right to water: "[The] DFID sees human rights as central to the development agenda and the fight against poverty. We are committed to working with developing country governments to assist them in implementing their human rights obligations and to empowering people living in poverty to claim their rights. We advocate a 'rights based approach' to development, which incorporates the human rights principles of participation, inclusion and fulfilling obligation" (DFID 2006c, sec. 4, par. 12).

This position would seem to be one that views international assistance as inclusive of "supporting fulfillment" of human rights obligations generally and that this includes assisting other states in fulfilling their obligations regarding the right to water, even though the legal basis for this right is disputed. Significantly though, this assistance does not appear to be based upon an extraterritorial legal obligation but rather is considered as a policy commitment as part of the DFID's development strategy.

In sum, the announcement of the recognition of the right to water amounts to just that—an announcement. As Henry Shue notes, it is important to understand that "a proclamation of a right is not the fulfilment of a right, anymore than an airplane schedule is a flight. A proclamation may or may not be an initial step toward the fulfilment of the rights listed. It is frequently the substitute of the promise in the place of the fulfilment" (Shue 1980, 15).

Moreover, in 2006 the IDC commissioned a report on the work of the DFID concerning sanitation and water. The IDC states that "whilst the UK's recognition of water as a basic human right sets a good example and underlines the UK's commitment to the sector internationally, ascertaining what recognition of the right means in practical terms . . . is quite difficult" (IDC 2007a, 24, par. 61).

In other words, without understanding and clarifying what entitlements and duties the right to water entails, this recognition of the "right" to water can be considered little more than well-meaning rhetoric, which does little to advance the right other than raising the public profile of its existence and reinforcing the policy focus of the DFID on water.

Positively regarding the human right to water, in its report the IDC notes that although a rights framework does not ensure universal access to water, it does serve as a "powerful moral claim" and a tool for "poor people to mobilise around their entitlements" (IDC 2007a, 24, par. 63). However, a moral entitlement is not equivalent to a legal entitlement, the latter of which is not explicitly clarified by the DFID or the IDC. Despite the acknowledgment that actual realization of the right is "difficult," the IDC does not elaborate further as to what action the DFID should take to tackle this particular issue. Rather, the IDC urges the DFID to "encourage developing countries to go beyond recognition to quantify and legislate for the right to water. Only then can citizens hold their providers accountable for their entitlement to water. This should include a complementary strategy of increasing demand for water services by helping to raise public knowledge of existing entitlements, as well as of gaps in legislation and policies" (IDC 2007a, 24, par. 63). Notwithstanding the beneficial and positive nature of these recommendations, they are problematic from the outset. The U.K. government itself has not clarified the content and understanding of the right to water, or adopted relevant legislation; and it could be problematic for it to assist other countries in realizing this particular right. As such, the government needs to recognize the content of the right, the necessary legal and political structures through which people can claim their entitlement to the right, and finally, the financial and technical ability needed to deliver the right.

The DFID's response to the recommendations of the IDC was thus: "We are committed to supporting partner countries to ensure that people enjoy their human right to water. How we do this will depend on the country context. Where appropriate, we will work with partner governments to define people's right to water, support efforts to increase people's knowledge of their entitlements, promote greater accountability in water services and strengthen the mechanisms by which people can claim their right to water" (IDC 2007b, 7–8).

This position would seem to imply that the definition of the right to water would vary according to the state. However, the definition and content of the right is universal, and it is only how the right is implemented that should vary according to the national context.

In sum, if the human right to water is not enshrined in U.K. law, it is difficult for the United Kingdom to tell other governments to do so, even if the right has been "recognized" by the government. In fact, the

CESCR has criticized the United Kingdom for not enshrining any of the economic and social rights contained within the ICESCR in its domestic law: "The Committee deeply regrets that . . ., the Covenant has still not been incorporated into the domestic legal order and that there is no intention by the State party to do so in the near future. The Committee reiterates its concern about the State party's position that the provisions of the Covenant . . . constitute principles and programmatic objectives rather than legal obligations that are justifiable" (UN Committee on Economic, Social, and Cultural Rights 2002a, par. 11).

This presents two issues: first, that the U.K. government's position concerning economic and social rights generally seems to imply that it interprets the rights contained in the ICESCR as aims rather than legal entitlements, which does not bode well for compliance with legal obligations; and second, that in relation to the right to water specifically, the issue is further complicated by the lack of clarification on the part of the government of the United Kingdom as to what entitlements follow the human right to water. Consequently, in order to comply with extraterritorial obligations regarding the right to water, as recognized under the ICESCR, the government of the United Kingdom needs to clarify its legal interpretation of the right and elaborate its understanding of the normative content and corresponding obligations.

The Practice of the U.K. Government via the DFID

Aside from the limiting legal and theoretical background on the human right to water, the actual practice of the DFID in relation to improving water and sanitation is encouraging. Notwithstanding the three levels of extraterritorial obligations discussed, the aim of the DFID's work is international development or assistance. Therefore, the focus of its extraterritorial obligations is at the level of the obligation to facilitate and support the fulfillment of the right to water. This does not imply that the other two levels of obligation are irrelevant, but rather, that they may be more relevant to other aspects of the United Kingdom's foreign policy, such as military and security assistance or trade. In addition, compliance with these levels of obligations is harder to assess, as it is only the proactive work that is publicized. It is only when the right to water is being violated in a third state due to the actions of the U.K. government that we become aware of the violation of the obligation to respect. Similarly, when a U.K. company violates human rights in a foreign state, awareness is raised concerning the lack of protection on the part of the government of the United Kingdom.

However, in terms of an extraterritorial obligation to support fulfillment and facilitate, even though the DFID does not frame its actions in terms of compliance with extraterritorial obligations, the projects may result in de facto compliance with these obligations. For example, the DFID's work in Nigeria is extensive. Working with UNICEF alongside 46 local government authorities in order to reach 165 communities, the DFID aims to drill 1,380 boreholes, install water pumps, rehabilitate 280 water supply systems, and construct latrines and urinals in 600 schools in 2007. Again, through UNICEF, the DFID funds the Federal Ministry of Water Resources' staff training program, and in 2006, supported Nigeria's first national water and sanitation forum, as well as supporting the NGO WaterAid, which is based in the United Kingdom, in a pilot study on community-led total sanitation. Moreover, through a state and local government project, the DFID supported a pilot program to improve the water supply to health clinics in three states (DFID 2007a, 9). These activities fulfill the duties as provided for in *General Comment 15* (par. 34) to facilitate the right to water through provisions of water resources and technical and financial assistance. Other examples of practice that is in compliance with the extraterritorial obligations to facilitate and support fulfillment can be seen in Ghana, where the DFID is working with partner governments from Germany, the Netherlands, and Denmark, and a co-funded research project into how Community Led Total Sanitation (CLTS) projects have been successful in Bangladesh and India (the DFID working with NGOs and civil society) and how similar projects can be implemented in Africa (the DFID 2007a, 10).

One very interesting project reflects the link between extraterritorial obligations and the right to water and the existing extraterritorial aspects of international water law. The Nile Basin Initiative aims to build greater cooperative management and development of the River Nile's water resources between the ten basin countries, including negotiating a new cooperative framework agreement on the Nile. The DFID is supporting regional investment projects and capacity-building projects, as well as civil society engagement with the project via a separate initiative: the Nile Basin Discourse (DFID 2007a, 13–14). This example illustrates the idea that there are aspects and principles of transboundary water law that support the concept of extraterritorial human rights obligations pertaining to the right to water, for the states concerned and for the DFID and other donors working on such projects.

A further example of the DFID's work is with the World Bank (the key partner), UNICEF, and the Chinese government. Here, the DIFD has spent £6 million on the water sector, focusing on water resources management. This has included supporting the government in implementation of a new water law (DFID 2007a, 16).

This example illustrates the multilateral nature of the majority of the DFID's work, which is part of the DFID's ongoing plan of action to carry out most of its work through financial and technical assistance with donor partners (including inter alia the World Bank, UNICEF, United Nations Relief and Works Agency For Palestine Refugees in the Near East (UNRWA), the Temporary International Mechanism (TIM), the African Development Bank, WaterAid, Oxfam, and other governments), moving away from individual small-scale projects. The reason given for this is to ensure that funding is spent effectively (DFID 2006c; IDC 2007a, 20, par. 48).

Significantly, the example given and the policy stated highlight the importance of the extraterritorial obligations regarding states parties' activities as part of international organizations (*General Comment 15*, par. 36), in this case as a member of the World Bank, in addition to its obligations as a state party acting through the DFID. Further, it is essential that the DIFD ensure that its "partner" organizations share the same objectives in regard to human rights obligations as the U.K. government does, otherwise the DFID's adherence to its extraterritorial obligations can be compromised. WaterAid has criticized the DFID for its lack of scrutiny in this regard (WaterAid 2006b, par. 3.2; 2007).

In addition to working in developing countries, the DFID also works in areas with water and sanitation problems created by conflict. Current examples can be seen in the assistance given in the Occupied Palestinian Territories, through the TIM, as well as in Iraq. In the latter case, the DFID has a £40 million infrastructure program, which includes several water projects that when completed will improve the water supply to over a million people in southern Iraq. In addition, the DFID funded and assisted in the establishment of a water-training center under the authority of the Basra Water Directorate, which as of 2007 was training 200 employees. Other completed projects include the refurbishment of a water filtration unit that provides the main source of drinking water for Basra, and the refurbishment of a pumping station, which has doubled the volume of water currently supplied to 500,000 people (DFID 2007b). An ongoing program is the building of three water towers and reservoirs to provide water to at least 250,000 of Basra's poorest people. However, the DFID states that "the security situation makes implementation difficult and has delayed the projects" (DFID 2007a, 18).

In the Occupied Palestinian Territories, the DFID has committed £1.5 million to fund essential operational, maintenance, and repair work to Palestinian water and sanitation services (DFID 2007a, 18). This has been part of the United Kingdom's contribution to the TIM, set up by the Quartet to continue international emergency aid to the Palestinians while imposing sanctions on the Hamas government (IDC 2007c, 40–44).

The DFID claims that the objectives of its Country Assistance Plan to the Palestinians (DFID 2006d) have not changed despite the election of Hamas and the establishment of the TIM. It has, however, reconfigured its program by supporting only institutions that report to the Office of the President or the PLO (IDC 2007c, 14; DFID 2006d, 1–4). These objectives are threefold: to enhance prospects for peace; to provide humanitarian and development assistance more effectively; and to support institutions of a Palestinian state, making them more effective, accountable, and inclusive. The DFID states that its support via the TIM has allowed for continued funding of public utilities, including water and sanitation services. However, the emphasis on emergency humanitarian assistance has meant that development and support for Palestinian institutions and infrastructure, including those concerned with water, has ceased. In fact, the practical effect of the TIM has been a contribution to the erosion of these institutions, which the DFID had previously been trying to build up (IDC 2007c, 14, par. 15). Moreover, not only is this incompatible with the objectives of the DFID's Country Assistance Plan for Palestinians, but this can also be viewed as a breach of its extraterritorial obligations correlative to the right to water. First, these measures can be seen as retrogressive to the progressive development of the right generally. Second, the effect of these sanctions can be seen as a violation of the obligation to respect by interfering with the enjoyment of the right to water under *General Comment 15* (par. 31). Furthermore, the financing and emphasis on humanitarian aid under the TIM is not sustainable in the long term, as noted by the IDC (IDC 2007c, 25, par. 52). As such, the TIM does not fulfill the obligation that international assistance should be sustainable, as contained in *General Comment 15* (par. 34).

Therefore, although these actions on face value can be seen as in line with the United Kingdom's extraterritorial obligations as set out in *General Comment 15*, the financial aid given by the DFID through the TIM is incompatible with its own objectives for the Occupied Palestinian Territories. Furthermore, its support for economic sanctions undermines compliance with its extraterritorial obligations regarding the right to water. As Dugard states,

In effect, the Palestinian people have been subjected to economic sanctions—the first time an occupied people have been so treated. This is difficult to understand. Israel is in violation of major Security Council and General Assembly resolutions dealing with unlawful territorial change and the violation of human rights and has failed to implement the 2004 advisory opinion of the International Court of Justice, yet it escapes the imposition of sanctions. Instead the Palestinian people, rather than the Palestinian Authority, have been subjected to possibly the most rigorous form of international sanctions imposed in modern times. (Dugard 2006, par. 70)

The DFID's response to these criticisms has been that the TIM serves as a useful "bridging mechanism" until full donor support can be reinstated (IDC 2007d, 11). It further states that it is "attempting to prevent the decay of PA institutions" through its support for the TIM via the Office of the President but "cannot provide assistance to a government committed to violence" (IDC 2007d, 12–13).

The example noted above of the DFID's policy on the Occupied Palestinian Territories and its commitment through the TIM highlights the possibility of contradictions between the aims of the DFID in realizing its extraterritorial obligations and wider political obligations and commitments of the government of the United Kingdom as a part of international or regional organizations such as the European Union, hence illustrating the need for adherence to extraterritorial obligations at the level of international organizations and the need for compatibility between actions taken unilaterally and multilaterally.

Furthermore and significantly, the work of the DFID is just one aspect of the United Kingdom's foreign policy and the largely positive effects of the practice of the DFID on the human right to water is only one area in which the United Kingdom has extraterritorial obligations concerning the right to water. Other governmental departments, as well as U.K. companies, also have obligations. For example, the practice of the Department for Trade and Industry would make an interesting comparison with that of the DFID. One policy that has been criticized is the United Kingdom's arms trade with Israel, which has had a negative impact on the human rights of the Palestinians living in the Occupied Palestinian Territories, including the right to water (Campaign against Arms Trade 2002, 2005; see also *Saleh Hasan v. U.K. Secretary of State*). These exports can be viewed in contrast to the stated policy and practice of the DFID, and this contrast highlights the need for cooperation across government departments in coordinating their compliance and policies regarding responsibility for human rights enjoyment in third states. In sum, coherent government is essential for the enjoyment of human rights and government compliance with its extraterritorial duties. Coherence is only possible by putting human rights standards at the center of all government foreign policy (Zeigler 2005, pars. 40–41), not just those departments that initially seem to have an explicit extraterritorial human rights remit, such as an element of a rights-based approach to development within the DFID, or as part of the ethical policy of the Foreign and Commonwealth Office.

In sum, this evaluation of U.K. policy illustrates that the work of the DFID in relation to improving water and sanitation, in the main, constitutes good practice and an increasing commitment in terms of policy and funding. However, despite this, there is a fundamental problem in that improving access to water and sanitation is seen as a foreign policy goal, not as a human rights obligation that must be realized. Even though the link between the work of the DFID and the realization of the MDGs is clearly and unequivocally stated as the main objective of its work, any legal commitment is absent from recognition. This conceptual difference is significant, as in essence the former position amounts to actions taken as good will or charitable activities rather than recognition of legal accountability. Without legal accountability, there can be no recourse for action by individuals in the third state, whose human rights have been violated by the actions or omissions of the United Kingdom acting unilaterally or as a member of an international organization.

In regard to the right to water specifically, if the government of the United Kingdom does not recognize the full scope of the human right to water as provided for in international law, this must surely affect its ability to comply with its international obligations in full under the ICESCR. Therefore, in terms of policy recommendations, there are several immediate measures that can be undertaken by the government of the United Kingdom. First, the DFID and other relevant governmental departments in the United Kingdom need to carry out further study as to their position on the human right to water and clarify what they consider their legal duties to be. Further, they should bring this position in line with the definition of the right to water as codified under international human rights law (as a state party to the ICESCR, the CRC, and the CEDAW). Only then, can they explicitly and clearly comply with their extraterritorial obligations under the ICESCR. Second, the right to water needs to be codified within U.K. domestic law (as do the rest of the rights contained within the ICESCR). This will confirm the United Kingdom's stated position that it affirms the human right to water, and it will also have the ensuing effect of encouraging foreign governments to take the right to water seriously, particularly in light of the fact that one of the DFID's stated aims is to assist foreign governments in implementing the right (DFID 2006b, pars. 12, 15, and 17).

If states parties continue to view water and sanitation as foreign policy targets alone, there is an enormous risk of the lack of any impetus. This, in turn, will lead directly to the failure to achieve MDGs, but with no penalties for the states involved, although with serious negative consequences for those living in poverty. As noted, the DFID seems to have comprehensive policies regarding adequate and safe water and it is improving its policy as regards sanitation. But in terms of fulfilling practical objectives, are these policies successfully operationalized? In several evaluation reports by WaterAid (WaterAid 2006a, 2006b, 2007), concern regarding a "gap" between rhetoric and implementation of policy at the operational level has been raised: "DFID needs to match the strong rhetoric around the importance attached to the sector at a senior level with actions in its Country Offices" (WaterAid 2006a, par. 1.3). It also states there is evidence of difficulties translating the commitment of the secretary of state into program delivery (WaterAid 2006a, par. 2.1; WaterAid 2007). This lack of local capacity and inadequate understanding of local circumstances has also been noted by the U.K. National Audit Office in its report of the DFID's work concerning water and sanitation prior to the new Global Plan and indicates a lack of progress concerning local delivery of programs (U.K. National Audit Office 2003). As a result of the present deliberate policy of the DFID, the increasing number of projects undertaken as multilateral donor projects, rather than those directly financed and implemented at the country level by the DFID itself, could exacerbate this problem.

Last, to improve operational practice and future policy, it is clear that there exists a need for more thorough evaluation of the DFID's work, both on the ground and at the head office to ensure that the comprehensive policies do not become just rhetoric, but are operationalized at the country level. Further research is required on how the human right to water can be incorporated as a central element of these policies at both the design and operational levels. There is also a need to incorporate a human rights impact assessment into all water and sanitation projects—unilateral and multilateral. This would assist the DFID in ensuring that all aspects of the right to water are considered in its projects. To assist them, *General Comment 15* could be used as a standard from which to work, thus ensuring a holistic approach and full coverage of the scope of the right to water within its work, including assisting with water resources management, water conflict and transboundary aspects, and non-discrimination and consideration of vulnerable groups, including gender issues and other related issues of education, health, water for agriculture, and of course sanitation.

How to Advance the Right to Water and Extraterritorial Obligations

If the right to water is accepted as an independent right, then the detailed provisions contained within *General Comment 15* provide clear and comprehensive guidance to states parties concerning their obligations for realizing the right within third states. The framework provided for extraterritorial obligations is brief but covers all three levels of obligations: to respect, protect, and fulfill the right to water. In the case of the obligation to fulfill, this can be interpreted as an obligation to facilitate or support fulfillment in partnership with or in the minimum with consent of the national government in question. Furthermore, the extraterritorial duties present within the current human rights framework for the right to water complement the established extraterritorial aspect present within existing environmental and international water law, connections to which are acknowledged in *General Comment 15*.

The inclusion of these recent developments in the understanding of the breadth of obligations as duties to be bound by, not just within national borders but also extraterritorially, represents an important strength of *General Comment 15*. However, further research is required in order to develop and implement states parties' international obligations and ensure they understand the nature of their responsibility for the enjoyment of the right to water and economic and social rights generally outside their national borders.

As such, in order to assist states parties in complying with their extraterritorial obligations regarding the right to water, work must continue to advance the understanding of extraterritorial obligations and economic and social rights in general, as well as to clarify those extraterritorial obligations specific to the right to water. Above all, compliance with extraterritorial obligations regarding water is even more difficult than that of other economic and social rights due to its relatively new and debated status as an independent right, and this can only compound existing confusion concerning what extraterritorial obligations the right entails. Subsequently, this will have consequences for how a state party interprets its extraterritorial obligations and for how seriously a national government will consider its obligations concerning the right. Therefore, it is imperative that in the first instance the legal status of the right is elucidated and strengthened, both internationally and domestically.

Current initiatives that work toward this goal and incorporate provisions for extraterritorial obligations and the right to water include an NGO alliance campaigning for a comprehensive new water treaty, which covers all aspects of water, including provisions for the human right to water as well as incorporating established principles of international water law and environmental law. Moreover, some of these entail extraterritorial elements, for example, the prohibition of harm. The draft "Key Principles for an International Treaty on the Right to Water" (Friends of the Right to Water 2005) includes several paragraphs pertaining to extraterritorial obligations. These principles reiterate provisions for extraterritorial obligations as set out in *General Comment 15*. For example, the first paragraph provides that "states shall respect the right to water by refraining from cutting off access to water sources that satisfy vital human needs in other countries." Furthermore, states are required to fulfill the right by providing appropriate international assistance. States are also required to protect the right to water by ensuring that their citizens and companies do not violate the right to water in other countries. Most significantly though, this provision includes an obligation to provide a remedy for victims of violations: "States shall provide a remedy in their own jurisdiction for complaints by affected people about the actions of their citizens or corporations" (principle 9). This constitutes another approach to the problem of making compliance with extraterritorial obligations justifiable, where redress would be through a domestic mechanism, rather than at the international level.

Although these principles have yet to be adopted or taken up by the United Nations as a possible international instrument, they do add impetus to the call for further legal clarification of the right in general, including extraterritorial obligations, which is imperative if the right is to be implemented successfully. Moreover, with regard to compliance and remedy for extraterritorial obligations, the provision in the draft principles suggests an approach worth investigating further.

Another crucial development for economic and social rights in general is the establishment of an individual complaints procedure for the ICESCR. The proposed Optional Protocol to the ICESCR will provide for a remedy otherwise lacking at present (See UN Commission on Human Rights 2006b; Arambulo 1999). Research by the commission's Working Group includes lengthy discussions as to the obligation for international assistance and the difficulties in assessing compliance with this obligation, for example, in deciding whether maximum available resources have been utilized (UN Commission on Human Rights 2006b, pars. 77–88). However, there is no apparent explicit discussion or examination of extraterritorial obligations at any level—respect, protect, or fulfill. Neither is there evidence of debate as to whether a mechanism is to be included as a part of this protocol, which allows for individual complaints against a third state, thus allowing for redress against extraterritorial violations of economic and social rights, including the right to water. None of the published reports mention extraterritorial obligations (see ibid.; UN Commission on Human Rights 2005b, pars. 48–56) and the revised draft (UN Human Rights Council 2007b) does not provide for any explicit consideration of complaints against third states' actions under their extraterritorial obligations. However, article 2 does include jurisdictional, but not territorial, limitations. There could, therefore, be potential for complaints on the basis of a breach of extraterritorial obligations when the protocol enters into force. It would, nevertheless, seem that we are a long way off from making extraterritorial obligations justiciable and offering remedies for non-compliance with extraterritorial obligations. However, such remedies would seem an essential component of the new protocol if extraterritorial obligations are to be taken seriously (Kunneman 2004). Therefore, research and study into the practicality of a procedure at the international level that would deal with individual communications concerning violations by third states requires urgent attention.

In conclusion, although the DFID has done a great deal to assist, support the fulfillment, and promote conditions necessary to realize individuals' human right to water in third states, these actions, as the DFID views them, are not based upon a legal obligation. As such, the subsequent effects are that there is no accountability in times of failure and no remedy for those harmed by the omissions or actions of the United Kingdom.

The rhetoric of a rights-based approach to development has long been used, but as highlighted, human rights standards need to be at the center of all foreign policy, not just development, to ensure that states are aware of and compliant with their extraterritorial duties concerning the right to water and other human rights. Although the focus for this chapter has been on international development, it is important to remember that international assistance is only one area where states must be held accountable for their actions outside their national borders. Similarly, extraterritorial obligations need to be developed and firmly complied with in relation to the entirety of a state's foreign policy. Although the concept of extraterritorial obligations is in its infancy, the legal basis for such a concept is clear. Further development of a framework for extraterritorial obligations at the international and national levels is now required so that states can be held accountable for all of their actions in third states, including trade and industry and military and security cooperation. Only by establishing and holding states parties accountable for breaches of their extraterritorial obligations can remedy be offered to individuals who have had their right to water (or any other right) violated by a foreign state. The development of this mechanism is essential if the rights of those in foreign states are to be given protection equal to those of citizens in a domestic state.

Finally, it is clear that the right to water will benefit from the development of economic and social rights generally, for example, improvements in remedy, as well as further progress in devising and implementing a legal framework for extraterritorial obligations. However, in order to benefit fully from these developments, simultaneously the legal status of the right must be clarified and consensus gained internationally with all states parties. Only then can the extraterritorial aspect of obligations correlative to the right be fully developed and established.

Notes

Chapter 1. Obligations of States to Prevent and Prohibit Torture in an Extraterritorial Perspective

The author expresses his gratitude to Julia Kozma for editing the article.

1. See also the first chapter on human dignity of the Charter of Fundamental Rights of the European Union, which contains both a general right to integrity (art. 3) and the prohibition of torture and ill-treatment (art. 4).

2. For more on the drafting background, see Burgers and Danelius 1988, 124 et seq.; Nowak and McArthur 2008, art. 2, ch. 2.

3. See the U.S. report in accordance with art. 19 of the CAT of 3 January 2006, UN Doc. CAT/C/48/Add.3/Rev.1.

4. See U.S. Department of Justice, Office of Legal Counsel, Memorandum for Alberto R. Gonzales, Counsel to the President, dated 1 August 2002 (the "Bybee Memorandum"), 2 et seq. Cf. Nowak 2006; Rouillard 2005; Goldman 2004.

5. On 14 February 2008, the U.S. Senate had voted for legislation aimed at barring the CIA from using harsh interrogation techniques such as water-boarding. On 8 March 2008, President Bush made use of his veto for the first time in order to avert the bill (BBC 2008).

6. Cf. UN Commission on Human Rights 2005c, secs. 40–52; UN Commission on Human Rights 2005d, secs. 31–32. the reports of the special rapporteur on torture submitted in 2005 to the General Assembly and the Commission on Human Rights, UN Docs. A/60/316, sec. 40–52 and E/CN.4/2006/6, sec. 31 and 32.

7. See the Council of Europe, Group of Specialists on Human Rights and the Fight against Terrorism (DH-S-TER) 2006.

8. But see the contrary position of the U.K. government in UN Committee Against Torture 2005, sec. 25. See also Nowak and McArthur 2008, art. 3, ch. 4.3.

9. Under the U.S. Alien Tort Claims Act 1789, such litigation is possible. See the well-known case of *Filartiga v. Pena-Irala*, which concerns a successful litigation by the relatives of a Paraguayan torture victim against his Paraguayan torturers, both living in the United States. See also Aceves 2007.

10. See, for example, a statement by Charles Clarke, the former British home secretary, in *The Guardian*, 13 December 2005: "[The House of Lords] held that there is an 'exclusionary' rule precluding the use of evidence obtained by torture. However, they held it was perfectly lawful for such information to be relied on operationally, and also by the home secretary in making executive decisions." See also a statement made by Wolfgang Schäuble, the German minister of the interior, in the *Süddeutsche Zeitung*, 16 December 2005: "It would be completely irresponsible if we were to say that we don't use information where we cannot

be sure that it was obtained in conditions that were wholly in line with the rule of law. We have to use such information." See also the discussion in the Danish newspaper *Politiken* of 9 October 2007, "FN støtter brug af tortur-oplysninger," available at http://politiken.dk/indland/article391136.ece [5 March 2008].

Chapter 2. Obligations to Protect the Right to Life

1. The resolution encompasses all arms transfers, including conventional weapons as well as small arms and light weapons. There were twenty-four abstentions, and one government, the United States, voted against the resolution.

2. "Arms transfer" refers to any type of transfer beyond a state's territory; it includes not only commercial sales but all exchanges of arms, including exchanges under aid programs and military alliances, exchanges between non-state actors, including private civilians, and non-monetary arrangements.

3. I have adopted the definition of small arms and light weapons used by the UN Panel of Governmental Experts on Small Arms, 1997. I use the terms "small arms," "weapons," "guns," and "firearms" interchangeably in this chapter.

4. Self-defense is another widely recognized, yet legally proscribed, exception to the universal duty to respect the right to life of others. Self-defense is broadly recognized in customary international law as grounds for exemption from criminal responsibility. Using lethal force in self-defense, subject to the principles of necessity and proportionality, is more properly characterized as a means of *protecting* the right to life and, as such, a basis for avoiding responsibility for violating the rights of another.

5. The UN Security Council currently has territorial embargoes in place against the Ivory Coast and Somalia. There are also embargoes from arms transfers to non-state actors in the Democratic Republic of Congo, Liberia, Sierra Leone, and in Sudan, as well as to Al Qaeda and associated persons. The Security Council has recently lifted arms embargoes against the government of Liberia and non-state actors in Rwanda.

Chapter 3. Growing Barriers

1. See, for example, the preamble of the UN Declaration on Territorial Asylum, UNGA resolution 2312 (XXII), 14 December 1967.

2. UN Doc. A/CONF.2/SR.16.

3. UN Doc. A/CONF.2/SR.35, p. 21

4. UN Doc. E/AC.32/SR.21, par 13–26.

5. UN Doc. E/AC.32/SR.20, par 14.

6. See in particular the dissent to the *Sale* verdict by Justice Blackmun.

7. Conclusion no. 6 (XXVIII) 1977, par. c; Conclusion no. 22 (XXXII) 1981, par. II.A.2; Conclusion no. 81 (XLVIII) 1997, par. h; Conclusion no. 85 (XLIX) 1998, par. q; and Conclusion no. 99 (LV) 2004, par. l.

8. Conclusion no. 97 (LIV) 2003, par. a(iv); Conclusion no. 74 (XLV) 1994, par. g, respectively.

9. Executive Order no. 12807, Interdiction of Illegal Aliens, 57 Federal Register 20627, 14 May 1992.

10. See also Schengen Convention, article 26, as reinforced by Council Directive 2001/51 (OJ 2001 L 187/45, 10.07.2001).

11. Council Directive 2005/85/EC (OJ 2005 L 326, 13.12.2005, art. 35).

12. In this context, the term is employed separately of its usage within international maritime law. See, for example, Gavouneli 2007.

13. The Human Rights Committee employed the formulation almost identically in *López Burgos v. Uruguay,* par. 12.3.

14. Immigration, Asylum, and Nationality Act 2006, secs. 40 and 41.

15. See, in particular, the commentaries to articles 4, 5, 6, 8, 9, and 11 in Crawford2002. See also Lauterpacht and Bethlehem 2003.

16. See the International Court of Justice's *Case of the S.S. "Lotus."* See also Ross 1961, 172.

17. Whether this is a legitimate argument could again be contested; as long as ships fly under the flag and are captained by officials of European States these officials could be claimed to hold effective authority.

18. UN Doc. E/AC.32/SR.20, par. 54.

19. Conclusion no. 97 (LIV) (2003).

Chapter 5. The Human Rights Responsibility of International Assistance and Cooperation in Health

The authors wish to acknowledge and thank Simon Walker, Lisa Oldring, and Dragana Korljan for contributions to this chapter, and also, in particular, Octavio Ferraz for his research on the human rights responsibility of international assistance and cooperation in health (Ferraz and Bueno de Mesquita 2006).

1. See section below called "The International Response."

2. In 2002 the UN Commission on Human Rights appointed Paul Hunt of New Zealand as a UN special rapporteur for a period of three years. In 2005, the commission extended his mandate for another three years. The UN practice is for special rapporteurs to serve two three-year terms. Accordingly, in 2008, Anand Grover of India was appointed special rapporteur. This chapter focuses on the work of the first special rapporteur regarding the human rights responsibility of international assistance and cooperation in health.

3. Regarding international obligations, see, in particular, pars. 38–42.

4. See, in particular, Hunt 2008. Several other commentators have given attention to the human rights responsibility of international assistance and cooperation in health, for example, Ferraz and Bueno de Mesquita 2006; Hammonds and Ooms 2004.

5. The text draws from a selection of the special rapporteur's reports and press releases and highlights those recommendations relating to international assistance and cooperation. Other missions, reports, and interventions of the rapporteur have also considered international assistance and cooperation. For example, in 2007 the rapporteur undertook a mission to Ecuador and Colombia with a view to examining the health impact in Ecuador of Colombian crop spraying. In 2006, he undertook a joint mission to Lebanon and Israel to examine the conflict between Israel and Hezbollah (UN Human Righs Council 2006a). In 2005, he submitted a report on the migration of health professionals, which includes the migration of health professionals from developing to developed countries. In this form the skills drain is a perverse subsidy by the poor to the rich and is inconsistent with developed states' human rights responsibilities of international assistance and cooperation in health (A/60/348). Because of space constraints, however, our analysis does not draw upon these—and some

other—initiatives undertaken by the rapporteur relating to international assistance and cooperation.

Chapter 6. The World Food Crisis and the Right to Adequate Food

1. Less than 10 percent of global cereal production is traded. Still, most of the cereals are consumed in the region where they are produced. The trend is similar for most staple foods.

2. The cases come from several research projects being carried out by Bread for the World, the development aid agency of the Protestant Church of Germany. Since 2001, Bread for the World has been engaged in a joint project with eed and FIAN-International in which such violations of extraterritorial obligations by Germany have been researched and reported on. At the time of this writing, over eighty cases have been analyzed and the material will be used for a civil society report to the UN Committee on Economic, Social, and Cultural Rights when Germany will be in the state-reporting process. Nine cases have been published in two booklets in November 2006.

3. The task force was convened on 29 April 2008 in Bern. A first draft report of the High-Level Task Force was presented during the FAO High Level Summit at the beginning of June. The final document, the so-called Comprehensive Framework for Action, was handed over by UN Secretary-General Ban Ki-moon to the General Assembly on 18 July 2008.

4. The concept is called trade-based food security. The policy advice was to earn hard currency with cash crops and to import other (cheap) foodstuffs on the world market. Now with increasing prices, the equation looks different for many developing countries.

5. These qualifications were first developed in the *Limburg Principles* from 1986. The *Limburg Principles* are the result of an international law conference that addressed the nature of the realization of economic, social, and cultural rights.

6. Article 2 of the ICESCR requires that state parties use the "maximum" of available resources to progressively implement all rights enshrined in the covenant. Determining what constitutes "available resources" is no easy matter.

7. The law 234/93 is the implementation of ILO Convention 169 on indigenous communities, which was ratified by Paraguay.

8. Such a note of clarification has been drafted between Austria and Paraguay, which have a similar BIT.

Chapter 8. A Sort of Homecoming

1. Article 1 in both covenants provides:
   1. All peoples have the right to self-determination. By virtue of that right they freely determine their political status and freely pursue their economic, social and cultural development.
   2. All peoples may, for their own ends, freely dispose of their natural wealth and resources without prejudice to any obligations arising out of international economic co-operation, based upon the principle of mutual benefit, and international law. In no case may a people be deprived of its own means of subsistence.
   3. The State Parties to the present Covenant, including those having respon-

sibilities for the administration of Non-Self-Governing and Trust Territories, shall promote the realization of the right to self-determination, and shall respect that right, in conformity with the provisions of the Charter of the United Nations.

2. For the application of the Convention against Torture to housing, see the decision by the UN Committee against Torture in *Hijirizi v. Yugoslavia.*

3. Chad-Cameroon Petroleum and Pipeline Project (Loan no. 4558-CD); Petroleum Sector Management Capacity Building Project (Credit no. 3373-CD); and Management of the Petroleum Economy (Credit no. 3316-CD).

4. Clark (2008, 639) notes that "in response to the Inspection Panel claim, the Indian government implemented an improved compensation package for about 1,200 families. While this revision to the compensation package was not enough to bring the project into compliance with the requirements of the resettlement policy, it was seen as a critically important step for those families that did receive the package."

5. For a largely contrary view in the case of the IMF, see Gianviti 2005, 113–40 and a response by Clapham 2006, 145–49.

6. Originally written and submitted for *Doe v. Unocal,* 110 F. Supp. 2d 1294 (C.D. Cal. 2000).

7. Cf. Government of Kenya, UNEP, KFWG, and KWS 2005; and Amnesty International et al. 2007.

8. Another example is UN-Habitat's model slum upgrading project in Kibera, Kenya, which has been accused of assisting eviction of tenants (Centre on Housing Rights and Evictions 2006). No secure tenure zone was created or enforced as called for in the project documentation and there is some evidence that slum landlords were replacing tenants with family members in order to gain the benefits from the project, which is meant to be pro-resident and not provide land to the large-scale informal "structure owners." No legal action has been taken against UN-Habitat or its government partner so far on this project, although some tenancy cases have been taken to residential tribunals against the landlords responsible.

9. This information is taken from the websites for both institutions: http://www.theglobalfund.org and http://www.citiesalliance.org.

Bibliography

Books, Articles, and Reports

Aceves, William C. 2007. *The Anatomy of Torture: A Documentary History of Filartiga v. Pena-Irala.* Leiden and Boston: Transnational Publishers.

African Development Bank, Austria, Germany, The Netherlands, Norway, Sweden, UK Department for International Development, and World Bank. 2005–9. *Joint Assistance Strategy for the Republic of Uganda.* Kampala: UJAS.

Alston, Philip. 2005a. "A Human Rights Perspective on the Millennium Development Goals." Paper prepared as a contribution to the work of the UN Millennium Project Task Force on Poverty and Economic Development, Geneva, 14–18 November.

———. 2005b. "Ships Passing in the Night: The Current State of the Human Rights and Development Debate Seen Through the Lens of the Millennium Development Goals." *Human Rights Quarterly* 27: 755–829.

Alvarez, I. J. 2003. "The Right to Water as a Human Right." In *Linking Human Rights and the Environment,* ed. Romina Piccolotti and Daniel Taillent. Tucson: University of Arizona Press.

Amnesty International et al. 2007. "Nowhere to Go: Forced Evictions in Mau Forest, Kenya." Briefing Paper. London: Amnesty International. Available at www.coher.org/kenya.

Amsterdam International Law Clinic. 2007. *Possibilities for Criminal & State Responsibility in Relation to the Operation Murambatsvina Case* (May).

Annan, Kofi. 2000. *We the Peoples: The Role of the United Nations in the Twenty-first Century.* New York: United Nations.

Arambulo, Kitty. 1999. *Strengthening the Supervision of the International Covenant on Economic, Social, and Cultural Rights: Theoretical and Procedural Aspects.* Antwerp: Intersentia.

Arms Trade Treaty Steering Committee. 2006. *A Guide to the Global Principles for Arms Transfers.* London: Amnesty International.

Associated Press. 2007. "Cambodian Leader Slams ILO for 'Untruthful' Reports about Garment Factories," 24 January.

Barratt-Brown, Elizabeth. 1991. "Building a Monitoring and Compliance Regime Under the Montreal Protocol." *Yale Journal of International Law* 16: 519–70.

Bailey, James, et al. 2007. "Risk Factors for Violent Death of Women in the Home." *Archives of Internal Medicine* 157: 777–82.

Bassett, Ellen. 2007. "The Persistence of the Commons: Economic Theory and Community Decision-Making on Land Tenure in Voi, Kenya." *African Studies Quarterly* 9. Available at http://web.africa.ufl.edu/asq/v9/v9i3a1.htm.

Baue, Bill. 2006. "Revised Equator Principles Fall Short of International Best

Practice for Project Finance." *Sustainability Investment News*, 12 July. Available at http://www.socialfunds.com/news/article.cgi/2055.html.

BBC. 2008a. "Bush Vetoes Interrogation Limits," 8 March.

———. 2008b. BBC News, "Angola to Allow Arms Ship to Dock." Available at http://news.bbc.co.uk/2/hi/africa/7368208.stm (accessed 28 May 2008).

———. 2009. "Evidence of Torture 'Buried' by Ministers." BBC News, 4 February. Available at http://www.guardian.co.uk/world/2009/feb/04/guantanamo-bay-torture (last accessed 5 February 2009).

Bello, Judith Hippler, and Juliane Kokott. 1997. "Amuur v. France." *American Journal of International Law* 91: 147–52.

Bethlehem, Daniel. 2003. "The Existing Responsibilities of States under Relevant International Law." Paper presented at the meeting "Implementing UN Programme of Action Commitments on Small Arms Transfers: Exchanging Ideas on the Way Forward," Cambridge University, 8 July 2003.

Bluemel, Eric B. 2004. "The Implications of Formulating a Human Right to Water." *Ecology Law Quarterly* 31: 957–1006.

Bohr, Niels. 1957. *Atomfysik og Menneskelig Erkendelse*. København: Schultz.

Bolton, John. 2001. Statement to the Plenary Session of the UN Conference on the Illicit Trade in Small Arms and Light Weapons in All Its Aspects, 9 July. Available at http://www.un.int/usa/01_104.htm.

Boswell, Christina. 2003. "The 'External Dimension' of EU Immigration and Asylum Policy." *International Affairs* 79: 619–38.

Boulesbaa, Ahcene. 1999. *The UN Convention on Torture and the Prospects for Enforcement*. The Hague: Martinus Nijhoff.

Boyle, Alan. 1996. "The Role of International Human Rights Law in the Protection of the Environment." In *Human Rights Approaches to Environmental Protection*, ed. Alan Boyle and Michael Anderson. Oxford: Oxford University Press.

Bradlow, Daniel. 1996. "The World Bank, the IMF, and Human Rights." *Transnational Law and Contemporary Problems* 6: 48–89.

Bread for the World, FIAN, eed. 2006a. *Germany's Extraterritorial Human Rights Obligations: Introduction and Six Case Studies*.

———. 2006b. *Germany's Extraterritorial Human Rights Obligations in Multilateral Development Banks: Introduction and Case Study of Three Projects in Chad, Ghana, and Pakistan.*

Brody, Reed. 2001. "The Prosecution of Hissein Habré—An 'African Pinochet.'" *New England Law Review* 35: 321–35.

Brody, Reed, and Michael Ratner. 2000. *The Pinochet Papers: The Case of Augusto Pinochet in Spain and Britain*. The Hague: Kluwer Law.

Bueno de Mesquita, Judith, and Matt Gordon. 2005. *The International Migration of Health Workers: A Human Rights Analysis*. London: Medact.

Burbach, Roger. 2004. *The Pinochet Affair: State Terrorism and Global Justice*. London: Zed Publishers.

Burgers, Herman, and Hans Danelius. 1988. *The United Nations Convention against Torture: A Handbook on the Convention against Torture and Other Cruel, Inhuman, or Degrading Treatment*. Dordrecht: Kluwer Law.

Byers, Michael. 2000. "The Law and Politics of the Pinochet Case." *Duke Journal of Comparative and International Law* 10: 415–41.

Byrne, Rosemary, et al. 2002. "New Asylum Countries? Migration Control and Refugee Protection in an Enlarged European Union." In *Immigration and Asylum Law and Policy in Europe*, ed. Elspeth Guild and Jan Niessen. The Hague: Kluwer Law International.

Byrnes, Andrew. 2001. "Civil Law Remedies for Torture Committed Abroad: An Obligation under the Convention against Torture." In *Torture as Tort: Comparative Perspectives on the Development of Transnational Human Rights Litigation*, ed. Craig Scott. Oxford: Hart Publishing.

Cahill, Amanda. 2005. "The Human Right to Water—A Right of Unique Status: The Legal Status and Normative Content of the Right to Water." *International Journal of Human Rights* 9: 389–410.

———. 2007. "The Human Right to Water and Its Application in the Occupied Palestinian Territories." Ph.D. thesis (unpublished, on file with author), Lancaster University, UK.

Campaign against Arms Trade. 2002. *Arming the Occupation: Israel and the Arms Trade.* London: Campaign against Arms Trade.

———. 2005. *Arms Exports and Collaborations: The UK and Israel; Developments since CAAT's "Arming the Occupation" Report, October 2002.* London: Campaign against Arms Trade.

Cassel, Douglas. 2004. "Extraterritorial Application of Inter-American Human Rights Instruments." In *Extraterritorial Application of Human Rights Treaties*, ed. Fons Coomans and Menno T. Kamminga. Antwerp: Intersentia.

Cassese, Antonio. 1999. *Self-determination of Peoples: A Legal Reappraisal.* New York: Cambridge University Press.

———. 2002. "When May Senior State Officials Be Tried for International Crimes? Some Comments on the Congo v. Belgium Case." *European Journal of International Law* 13: 853–75.

Center for Reproductive Rights. 2000. *The Bush Global Gag Rule: A Violation of International Human Rights.* New York: Center for Reproductive Rights.

Centre on Housing Rights and Evictions. 2004. Petition Submitted by the Centre on Housing Rights and Evictions (COHRE) on Behalf of the Survivors of the Río Negro Community and Similarly Situated Communities in Guatemala (Petitioners) to the Inter-American Commission on Human Rights.

———. 2006. *Listening to the Poor: Housing Rights in Nairobi, Kenya.* Geneva: COHRE.

———. 2007. *Fair Play for Housing Rights: Mega-Events, Olympic Games, and Housing Rights; Opportunities for the Olympic Movement and Others.* Supported by the Geneva International Academic Network (GIAN). Geneva: COHRE.

Centre for Studies and Research in International Law and International Relations, Hague Academy of International Law. 2002. *Water Resources and International Law 2001.* The Hague: Martinus Nijhoff.

Cerna, Christina. 2004. "Extraterritorial Application of the Human Rights Instruments of the Inter-American System." In *Extraterritorial Application of Human Rights Treaties*, ed. Fons Coomans and Menno T. Kamminga. Antwerp: Intersentia.

Cerone, John. 2002. "The Human Rights Framework Applicable to Trafficking in Persons and Its Incorporation into UNMIK Regulation 2001/4." *International Peacekeeping, the Yearbook of International Peace Operations* 7: 43–98.

———. 2005. "The Application of Regional Human Rights Law beyond Regional Frontiers: The Inter-American Commission on Human Rights and US Activities in Iraq." *ASIL Insight*, 5 October. Available at http://www.asil.org/insights/2005/10/insights051025.html.

Chander, Ramesh. 1999. "Can Dams and Reservoirs Cause Earthquakes? Triggering of Earthquakes." *Resonance* (November): 1–13.

Chayes, Abram, and Antonia Handler Chayes. 1995. *The New Sovereignty: Compliance with International Regulatory Agreements.* Cambridge, Mass.: Harvard University Press.

Chimni, B. S. 1999. "The Geopolitics of Refugee Studies and the Practice of International Institutions: A View from the South." *Journal of Refugee Studies* 11: 350–74.

Clapham, Andrew. 2006. *Human Rights Obligations of Non-State Actors.* Oxford: Oxford University Press.

Clark, Dana. 2002. "The World Bank and Human Rights: The Need for Greater Accountability." *Harvard Human Rights Journal* 15: 205–26.

———. 2008. "World Bank Inspection Panel." In *Social Rights Jurisprudence: Emerging Trends in International and Comparative Law,* ed. Malcolm Langford. New York: Cambridge University Press.

Commission of the Legal Empowerment of the Poor. 2008. *Making the Law Work for Everyone.* Vol. 1, *Report of the Commission of the Legal Empowerment of the Poor.* New York.

Commission on Macroeconomics and Health. 2001. *Investing in Health for Economic Development.* Geneva: World Health Organization.

Coomans, Fons. 2004. "Some Remarks on the Extra-territorial Application of the International Covenant on Economic, Social, and Cultural Rights." In *Extraterritorial Application of Human Rights Treaties,* ed. Fons Coomans and Menno T. Kamminga. Antwerp: Intersentia.

Coomans, Fons, and Menno T. Kamminga, eds. 2004. "Comparative Introductory Comments on the Extraterritorial Application of Human Rights Treaties." In *Extraterritorial Application of Human Rights Treaties,* ed. Fons Coomans and Menno T. Kamminga. Antwerp: Intersentia.

Council of Europe. 1965. *Report on the Granting of the Right of Asylum to European Refugees.* Doc. 1986 (29 September).

———. 1968. Consultative Assembly of the Council of Europe, Twentieth Session, 1968–69. Doc. 2359 (7 March).

———. 2006. *Secretary-General's Report under Article 52 ECHR on the Question of Secret Detention and Transport of Detainees Suspected of Terrorist Acts, Notably by or at the Instigation of Foreign Agencies,* 28 February.

Council of Europe, European Commission for Democracy through Law (Venice Commission). 2006. *Opinion on the International Legal Obligations of Council of Europe Member States in Respect of Secret Detention Facilities and Inter-State Transport of Prisoners,* 17 March.

Council of Europe, Group of Specialists on Human Rights and the Fight Against Terrorism (DH-S-TER). 2006. Meeting Report. Second Meeting, Strasbourg, 29–31 March 2006, Doc. DH-S-TER(2006)005, of 3 April.

Courtis, Christian and Magdalena Sepúlveda. 2009. "Are Extra-Territorial Obligations Reviewable under the Optional Protocol to the ICESCR?" *Nordic Journal of Human Rights* 27: 1-28.

Craven, Matthew. 1993. "The Domestic Application of the International Covenant on Economic, Social, and Cultural Rights." *Netherlands International Law Review* 40: 367–404.

———. 1995. *The International Covenant on Economic, Social, and Cultural Rights: A Perspective on Its Development.* Oxford: Clarendon Press.

———. 2005. "Assessment of the Progress on Adjudication of Economic, Social, and Cultural Rights." In *Road to a Remedy: Current Issues in Litigation of Economic, Social, and Cultural Rights,* ed. John Squires, Malcolm Langford, and Bret Thiele. Sydney: Australian Human Rights Centre and University of NSW Press.

Crawford, James. 2002. *The International Law Commission's Articles on State Responsibility: Introduction, Text, and Commentaries.* Cambridge: Cambridge University Press.

Dañino, Roberto. 2006. *Human Rights and the Work of the World Bank.* Legal opinion by the senior vice president and general counsel, 27 January.

Darrow, Mac. 2003a. "Human Rights Accountability of the World Bank and IMF: Possibilities and Limits of Legal Analysis" (Review essay). *Social and Legal Studies* 12: 133–44.

———. 2003b. *Between Light and Shadow: The World Bank, the International Monetary Fund, and International Human Rights Law.* Oxford: Hart Publishing.

Davis, Madeleine. 2003. *The Pinochet Case: Origins, Progress, and Implications.* London: Institute of Latin American Studies.

Davy, Ulrike. 1996. *Asyl und internationales Flüchtlingsrecht.* Vol. 1, *Völkerrechtlicher Rahmen.* Wien: Österreichische Staatsdruckerei.

De Alba, Luis Alfonso. 2006–7. "The Human Rights Council and Efforts to Reduce Small Arms and Lights Weapons Related Violence." *Small Arms and Human Security Bulletin* 8.

de Albuquerque, Catarina. 2005. *Report of the Open-ended Working Group to Consider Options Regarding the Elaboration of an Optional Protocol to the International Covenant on Economic, Social, and Cultural Rights on Its Second Session.* UN Doc. E/CN.4/2005/52.

———. 2006. *Report of the Open-ended Working Group to Consider Options Regarding the Elaboration of an Optional Protocol to the International Covenant on Economic, Social and Cultural Rights on Its Third Session.* UN Doc. E/CN.4/2006/47, 14 March.

Del Carmen Marquez Carrasco, Maria, and Joaquin Alcaide Fernandez. 1999. "*In Re* Pinochet." *American Journal of International Law* 93: 690–96.

Dennis, Michael J. 1998. "The Fifty-Third Session of the UN Commission on Human Rights." *American Journal of International Law* 92: 112–24.

de Schutter, Oliver. 2008. "The Negative Impact of the Worsening of the World Food Crisis on the Realization of the Right to Adequate Food." Statement of the UN Special Rapporteur during the Seventh Special Session of the UN Human Rights Council, Geneva, 22 May. UN Doc. A/HRC/S-7/L.2.

Deshmukh, Smita. 2006. "State Spurns World Bank, Looks for Love in Tokyo." *DNA Mumbai*, 18 May, p. 5.

Diabes-Murad, Fadia. 2005. *A New Legal Framework for Managing the World's Shared Groundwaters: A Case Study from the Middle East.* London: IWA.

Dugard, John. 2006. *Report of the Special Rapporteur on the Situation of Human Rights in the Palestinian Territories Occupied Since 1967.* UN Doc. A/HRC/2/5.

European Commission. 2008. *Communication on Tackling the Challenge of Rising Food Prices,* COM (2008) 321 final (20 May). Brussels.

European Commission TIM-Management Unit/EuropeAid. 2006. *Temporary International Mechanism-TIM: Direct Support to the Palestinian Population in the West Bank and Gaza, Operational and Financial Report.* Brussels: European Commission.

European Union. 2002. *Council Joint Action of 12 July 2002 on the European Union's Contribution to Combating the Destabilising Accumulation and Spread of Small Arms and Light Weapons and Repealing Joint Action 1999/34/CFSP.* (2002/589/CFSP).

FAO. 1996. *Rome Declaration on World Food Security and World Food Summit Plan of Action.* Available at http://www.fao.org/docrep/003/w3613e/w3613e00.HTM

————. 2003. *Climate Change and Agriculture: Physical and Human Dimension*. World Agriculture 2015/2030; FAO, Rome.

Fava, Giovanni Claudio. 2007. *Report on the Alleged Use of European Countries by the CIA for the Transportation and Illegal Detention of Prisoners*, 26 January. EU Temporary Committee on the Alleged Use of European Countries by the CIA for the Transportation and Illegal Detention of Prisoners, Doc. A6-9999/2007.

Ferraz, Octavio, and Judith Bueno de Mesquita. 2006: *The Right to Health and the Millennium Development Goals in Developing Countries: A Right to International Assistance and Cooperation?* Available at http://www2.essex.ac.uk/human_rights_centre/rth/docs/IAC_H_final.doc.

FIAN. 2008a. *Peru: Water Contamination by Oil Company Pluspetrol S.A. in the Area of the Indigenous Communities*. Available at http://www.fian.org.

————. 2008b. *Ecuador: Planned Dam Threatens Peasants' Access to Land and River Water*. Available at http://www.fian.org.

FIAN/Brot für die Welt. 2006. *Identifying and Addressing Violations of the Human Right to Water Applying the Human Rights Approach*. Stuttgart: FIAN.

FIAN. Brot für die Welt, eed. 2006. *Globalizing Economic and Social Human Rights by Strengthening Extraterritorial Human Rights Obligations: Germany's Extraterritorial Human Rights Obligations*.

Fitzpatrick, Joan. 1996. "Revitalizing the 1951 Refugee Convention." *Harvard Human Rights Journal* 9: 229–53.

Frey, Barbara. 2006. *Final Report on the Prevention of Human Rights Violations Committed with Small Arms and Light Weapons*. UN Doc. A/HRC/Sub.1/58/27.

Friends of the Right to Water. 2005. "Key Principles for an International Treaty on the Right to Water—Draft Work in Progress for Consultation and Revision," 14 April. Friends of the Right to Water (including COHRE, FIAN, and Brot für die Welt).

Frontex. 2006. *Longest Frontex Coordinated Operation: HERA, the Canary Islands*. Available at http://frontex.europa.eu (accessed 16 March 2007).

Gammeltoft-Hansen, Thomas. 2006. "Outsourcing Migration Management: EU, Power, and the External Dimension of Asylum and Immigration Policy." DIIS Working Paper no. 2006/1. Copenhagen: Danish Institute for International Studies.

————. 2007. "The Extraterritorialisation of Asylum and the Advent of 'Protection Lite.'" DIIS Working Paper no. 2/2007. Copenhagen: Danish Institute for International Studies.

Gasper, Brandie. 2005. "Examining the Use of Evidence Obtained Under Torture: The Case of the British Detainees May Test the Resolve of the European Convention in the Era of Terrorism." *American University International Law Review* 21: 277–325.

Gatev, Ivalyo. 2006. "Very Remote Control: Policing the Outer Perimeter of the EU Neighbourhood." Paper presented at the External Dimension of European Immigration Policies, European University Institute, Florence, 23–24 November.

Gavouneli, Maria. 2007. *Functional Jurisdiction in the Law of the Sea*. The Hague: Martinus Nijhoff Publishers.

Gianviti, François. 2005. "Economic, Social, and Cultural Rights and the International Monetary Fund." In *Non-State Actors and Human Rights*, ed. Philip Alston. Oxford: Oxford University Press.

Gillard, Emmanuela. 200. "What Is Legal? What Is Illegal? Limitations on Transfers of Small Arms under International Law." Cambridge: Lauterpacht Research Centre for International Law. Available at http://www.armstradetreaty. org/att/what.is.legal.what.is.illegal.pdf.

Giovannetti, Frédéric. 2005. "Newmont Ghana Gold Ltd.: Ahafo South Project; Independent Monitoring of Resettlement Implementation, 2nd Review—December 2005." Available at http://www.newmont. com/en/operations/projectpipeline/ahafo.

Gleick, Peter H. 1999. "The Human Right to Water." *Water Policy* 1: 487–503.

Goldman, Robert K. 2004. "Trivializing Torture: The Office of Legal Counsel's 2002 Opinion Letter and International Law against Torture." *Human Rights Brief* 12: 1–14.

Goodwin-Gill, Guy. 1994. "The Haitian Refoulement Case: A Comment." *International Journal of Refugee Law* 6: 103–9.

———. 1996. *The Refugee in International Law*. 2nd ed. Oxford: Oxford University Press.

Goodwin-Gill, Guy, and Jane McAdam. 2007. *The Refugee in International Law*. 3rd ed. Oxford: Oxford University Press.

Gormley, Paul. 1985. "The Right to Life and the Rule of Non-Derogability: Peremptory Norms of *Jus Cogens*." In *The Right to Life in International Law*, ed. B. G. Ramcharan. Dordrecht: Martinus Nijhoff.

Government of Kenya, UNEP, KFWG, and KWS. 2005. *Maasai Mau Forest Status Report*. Available at http://www.iapad.org/publications/maasai_mau_report. pdf (accessed 1 June 2009).

Government of Sweden. Forthcoming. *Country Strategy for Development Cooperation, Uganda*.

———. 2001. *Country Strategy for Development Cooperation, Uganda: 2001–2005*. UD 01.013.

———. 2003a. *Human Rights in Swedish Foreign Policy*. Government Communications 1997–98:89 and 2003–4:20.

———. 2003b. *Shared Responsibility: Sweden's Policy for Global Development*. Government Bill 2002/03.122.

Government of Vietnam. 2005. *Vietnam Achieving the Millennium Development Goals*. Hanoi: UNDP. .

Graduate Institute of International Studies. 2002. *Small Arms Survey 2002: Counting the Human Cost*. Oxford: Oxford University Press.

Grahl-Madsen, Atle. 1997. *Commentary on the Refugee Convention 1951 Articles 2–11, 13–37*. Geneva: Division of International Protection of the UN High Commissioner for Refugees.

Greene, Owen. 1998. "The System for Implementation Review in the Ozone Regime." In *The Implementation and Effectiveness of International Environmental Commitments: Theory and Practice*, ed. David G. Victor et al. Cambridge, Mass.: MIT Press.

Guiraudon, Virginie. 2002. "Before the EU Border: Remote Control of the 'Huddled Masses.'" In *In Search of Europe's Borders*, ed. K. Groenendijk et al. The Hague: Kluwer Law International.

Gyau-Boakye, Philip. 2001. "Sources of Rural Water Supply in Ghana." *Water International* 26: 96–104.

Gwam, Cyril Uchenna. 2002. "Adverse Effects of the Illicit Movement and Dumping of Hazardous, Toxic, and Dangerous Wastes and Products on the Enjoyment of Human Rights." *Florida Journal of International Law* 14: 427–73.

Gwatkin, Davidson, Abbas Bhuiya, and Cesar Victora. 2004. "Making Health Systems More Equitable." *The Lancet* 364: 1273–80.

Hammonds, Rachel, and Gorik Ooms. 2004. "World Bank Policies and the Obligation of Its Members to Respect, Protect, and Fulfil the Right to Health." *Health and Human Rights* 8: 26–60.

Hancock, Graham. 1989. *Lords of Poverty*. London: Mandarin.

Handl, Günther. 1995. "Human Rights and Protection of the Environment: A Mildly 'Revisionist' View." In *Derechos Humanos, Desarrollo Sustentable y Medio Ambiente*, 2nd ed., ed. Antonio Augusto Cançado Trindade. Available at http://www.bibliojuridica.org/libros/libro.htm?l=1985.

Harris, Richard, and Godwin Arku. 2007. "The Rise of Housing in International Development: The Effects of the Economic Discourse." *Habitat International* 31: 1–11.

Hathaway, James (ed.). 1997. *Reconceiving International Refugee Law*. The Hague: Kluwer Law International.

———. 2005. *The Rights of Refugees under International Law*. Cambridge: Cambridge University Press.

———. 2007. "Forced Migration Studies: Could We Agree Just to 'Date'?" *Journal of Refugee Studies* 20: 349–69.

Haug, L., M. Langvandslien, L. Lumpe, and N. Marsh. 2002. "Shining a Light on Small Arms Exports: The Record of State Transparency." Norwegian Initiative on Small Arms Transfers and Small Arms Survey, Occasional Paper #4.

Henkin, Louis. 1993. "Notes from the President." *ASIL Newsletter* (September/October).

Huchzermeyer, Marie. 2008. "Slums Law Based on Flawed Interpretation of UN Goals." *Business Day*, 19 May.

Human Rights Watch. 2004. "Between a Rock and a Hard Place: Civilians Struggle to Survive in Nepal's Civil War." Available at http://www.hrw.org/reports/2004/nepal1004/index.htm (accessed 3 March 2008).

———. 2005. *Still at Risk: Diplomatic Assurances No Safeguard against Torture*. Available at http://www.hrw.org/reports/2005/eca0405/.

Hunt, Paul. 2004. *Report of the Special Rapporteur on the Right to the Enjoyment of the Highest Attainable Standard of Physical and Mental Health: Addendum—Mission to the World Trade Organization*. UN Doc. E/CN.4/2004/49/Add.1.

———. 2005a. *Report of the Special Rapporteur on the Right to the Enjoyment of the Highest Attainable Standard of Physical and Mental Health*. UN Doc. E/CN.4/2005/51.

———. 2005b. *Report of the Special Rapporteur on the Right to the Enjoyment of the Highest Attainable Standard of Physical and Mental Health: Addendum—Mission to Peru*. UN Doc. E/CN.4/2005/51/Add.3.

———. 2006. "UN Health Rights Expert Criticizes Donors for Failing to Fulfil the Humanitarian Responsibilities in the Occupied Palestinian Territories." UN press release, 22 June.

———. 2007. *Report of the Special Rapporteur on the Right to the Enjoyment of the Highest Attainable Standard of Physical and Mental Health: Addendum—Mission to Sweden*. UN Doc. A/HRC/7/11/Add.2.

———. 2008. *Report of the Special Rapporteur on the Right to the Enjoyment of the Highest Attainable Standard of Physical and Mental Health: Addendum—Mission to the World Bank and International Monetary Fund in Washington, D.C. (20 October 2006) and Uganda (4–7 February 2007)*. UN Doc. A/HRC/7/11/Add.2.

Ingelse, Chris. 2001. *The UN Committee against Torture: An Assessment*. The Hague: Kluwer Law.

Inter-American Commission on Human Rights. 1997. *Report on the Situation of Human Rights in Ecuador*. OEA/Ser.L/V/II.96, Doc. 10 rev. 1.

International Assessment of Agriculture, Science, and Technology for Development (IAASTD). 2008. *Final Report.* Available at http://www.agassessment. org.

International Commission on Intervention and State Sovereignty (ICISS). 2001. *The Responsibility to Protect.* Ottawa: International Development Research Centre.

International Committee of the Red Cross. 2007. *Arms Transfer Decisions: Applying International Humanitarian Law Criteria.* Geneva. International Committee of the Red Cross.

International Council for Human Rights Policy (ICHRP). 2003. *Duties sans Frontiers.* ICHRP: Geneva.

International Labour Organization. 2006. *Seventeenth Synthesis Report on Working Conditions, Cambodia's Garment Sector.* Kingdom of Cambodia, ILO, Better Factories Cambodia (31 October).

———. 2007a. *Press Bulletin on the Better Factories Project 2007.*

———. 2007b. *ILO/IFC Programme Information Bulletin.*

———. 2007c. Press release. Available at http//betterworkILO.ziplo.com/better work/public/global/public-files/news.2007.

———. 2008. Press release. Available at http://www.ilo.org/global/About_the_ILO/Media_and_public_information/Feature_stories/lang—en/WCMS_092231/index.htm

International Law Commission. 1978. Yearbook of the International Law Commission: Report of the Commission to the General Assembly on the Work of Its Thirtieth Session. UN Doc. A/CN.4/SER.A/1978/Add.l (Part 2).

Joseph, Sarah. 2008. "Liability of Multinational Corporations." In *Social Rights Jurisprudence: Emerging Trends in International and Comparative Law,* ed. Malcolm Langford. New York: Cambridge University Press.

Kaul, Inge, Isabelle Grunberg, and Marc Stern. 2007. *Global Public Goods: International Cooperation in the Twenty-first Century.* New York: Oxford University Press.

Kiefer, Thorsten, and Catherine Brolmann. 2005. "Beyond State Sovereignty: The Human Right to Water." *Non-State Actors and International Law* 5: 183–208.

Kindhauser, Mary Kay. 2003. *Communicable Diseases 2002: Global Defence against the Infectious Disease Threat.* Geneva: World Health Organization.

Kinney, Eleanor, and Brian Clark. 2004. "Provisions for Health and Health Care in the Constitutions of the Countries of the World." *Cornell International Law Journal* 37: 285–355.

Klein, Pierre. 1999. "Les institutions financières internationales et les droits de la personne." *Revue belge de droit international* 1: 97–114.

Kneebone, Susan. 2006. "The Pacific Plan: The Provision of 'Effective Protection'?" *International Journal of Refugee Law* 18: 696–722.

Knox, John H. 2001. "A New Approach to Compliance with International Environmental Law: The Submissions Procedure of the NAFTA Environmental Commission." *Ecology Law Quarterly* 28: 1–122.

———. 2002. "The Myth and Reality of Transboundary Environmental Impact Assessment." *American Journal of International Law* 96: 291–319.

———. 2008. "Horizontal Human Rights Law." *American Journal of International Law* 102: 1–47.

Koch, Ida. 2005. "Dichotomies, Trichotomies, or Waves of Duties?" *Human Rights Law Review* 5: 81–103.

Koh, Harold Hongju. 1994. "The 'Haiti Paradigm' in United States Human Rights Policy." *Yale Law Journal* 103: 2391–2435.

————. 2003. "A World Drowning in Guns." *Fordham Law Review* 71: 2333–62.

Kravchenko, Svitlana. 2007. "The Aarhus Convention and Innovations in Compliance with Multilateral Environmental Agreements." *Colorado Journal of International Environmental Law and Policy* 18: 1–50.

Kunnemann, Rolf. 2004. "Extraterritorial Application of the International Covenant on Economic, Social, and Cultural Rights." In *Extraterritorial Application of Human Rights Treaties*, ed. Fons Coomans and Menno T. Kamminga. Antwerp: Intersentia.

Lancet. 2006. "Making Health a G8 Priority." *Lancet* 368: 259.

Langford, Malcolm. 2007. "Beyond Formalisation: The Role of Civil Society in Reclaiming the Legal Empowerment Agenda." *Legal Empowerment: A Way out of Poverty* 4: 41–66.

————, ed. 2008. *Social Rights Jurisprudence: Emerging Trends in International and Comparative Law.* New York: Cambridge University Press.

————. 2009a. "Closing the Gap? An Introduction to the Optional Protocol to the International Covenant on Economic, Social and Cultural Rights," *Nordic Journal of Human Rights* 27: 1-28.

————. 2009b. "Keeping Up with the Fashion: Human Rights and Global Public Goods." *International Journal on Minority and Group Rights* 16: 165–78.

Langford, Malcolm, and Jeff King. 2008. "Committee on Economic, Social, and Cultural Rights: Past, Present, and Future." In *Social Rights Jurisprudence: Emerging Trends in International and Comparative Law*, ed. Malcolm Langford. New York: Cambridge University Press.

Langford, Malcolm, and Aoife Nolan. 2006. *Litigating Economic, Social, and Cultural Rights: Legal Practitioners Dossier (Revised).* Geneva: Centre on Housing Rights and Evictions.

Lauterpacht, Elihu, and Daniel Bethlehem. 2003. "The Scope and Content of the Principle of *Non-refoulement:* Opinion." In *Refugee Protection in International Law: UNHCR's Global Consultations on International Protection*, ed. E. Feller et al. Cambridge: Cambridge University Press.

Lawson, Rick. 2004. "Life after Bankovic: On the Extraterritorial Application of the European Convention on Human Rights." In *Extraterritorial Application of Human Rights Treaties*, ed. Fons Coomans and Menno T. Kamminga. Antwerp: Intersentia.

Leckie, Scott. 2008. "The Human Rights Implications of Climate Change: What Next?" Paper delivered at the UN building, Mále, Maldives, 5 March.

Legomsky, Stephen H. 2006. "The USA and the Caribbean Interdiction Program." *International Journal of Refugee Law* 18: 677–96.

Limburg Principles on the Nature and Scope of the Obligations of State Parties to the International Covenant on Economic, Social, and Cultural Rights. 1986. Adopted by a group of distinguished experts in international law, in Maastricht on 2–6 June.

Lowe, Vaughan. 2007. *International Law.* Oxford: Oxford University Press.

Lutterbeck, Derek. 2006. "Policing Migration in the Mediterranean." *Mediterranean Politics* 11: 59–82.

Mahon, Claire. 2008. "Progress at the Front: The Draft Optional Protocol to the International Covenant on Economic, Social and Cultural Rights." *Human Rights Law Review* 8: 617–646.

Magraw, Daniel Barstow. 1995. *NAFTA & the Environment: Substance and Process* Washington D.C.: American Bar Association Section of International Law and Practice.

Marks, Stephen P. 2005. "The Hissene Habré Case: The Law and Politics of Universal Jurisdiction." In *Universal Jurisdiction: National Courts and the Prosecution of Serious Crimes under International Law,* ed. Stephen Macedo. Philadelphia: University of Pennsylvania Press.

Marty, Dick. 2006. *Alleged Secret Detentions and Unlawful Inter-state Transfers of Detainees Involving Council of Europe Member States.* Strasbourg: Council of Europe Committee on Legal Affairs and Human Rights Report (12 June).

———. 2007. *Secret Detentions and Illegal Transfers of Detainees Involving Council of Europe Member States: Second Report.* Strasbourg: Council of Europe Committee on Legal Affairs and Human Rights Report Explanatory Memorandum (7 June).

Maxwell, Simon. 2007. *Can the International Health Partnership Deliver a New Way of Health Spending?* London: Overseas Development Institute.

McCaffrey, Stephen C. 1992. "A Human Right to Water: Domestic and International Implications." *Georgetown International Environmental Law Review* 5: 1–24.

———. 2004. "The Human Right to Water Revisited." In *Fresh Water and International Economic Law,* ed. Edith Weiss, Laurance DeChazournes Boisson, and Nathalie Bernasconi-Osterwalder. Oxford: Oxford University Press.

McGoldrick, Dominic. 2004. "Extraterritorial Application of the International Covenant on Civil and Political Rights." In *Extraterritorial Application of Human Rights Treaties,*" ed. Fons Coomans and Menno T. Kamminga. Antwerp: Intersentia.

Moore, Jonathan. "Refugees and Foreign Policy: Immediate Needs and Durable Solutions." Address delivered at the Kennedy School of Government, Harvard University, 6 April.

Mukhija, Vinit. 2005. "Challenges for International Development Planning: Preliminary Lessons from the Case of the Cities Alliance." *International Journal of Urban Policy and Planning* 23: 56–62.

Mutua, Makau. 2002. *Human Rights: A Cultural and Political Critique.* Philadelphia: University of Pennsylvania Press.

Nakani, Gobind, John Page, and Lindsay Judge. 2005. "Human Rights and Poverty Reduction Strategies: Moving Towards Convergence?" In *Human Rights and Development: Towards Mutual Reinforcement,* ed. Philip Alston and Mary Robinson. Oxford: Oxford University Press.

Nicholson, Frances. 1997. "Implementation of the Immigration (Carriers' Liability) Act 1987: Privatising Immigration Functions at the Expense of International Obligations." *International and Comparative Law Quarterly* 46: 586–634.

Noll, Gregor. 2003. "Visions of the Exceptional: Legal and Theoretical Issues Raised by Transit Processing Centres and Protection Zones." *European Journal of Migration Law* 5: 303.

Nowak, Manfred. 2003. *Introduction to the International Human Rights Regime.* The Hague: Martinus Nijhoff.

———. 2006. "What Practices Constitute Torture? US and UN Standards." *Human Rights Quarterly* 28: 809–41.

Nowak, Manfred, and Elizabeth McArthur. 2008. *The United Nations Convention against Torture: A Comment.* Oxford: Oxford University Press.

Nyamu-Musembi, Celestine. 2006. "Breathing Life into Dead Theories about Property Rights: De Soto and Land Relations in Rural Africa." Brighton: IDS Working Paper.

Organisation for Economic Co-operation and Development (OECD). 1977. *Legal Aspects of Transfrontier Pollution.* Paris: OECD.

———. 1986. *OECD and the Environment.* Paris: OECD.

———. 2007. *The OECD Guidelines for Multinational Enterprises and the Equator Principles, Similarities, Differences, and Synergies,* by Paul Watchman and Angela Delfino. Annual Meeting of the National Contact Points for the OECD Guidelines for Multinational Enterprises, Daf/Inv/Ncp. (20 July).

———. 2008a. *Debt Relief Is Down: Other ODA Rises Slightly.* Available at http://www.oecd.org.

———. 2008b. *Rising Food Prices: Causes and Consequences.* Paris: OECD.

OECD-FAO. 2008. *OECD-FAO Agricultural Outlook 2008–2017.* Paris: OECD-FAO. Available at http://www.oecd.org/documents/29/0.3343.en.

Okoampa-Ahoofe, Kwame. 2007. "NPP Cuts Sod for Bui Dam." *The Statesman* (28 August). Available at http://www.thestatesmanonline.com/pages/news_detail.php?section=11&newsid=4580.

Okoth-Obbo, Georges. 1996. "Coping with a Complex Refugee Crisis in Africa: Issues, Problems, and Constraints for Refugee and International Law." In *The Problem of Refugees in the Light of Contemporary International Law: Papers Presented at the Colloquium Organized by the Graduate Institute of International Studies in Collaboration with the United Nations High Commissioner for Refugees, Geneva 26 and 27 May 1994,* ed. Vera Gowlland-Debbad. Dordrecht: Martinus Nijhoff.

O'Neill, Tam, Marta Foresti, Tim Braunholtz, and Bavna Sharma. 2007. *DFID's Human Rights Policy: Scoping Study.* London: Overseas Development Institute.

Ooms, Gorik, and Ted Schrecker. 2005. "Expenditure Ceilings, Multilateral Financial Institutions, and the Health of Poor Populations." *The Lancet* 365: 1821–23.

Organisation of African Unity (OAU). 2001. *Abuja Declaration on HIV/AIDS, Tuberculosis, and Other Related Infectious Diseases.* Adopted by the Heads of State and Government of the Organisation of African Unity, Abuja, Nigeria. OAU Doc. OAU/SPS/ABUJA/3.

Oxfam. 2005. "Kicking down the Door: How Upcoming WTO Talks Threaten Farmers in Poor Countries." Oxfam Briefing Paper 72. London: Oxfam

———. 2006. *Patents versus Patients: Five Years after the Doha Declaration.* Oxford.

Paasch, Armin, Frank Garbers, and Thomas Hirsch, eds. 2007. *The Impact of Trade Liberalization on the Right to Food of Rice Farming Communities in Ghana, Honduras, and Indonesia.* Geneva: Ecumenical Advocacy Alliance.

Palan, Ronen. 2003. *The Offshore World: Sovereign Markets, Virtual Places, and Nomad Millionaires.* Ithaca, N.Y.: Cornell University Press.

Parker, Sarah. 2007. *Analysis of States' Views on an Arms Trade Treaty.* Geneva: UN Institute for Disarmament Research.

Parlett, Kate. 2007. "Universal Civil Jurisdiction for Torture." *European Human Rights Law Review* 4: 385–403.

Patel, Sheela. 2007. "Towards the Legal Empowerment of the Poor: Article Written in Response to Kumi's Article on the Commission on Legal Empowerment of the Poor." July. Available at http://www.undp.org/legalempowerment/docs/SheelaPatel_towards_LEP.doc.

Payne, Geofreey, Alain Duran-Lasserve, and Carole Rakodi. 2007. "Urban Land Titling Programmes." *Legal Empowerment: A Way out of Poverty* 3: 11.

Pitea, Cesare. 2005. "NGOs in Non-Compliance Mechanisms under Multilateral Environmental Agreements: From Tolerance to Recognition?" In *Civil Society, International Courts, and Compliance Bodies,* ed. Tullio Treves et al. Cambridge: Cambridge University Press.

Plender, Richard, and Nuala Mole. 1999. "Beyond the Geneva Convention: Constructing a De Facto Right of Asylum from International Human Rights Instruments." In *Refugee Rights and Realities*, ed. F. Nicholson and P. Twomey. Cambridge: Cambridge University Press.

Pogge, Thomas, ed. 2007. *Freedom from Poverty as a Human Rights; Who Owes What to the Very Poor?* Oxford: Oxford University Press.

Polaski, Sandra. 2004. "Protecting Labor Rights through Trade Agreements: An Analytical Guide." *Journal of International Law and Policy* 10: 13–25.

———. 2006. "Combining Global and Local Forces: The Case for Labor Rights in Cambodia." *World Development* 34. Reprint, Washington, D.C.: Carnegie Endowment for International Peace.

Pugh, Michael. 2004. "Drowning Not Waving: Boat People and Humanitarianism at Sea." *Journal of Refugee Studies* 17: 50–68.

Rajagopal, Balakrishnan. 2003. *International Law from Below: Development, Social Movements, and Third World Resistance* Cambridge: Cambridge University Press.

Reydams, Luc. 2003. *Universal Jurisdiction: International and Municipal Legal Perspectives* Oxford: Oxford University Press.

Rizvi, Haider. 2006. "UN Passes Arms Trade Treaty over US Opposition." Inter Press Service, 27 October. Available at http://www.commondreams.org/headlines06/1027-01.htm.

Robinson, Nehemiah. 1953. *Convention Relating to the Status of Refugees: Its History, Contents, and Interpretation; A Commentary*. New York: Institute for Jewish Affairs.

Rosenthal, Eric, and Éva Szeli. 2002. *Not on the Agenda: Human Rights of People with Mental Disabilities in Kosovo*. Washington, D.C.: Mental Disability Rights International. Available at http://www.mdri.org/pdf/KosovoReport.pdf.

Ross, Alf. 1961. *Lærebog i Folkeret*. 4th ed. København: Munksgaards Forlag.

Rouillard, Louis-Philippe F. 2005. "Misinterpreting the Prohibition of Torture under International Law: The Office of the Legal Counsel Memorandum." *American University International Law Review* 21: 9–41.

Roxstrom, Erik, et al. 2005. "The NATO Bombing Case (Bankovic et al. v. Belgium et al.) and the Limits of Western Human Rights Protection." *Boston University International Law Journal* 23: 56–136.

Rozental, Stefan. 1955. "Om komplementaritet i atomfysikken." *Fysisk Tidsskrift* 325–42.

Saith, Ashwani. 2006. "From Universal Values to Millennium Development Goals: Lost in Translation." *Development and Change* 37: 1167–99.

Salomon, Margot E. 2007. *Global Responsibility for Human Rights: World Poverty and the Development of International Law*. Oxford: Oxford University Press.

Sands, Philippe J. 1989. "The Environment, Community, and International Law." *Harvard International Law Journal* 30: 393–420.

Scanlon, John, Angela Cassar, and Noemi Nemes. 2003. "Water as a Human Right?" Paper presented at the Seventh International Conference on Environmental Law titled "Water and the Web of Life," São Paulo, Brazil, 2–5 June.

Scheinin, Martin. 2004. "Extraterritorial Effect of the International Covenant on Civil and Political Rights." In *Extraterritorial Application of Human Rights Treaties*, ed. Fons Coomans and Menno T. Kamminga. Antwerp: Intersentia.

———. 2008. "Human Rights Committee: Not Only a Committee on Civil and Political Rights." In *Social Rights Jurisprudence: Emerging Trends in International and Comparative Law*, ed. Malcolm Langford. New York: Cambridge University Press.

Scudder, Thayer. 2005. *The Future of Large Dams: Dealing with the Social, Environmental, Institutional, and Political Costs.* London: Earthscan.

Sepúlveda, Magdalena. 2006. "Obligations of 'International Assistance and Cooperation' in an Optional Protocol to the International Covenant on Economic, Social, and Cultural Rights." *Netherlands Quarterly of Human Rights* 24: 271–303.

———. 2008. "The Constitutional Court's Role in Addressing Social Injustice." In *Social Rights Jurisprudence: Emerging Trends in International and Comparative Law,* ed. Malcolm Langford. New York: Cambridge University Press.

Shelton, Dinah. 2003. "The Environmental Jurisprudence of International Human Rights Tribunals." In *Linking Human Rights and the Environment,* ed. Romina Picolotti and Jorge Daniel Taillant. Tucson: University of Arizona Press.

Shihata, Ibrahim. 1995. *Prohibition of Political Activities in the World Bank's Work.* Legal opinion by the senior vice president and general counsel, 12 July.

Shiva, Vandana. 2002. *Water Wars.* London: Pluto Press.

Shue, Henry. 1979. "Rights in Light of Duties." In *Human Rights and U.S. Foreign Policy,* ed. Peter Brown and Douglas Maclean. Lexington, Mass.: Lexington Books.

———. 1980. *Basic Rights: Subsistence, Affluence, and U.S. Foreign Policy.* Princeton, N.J.: Princeton University Press.

Simma, Bruno, and Philip Alston. 1992. "The Sources of Human Rights Law, Custom, *Jus Cogens,* and General Principles." *Australian Yearbook of International Law* 12: 82–108.

Skogly, Sigrun. 2001. *The Human Rights Obligations of the World Bank and the International Monetary Fund.* London: Cavendish.

———. 2003a. "The Obligations of International Assistance and Cooperation in the International Covenant on Economic, Social, and Cultural Rights." In *Human Rights and Criminal Justice for the Downtrodden: Essays in Honour of Asbjørn Eide,* ed. Morten Bergsmo. Leiden: Martinus Nijhoff.

———. 2003b. "The Obligations of International Assistance and Cooperation in the International Covenant on Economic, Social, and Cultural Rights." In *Human Rights and Criminal Justice for the Downtrodden: Essays in Honour of Asbjørn Eide,* ed. Morten Bergsmo. Dordrecht: Kluwer Law International.

———. 2006. *Beyond National Borders: States' Human Rights Obligations in International Cooperation.* Antwerp: Intersentia.

Skogly, Sigrun, and Mark Gibney. 2002. "Transnational Human Rights Obligations." *Human Rights Quarterly* 24: 781–98.

———. 2007. "Economic Rights and Extraterritorial Obligations." In *Economic Rights: Conceptual, Measurement, and Policy Issues,* ed. Shareen Hertel and Lanse Minkler. New York: Cambridge University Press.

Smets, Henri. 2000. "The Right to Water as a Human Right." *Environmental Policy and Law* 30: 248–51.

Special Rapporteur to the UN Commission on Human Rights (Fatma-Zohra Ksentini). 1998. *Adverse Effects of the Illicit Movement and Dumping of Toxic and Dangerous Products and Wastes on the Enjoyment of Human Rights.* UN Doc. E/CN.4/1998/10 (20 January) [1998 Report].

———. (Fatma-Zohra Ouhachi-Vesely). 2001. *Adverse Effects of the Illicit Movement and Dumping of Toxic and Dangerous Products and Wastes on the Enjoyment of Human Rights.* UN Doc. E/CN.4/2001/55 (19 January) [2001 Report].

———. (Fatma-Zohra Ouhachi-Vesely). 2003a. *Adverse Effects of the Illicit Movement and Dumping of Toxic and Dangerous Products and Wastes on the Enjoyment of Human Rights.* UN Doc. E/CN.4/2003/56/Add.1 (10 January) [2003 Report].

———. 2003b. *Adverse Effects of the Illicit Movement and Dumping of Toxic and Dangerous Products and Wastes on the Enjoyment of Human Rights.* UN Doc. E/CN.4/2004/46 (15 December 2003) [2004 Report].

Stec, Stephen, and Susan Casey-Lefkowitz. 2000. *The Aarhus Convention: An Implementation Guide.* New York: United Nations.

Stohl, Rachel, Matt Schroeder, and Col. Dan Smith (USA ret.). 2007. *The Small Arms Trade.* Oxford: Oneworld Publications.

Swedish International Development Cooperation Agency (SIDA). 2002. *Health Is Wealth: Policy for Health and Development.* Stockholm.

Tams, Christian J. 2005. *Enforcing Obligations Erga Omnes in International Law.* New York: Cambridge University Press.

Technical Centre for Agriculture and Rural Cooperation ACP-EU. 2008. *Agritrade: Special Report; Policy Response to Food Crisis.* Brussels.

Thiele, Bret, and Mayra Gomez. 2005. "Suing the World Bank: The Chixoy Dam Case." In *Road to a Remedy: Current Issues in Litigation of Economic, Social, and Cultural Rights,* ed. John Squires, Malcolm Langford, and Bret Thiele. Sydney: Australian Human Rights Centre and University of NSW Press.

Tully, Stephen. 2005. "A Human Right to Access Water? A Critique of General Comment No. 15." *Netherlands Quarterly of Human Rights* 23: 35–64.

Ugandan Ministry of Finance, Planning, and Economic Development. 2003. *Partnership Principles between Government of Uganda and Its Development Partners.* Kampala.

U.K. Department for International Development. 2004. *DFID Country Assistance Plan for Palestinians.* London: DFID/Crown. Available at http://www.dfid.gov.uk.

———. 2006a. "UK Recognises the Right to Water as Hilary Benn Launches Call for Global Action Plan to Solve Water Crisis." Press release, DFID, 9 November. Available at http://www.dfid.gov.uk/news/files/pressreleases/human-dev-report06.asp.

———. 2006b. *Why We Need a Global Action Plan for Water and Sanitation.* London: DFID/Crown.

———. 2006c. "The Human Right to Water." Draft Position Paper, 9 November. Available at http://www.dfid.gov.uk/pubs/files/human-right-water.

———. 2006d. *DFID Palestinian Programme Interim Update.* London: DFID/Crown. Available at http://www.dfid.gov.uk.

———. 2007a. *Meeting Our Promises: A Third Update on DFIDs Work in Water and Sanitation since the 2004 Water Action Plan.* London: DFID/Crown.

———. 2007b. *Better Basra: Getting Clean Water to Southern Iraq.* Case Studies, 20 June. Available at http://www.dfid.gov.uk.

———. 2007c. *Working Together for Better Health.* London.

U.K. Home Office. 2003. "New Vision for Refugees" (7 March).

U.K. House of Commons Defence, Foreign Affairs, International Development, and Trade and Industry Committees. 2007. *Strategic Export Controls: 2007 Review.* First Joint Report of Session 2006–07, HC 117 (7 August). London: The Stationery Office Limited.

U.K. House of Commons International Development Committee. 2007a. *Sanitation and Water.* Sixth Report of Session 2006–7, vol. 1, HC 126-I (26 April). London: The Stationery Office Limited.

———. 2007b. *Sanitation and Water: Government Response to the Committee's Sixth*

Report of Session 2006–7. Seventh Special Report of Session 2006–7, HC 854 (10 July). London: The Stationery Office Limited.

———. 2007c. *Development Assistance and the Occupied Palestinian Territories.* Fourth Report of Session 2006–7, HC 114-I (31 January). London: The Stationery Office Limited.

———. 2007d. *Development Assistance and the Occupied Palestinian Territories: Government Response to the Committee's Fourth Report of Session 2006–7.* Fifth Special Report of Session 2006–7, HC 430 (29 March). London: The Stationery Office Limited.

U.K. National Audit Office. 2003. *DFID: Maximising Impact in the Water Sector.* Report by the Auditor General, Session 2002–3, HC351 (31 January). London: The Stationery Office Limited.

United Nations. 1994. United Nations Security Council Resolution 918 (Rwanda). UN Doc. S/Res/918, 17 May.

———. 1996. United Nations Security Council Resolution 1076 (the situation in Afghanistan). UN Doc. S/Res/1076, 22 October.

———. 1997. United Nations General Assembly. *Report of the Governmental Panel of Experts on Small Arms.* UN Doc A/52/298, 27 August.

———. 2001. *Report of the United Nations Conference on the Illicit Trade in Small Arms and Light Weapons in All Its Aspects.* UN Doc. A/Conf.192/15, 20 July.

———. 2003. Official Records of the General Assembly, Fifty-eighth Session, Supplement No. 10 (A/58/10), pars. 49–54, 5–9 May.

———. 2003. "UN Rights Expert Welcomes Canadian Initiative on Access to Low-Cost Drugs in Developing Countries." Press release, 7 November.

———. 2004. United Nations Security Council. Resolution 1556 (Sudan). UN Doc. S/Res/1556, 30 July.

———. 2005. "US-Peru Free Trade Pact Negotiations: Special Rapporteur on Right to Health Reminds Parties of Human Rights Obligations." Press release, 13 July.

———. 2006. *The Millennium Development Goals Report 2006.* New York: UN Department of Economic and Social Affairs (DESA).

———. 2006a. United Nations General Assembly. "Towards an Arms Trade Treaty: Establishing Common International Standards for the Import, Export and Transfer of Conventional Arms." Resolution 61/89. UN Doc. A/Res/61/89, 18 December.

———. 2006b. Report of the Chairperson-Rapporteur of the Working Group on Arbitrary Detention, *Situation of Detainees at Guantánamo Bay.* UN Doc. E/CN.4/2006/120.

———. 2007. *Millennium Development Goals Report 2007.* New York: UN Department of Economic and Social Affairs (DESA).

———. 2008. Report of the Secretary-General, *Small Arms.* UN Doc. S/2008/258, 17 April.

———. 2008. Report of the Secretary-General, *Toward an Arms Trade Treaty* (replies received from member states). UN Doc. A/62/278, 17 August.

UNAIDS and WHO. 2007. *AIDS Epidemic Update.* Geneva: United Nations.

UN Commission on Human Rights. 2002. *The Right of Everyone to the Enjoyment of the Highest Attainable Standard of Physical and Mental Health.* Commission on Human Rights Resolution 2002/31.

———. 2003. *The Prevention of Human Rights Violations Caused by the Availability and Misuse of Small Arms and Light Weapons.* UN Doc. E/CN.4/DEC/2003/112, 25 April.

————. 2005a. Report on the Sixty-first Session. Resolution 2005/15. UN Doc. E/2005/23, 14 March–22 April.

————. 2005b. Open-ended Working Group to Consider Options Regarding the Elaboration of an Optional Protocol to the International Covenant on Economic, Social, and Cultural Rights on Its Third Session, *Elements for an Optional Protocol to the International Covenant on Economic, Social, and Cultural Rights, Analytical Paper by the Chairperson-Rapporteur, Catarina de Albuquerque.* UN Doc. E/CN.4/2006/WG.23/2, 30 November.

————. 2005c. *Torture and Other Cruel, Inhuman or Degrading Treatment or Punishment: Interim Report of the Special Rapporteur (Manfred Nowak).* UN Doc. A/60/316, 30 August.

————. 2005d. *Civil and Political Rights, Including the Questions of Torture and Detention: Report of the Special Rapporteur (Manfred Nowak).* UN Doc. E/CN.4/2006/6, 23 December.

UN Committee against Torture. 2005. *Consideration of Reports Submitted by States Parties Under Article 19 of the Convention: Fourth Periodic Report of the United Kingdom of Great Britain and Northern Ireland.* UN Doc. CAT/C/SR.627, 24 November.

————. 2007. Consideration of Reports Submitted by States Parties Under Article 19 of the Convention. Comments by the Government of the United States of America to the conclusions and recommendations of the Committee against Torture. UN Doc. CAT/C/USA/CO/2, 6 November.

UN Committee on Economic, Social, and Cultural Rights. 1990a. *General Comment 2: International Technical Assistance Measures.* Fourth Session, UN Doc. E/1990/23, annex III at 86. Reprinted in *Compilation of General Comments and General Recommendations Adopted by Human Rights Treaty Bodies,* UN Doc. HRI/GEN/1/Rev.6 at 11 (2003).

————. 1990b. *General Comment 3: The Nature of States Parties Obligations (Art. 2, Para. 1 of the Covenant).* UN Doc. E/1991/23. Geneva: United Nations.

————. 1991. *General Comment 4: The Right to Adequate Housing.* Sixth Session. UN Doc. E/1992/23, annex III.

————. 1997a. *General Comment 7: The Right to Adequate Housing (Art. 11.1 of the Covenant); Forced Evictions.* UN Doc. E/1998/22, annex IV.

————. 1997b. *General Comment 8: The Relationship between Economic Sanctions and Respect for Economic and Social Rights.* UN Doc. E/C.12/1997/8.

————. 1999. *General Comment 12: The Nature to Adequate Food.* UN Doc. E/C.12/1999/5.

————. 2000. *General Comment 14: The Right to the Highest Attainable Standard of Health.* UN Doc. E/C.12/2000/4.

————. 2001. *Concluding Observations of the Committee on Economic, Social, and Cultural Rights: Germany.* Consideration of Reports Submitted by State Parties Under Articles 16 and 17 of the Covenant. UN Doc. E/C.12/1/Add.68.

————. 2001a. *Concluding Observations of the Committee on Economic, Social, and Cultural Rights: Sweden.* UN Doc. E/C.12/1/Add.70, 30 November.

————. 2001b. *Poverty and the International Covenant on Economic, Social, and Cultural Rights.* UN Doc. E/C.12/2001/10, 10 May.

————. 2002a. *Concluding Observations of the Committee on Economic, Social, and Cultural Rights: United Kingdom of Great Britain and Northern Ireland.* UN Doc. E/C.12/1Add.79.

————. 2002b. *General Comment 15: The Right to Water (arts. 11 and 12 of the Covenant).* UN Doc. E/C.12/2002/11.

————. 2003. *Concluding Observations Observations of the Committee on Economic, Social, and Cultural Rights: Israel.* UN Doc. E/C.12/1/Add.90.

————. 2005. *General Comment 18: The Right to Work (Art. 6).* UN Doc. E/C.12/GC/18.

————. 2006. *Concluding Observations of the Committee on Economic, Social, and Cultural Rights: Canada.* UN Doc. E/C.12/CAN/CO/4 E/C.12/CAN/CO5, 22 May.

————. 2008a. *Concluding Observations of the Committee on Economic, Social, and Cultural Rights: Belgium.* UN Doc. E/C.12/BEL/CO/3, 4 January.

————. 2008b. *Concluding Observations of the Committee on Economic, Social, and Cultural Rights: Finland.* UN Doc. E/C.12/FIN/CO/5, 16 January.

UN Development Programme (UNDP). 2005. *Human Development Report 2005: International Cooperation at a Crossroads; Aid, Trade, and Security in an Unequal World.* New York: UNDP.

UN Food and Agriculture Organization (FAO). 2006. *Briefs on Import Surges— Countries, No. 5 Ghana: Rice, Poultry, and Tomato Paste.* Rome: FAO.

UN-Habitat. 20009. *History of UN-Habitat.* Available at http://www.unhabitat.org/content.asp?typeid=19&catid=10&cid=927.

UN High Commissioner for Refugees. 1994. "Brief Amicus Curiae: The Haitian Interdiction Case 1993." *International Journal of Refugee Law* 6:85–102.

————. 2007. *Advisory Opinion on the Extraterritorial Application of Non-Refoulement Obligations under the 1951 Convention Relating to the Status of Refugees and Its 1967 Protocol,* 26 January.

UN High-Level Task Force on the Global Food Crisis. 2008. *Comprehensive Framework for Action.* New York: United Nations.

UN Human Rights Committee. 1982. *General Comment 6: The Right to Life (Art. 6)*

————. 1993. *Concluding Observations, Islamic Republic of Iran.* UN Doc. CCPR/C/79/Add.25.

————. 1994. *General Comment 24/52: Reservations and Declarations.* UN Doc. CCPR/C/21/Rev.1/Add.6.

————. 1995. *Concluding Observations, United States of America.* UN Doc. CCPR/C/79/Add.50, A/50/40.

————. 1999a. *Concluding Observations, Canada.* UN Doc. CCPR/C/79/Add.105.

————. 1999b. *General Comment 27: Freedom of Movement (Art. 12).* UN Doc. CCPR/C/21/Rev.1/Add.9

————. 2003. *Concluding Observations, Israel.* UN Doc. CCPR/C/SR.2128-2130

————. 2004. *General Comment 31/80: The Nature of the General Legal Obligation Imposed on States Parties to the Covenant.* UN Doc. CCPR/C/21/Rev.1/Add.13.

————. 2005. *Concluding Observations, Kenya.* UN Doc. CCPR/CO/83/KEN.

————. 2006. *Concluding Observations, United States of America.* UN Doc. CCPR/C/USA/CO/3.

UN Human Rights Council. 2006. Decision 2/104, *Human Rights and Access to Water,* Thirty-first Meeting, Second Session, 27 November.

————. 2006a. *Implementation of General Assembly Resolution 60/251 (Mission to Lebanon and Israel).* UN Doc. A/HRC/2/7, 2 October.

————. 2007a. Open-ended Working Group on an Optional Protocol to the International Covenant on Economic, Social, and Cultural Rights, Fifth Session. *Revised Draft Optional Protocol to the International Covenant on Economic, Social, and Cultural Rights* (advance unedited version). UN Doc. HRC/8/WG.4/2.

————. 2007b. Open-ended Working Group on an Optional Protocol to the International Covenant on Economic, Social, and Cultural Rights, Fourth Session. *Draft Optional Protocol to the International Covenant on Economic, Social, and Cultural Rights.* UN Doc. A/HRC/6/WG.4/2*.

———. 2007c. *Report of the United Nations High Commissioner for Human Rights on the Scope and Content of the Relevant Human Rights Obligations Related to Equitable Access to Safe Drinking Water and Sanitation under International Human Rights Instruments.* UN Doc. A/HRC/6/3, 16 August.

———. 2008. Seventh Special Session: Resolution S-7/1, "The Negative Impact of the Worsening of the World Food Crisis on the Realization of the Right to Adequate Food."

UNICEF. 2007. *State of the World's Children 2008: Child Survival.* New York: United Nations.

UN Millennium Project. 2005. *Who's Got the Power? Transforming Health Systems for Women and Children.* Task Force on Child Health and Maternal Health. New York: UN Development Programme.

UN Office of the High Commissioner for Human Rights. 2007. *Consultation on Human Rights and Access to Safe-Drinking Water and Sanitation.* Geneva: United Nations.

———. 2008. *Claiming the MDGS: A Human Rights Approach.* Geneva: OHCHR.

UN Sub-Commission on the Promotion and Protection of Human Rights. 2006. "Principles on the Prevention of Human Rights Violations Committed with Small Arms." UN Doc. A/HRC/Sub.1/58/L.11/Add.1.

UN Third Committee. 1957. Report. UN Doc. A/3525, 9 February.

Vandenhole, Wouter. 2007a. "EU and Development: Extraterritorial Obligations under the International Covenant on Economic, Social, and Cultural Rights." In *Casting the Net Wider: Human Rights Development and the New Duty-Bearers,* ed. Margot Salomon, Arne Tostensen, and Wouter Vandenhole. Antwerp: Intersentia.

———. 2007b. "Third State Obligations under the ICESCR: A Case Study of EU Sugar Policy." *Nordic Journal of International Law* 76: 73–100.

———. Forthcoming. "Economic, Social, and Cultural Rights in the CRC: Is There a Legal Obligation to Cooperate Internationally for Development?" *International Journal of Children's Rights.*

Vargha, Corinne. 2008. "Promouvoir le travail décent dans les chaînes de production mondiale: l'Expérienc de Better Factories Cambodia." In *Résponsabilité de enterprise transnationale et mondialisation de l'economie,* ed. Isabelle Daugareilh. Bruxelles: Editeur Bruylant-Bruxelles.

Wagner, Martin, and Donald M. Goldberg. 2004. *An Inuit Petition to the Inter-American Commission on Human Rights for Dangerous Impacts of Climate Change.* Available at http://www.ciel.org/Publications/COP10_Handout_EJCIEL.pdf.

Walker, Neil. 2003. "Late Sovereignty in the European Union." In *Sovereignty in Transition,* ed. Neil Walker. Oxford: Hart Publishing.

Wasem, Ruth Ellen. 2007. "Cuban Migration Policy and Issues." CRS Report for Congress RS20468. Washington, D.C.: Congressional Research Service.

WaterAid. 2006a. *DFIDs Organisational Capacity for Support to Water and Sanitation.* Available at http://www.wateraid.org.

———. 2006b. *WaterAid's Submission to the International Development Select Committee, Executive Summary, November 2006.* Available at http://www.wateraid.org.

———. 2007. "DFID Report Follows WaterAid Recommendations." Press release, 27 April. Available at http://www.wateraid.org.

Wates, Jeremy. 2005. "NGOs and the Aarhus Convention." In *Civil Society, International Courts, and Compliance Bodies*, ed. Tullio Treves. Cambridge: Cambridge University Press.

Watson, Chris. 2007. *Recent Trends and Labor Developments in Cambodia.* Washington, D.C.: U.S. Department of Labor, Bureau of International Labor Affairs.

Wells, Don. 2006. " 'Best Practice' in the Regulation of International Labor Standards: Lessons of the US-Cambodia Textile Agreement." *Comparative Labor Law and Policy Journal* 27, no. 20: 357.

WHO, UNICEF, UNFPA, and the World Bank. 2007. *Maternal Mortality in 2005: Estimates Developed by WHO, UNICEF, UNFPA, and the World Bank.* Geneva: World Health Organization.

Wirth, David. 1994. "Reexamining Decision-Making in International Environmental Law." *Iowa Law Review* 79: 769–802.

Wold, Chris, Lucus Ritchie, Deborah Scott, and Matthew Clark. 2004. "The Inadequacy of the Citizen Submission Process of Articles 14 and 15 of the North American Agreement on Environmental Cooperation." *Loyola of Los Angeles International and Comparative Law Review* 26: 415–44.

Wood, Brian. 2006. "Strengthening Compliance with UN Arms Embargoes." Occasional Paper No. 10, Department of Disarmament Affairs. Available at http://disarmament.un.org/DDApublications/OP10/4Wood.pdf.

World Bank. 2007. *World Development Report: Agriculture for Development.* Washington, D.C.

———. 2008. Speech by World Bank Group President Robert B. Zoellick at the International Labour Organization, Geneva, 17 March. Available at http://209.85.135.104/search?q=cache:UELY0bSRgCQJ:web.worldbank.org/WBSITE/EXTERNAL/EXTABOUTUS/ORGANIZATION/EXTPRESIDENT2007/0,,contentMDK:21690802~menuPK:64822311~pagePK:64821878~piPK:6482 1912~theSitePK:3916065,00.html+%22improve+labor+practices+and+competitiveness%22&hl=en&ct=clnk&cd=1&gl=uk.

World Health Organisation. 2000. *The Global Water Supply and Sanitation Assessment 2000.* Geneva: WHO.

———. 2003. *The Right to Water.* Geneva: WHO.

Wouters, Jan, and Leen de Smet. 2004. "The ICJ's Judgment in the Case Concerning the Arrest Warrant of 11 April 2000: Some Critical Observations." *2004 Yearbook of International Humanitarian Law* 4: 373–88.

Yihdego, Zeray. 2007. *The Arms Trade and International Law.* Oxford: Hart.

Zanetta, Cecilia. 2001. "The Evolution of the World Bank's Urban Lending in Latin America." *Habitat International* 25: 513–33.

Ziegler, Jean. 2005. *Report of the Special Rapporteur on the Right to Food.* UN Doc. E/CN.4/2005/47.

Cases

International Arbitration Panel

Trail Smelter Case (*U.S. v. Canada*), 3 R.I.A.A. 1905 (1941).

African Commission on Human and Peoples' Rights

Social and Economic Rights Action Center for Economic and Social Rights v. Nigeria. No. 155/96 (2001).

Colombian Court
Constitutional Court of Colombia, SU-383/97.

Commission for Environmental Cooperation
Secretariat Determination (Devils Lake). SEM-06-002 (2006).
Secretariat Determination (Great Lakes). SEM-98-003 (1999).
Secretariat Determination (Great Lakes). SEM-98-003 (2001).
Secretariat Determination (Ontario Power Generation). SEM-03-001 (2004).

European Court of Human Rights
Amuur v. France. Appl. no. 19776/92 (25 June 1996).
Banković and Others v. Belgium and 16 Other Contracting States. Appl. no. 52207/99 (19 December 2001), adm. dec. (12 December 2001).
Cyprus v. Turkey. Appl. no. 25781/94 (10 May 2001).
Guerra and Others v. Italy. No. 116/1996/735/932 (19 February 1998).
Ilascu and Others v. Moldova and Russia. Appl. no. 48787/99, adm. dec. (8 July 2004).
Ilascu and Others v. Moldova and the Russian Federation. Appl. no. 48787/99, judgment (8 July 2004).
Issa and Others v. Turkey. Appl. no. 31821/96, judgment (16 November 2004).
Loizidou v. Turkey. Appl. no. 15318/89, first judgment (23 March 1995), judgment on merits (18 December 1996).
Loizidou v. Turkey. 23 E.H.R.R. 513 (1997).
López Ostra v. Spain. No. 16798/90 (1994).
Öcalan v. Turkey. Appl. no. 46221/99, first judgment (12 March 2003), confirmed by the Grand Chamber judgment (12 May 2005).
Soering v. United Kingdom. Appl. No. 14038188 (7 July 1989).
T. I. v. United Kingdom. Appl. no. 43844/98, adm. dec. (7 March 2000).
Xhavara and Fifteen v. Italy and Albania. Appl. no. 39473/98, adm. dec. (11 January 2001).

Inter-American Commission on Human Rights
Armando Alejandro Jr. and Others v. Cuba ("Brothers to the Rescue"). Case 11.589, Report no. 86/99, Annual Report IACHR 1999, 586 (29 September 1999).
Haitian Center for Human Rights v. United States. Case 10.675, Report no. 51/96, Doc. OEA/Ser. L/V/II.95 7 rev. (13 March 1997), par. 156–57.
Maya Indigenous Community of the Toledo District v. Belize. Case 12.053, Report no. 40/04, Doc. OEA/Ser. L/V/II.122 5 rev. 1 at 727 (2004).
Rafael Ferrer-Mazorra and Others v. the United States. Case 9903, Report no. 51/01, Annual Report IACHR 2000, 1188 (4 April 2001), par. 179.
Saldano v. Argentina. No. 38/99 (11 March 1999).

Inter-American Court
Sawhoyamaxa Indigenous Community of the Enxet People v. Paraguay. Case 0322/2001, Report No. 12/03, Inter-Am. C.H.R., OEA/Ser.L/V/II.118 Doc. 70 rev. 2 at 378 (2003).

International Court of Justice
Barcelona Traction, Light and Power Company, Limited. Judgment. ICJ Reports (1970).
Case of the S.S. "Lotus." Permanent Court of International Justice. PCIJ Series A, no. 10 (7 September 1927), p. 14.

Corfu Channel Case. Judgment. ICJ Reports (1949).
Democratic Republic of the Congo v. Belgium. ICJ Reports (14 February 2002).
Legal Consequences of the Construction of a Wall in the Occupied Palestinian Territory. Advisory Opinion. ICJ Reports (9 July 2004), http://www.icj-cij.org/icjwww/idocket/imwp/imwpframe.htm.
Legal Consequences for States of the Continued Presence of South Africa in Namibia. Advisory Opinion. ICJ Reports (1971).
Legality of the Threat or Use of Nuclear Weapons, Advisory Opinion, 8 July 1996
Nicaragua v. United States of America. Judgment on merits. ICJ Reports (1986).
Reservations to the Convention on Genocide, Advisory Opinion. ICJ Reports (1951).

U.K. Courts

A and Others v. Secretary of State for the Home Department. EWCA Civ. 1123, judgment (11 August 2004). UKHL 71, judgment (8 December 2005).
Al-Skeini and Others v. Secretary of State for Defence. UKHL 26 (13 June 2006).
Jones v. Ministry of the Interior of the Kingdom of Saudi Arabia. EWCA Civ. 1394, judgment (28 October 2004). UKHL 26, judgment (14 June 2006).
R. (European Roma Rights Centre and Others) v. Immigration Officer at Prague Airport. Court of Appeal, QB 811 EWCA Civ. 666 (20 May 2003).
R. v. Zardad. High Court judgement (18 July 2005).
Regina v. Bartle and the Commissioner of Police for the Metropolis and Others Ex Parte Pinochet (On Appeal from a Divisional Court of the Queen's Bench Division). Judgment (24 March 1999).
Regina v. Evans and Another and the Commissioner of Police for the Metropolis and Others Ex Parte Pinochet (On Appeal from a Divisional Court of the Queen's Bench Division). Judgment (24 March 1999).
Saleh Hasan and Others v. U.K. Secretary of State for Foreign and Commonwealth Affairs (2006).

UN Committee against Torture

Agiza v. Sweden. Comm. no. 233/2003 (2005).
G. K. v. Switzerland. Comm. no. 219 (2002).
Guengueng and Others v. Senegal. Comm. no. 181 (2001).
Guridi v. Spain. Comm. no. 212 (2002).
Hijirizi et al v. Yugoslavia. Comm. no. 161 (2000).
Kindler v. Canada. Communication No. 470/1990, 30 July 1993.

UN Human Rights Committee

Alzery v. Sweden. Comm. no. 1416/2005 (2006).
Apirana Mahuika and Others v. New Zealand. Comm. no. 547 (1993).
Bernard Ominayak, Chief of the Lubicon Lake Band v. Canada. Comm. no. 167 (1984). Views (1990).
Jiménez Vaca v. Colombia. Comm. no. 859 (1999).
Judge v. Canada. Communication No. 829/98. U.N. Doc. CCPR/C/78/D/829/1998, 20 October 2003.
Länsman v. Finland (No. 2). Comm. no. 671 (1995).
Lilian Celiberti de Casariego v. Uruguay. Comm. no. 56 (1979). UN Doc. CCPR/C/OP/1 (1981).
López Burgos v. Uruguay. Communication No. 52/1979, CCPR/C/13/D/52/1979, 29 July 1981.
Marie-Hélène Gillot and Others. v. France. Comm. no. 932 (2000).

Ng v. Canada. Communication No. 469/1991, U.N. Doc. CCPR/C/49/ D/469/1991 (1994).
Passport Cases, Comm. nos. 31 (1978), 57 (1979), 77 (1980), 106 and 108 (1981), 125 (1982).

U.S. Courts

Doe v. Unocal. 110 F. Supp. 2d 1294 (C.D. Cal. 2000).
Filartiga v. Pena-Irala. 630 F.2d 876 (CA, 2d Cir. 1980).
Rasul v. Bush. 542 U.S. 466 (2004).
Sale, Acting Cmmr., Immigration and Naturalization Service v. Haitian Center Council, U.S. 113 S. Ct. 2549, 509 U.S. 155 (1993).
Wiwa v. Royal Dutch Petroleum Co. 226 F. 3d 88 (2d. Cir. 2000).

World Bank Inspection Panel

Decision on Chad-Cameroon Petroleum and Pipeline Project (Loan no. 4558-CD).
Decision on Management of the Petroleum Economy (Credit no. 3316-CD).
Decision on Petroleum Sector Management Capacity Building Project (Credit no. 3373-CD).

International and Regional Treaties and Declarations

Aarhus Convention on Access to Information, Public Participation in Decision-Making, and Access to Justice in Environmental Matters. Done at Aarhus, Denmark, 25 June 1998.
Additional Protocol to the American Convention on Human Rights in the Area of Economic, Social, and Cultural Rights (Protocol of San Salvador). Adopted in San Salvador, 17 November 1988, 28 I.L.M. 156 (1989).
African (Banjul) Charter on Human and Peoples' Rights. Adopted by the Organization of African Unity at Nairobi, 27 June 1981. Entered into force, 21 October 1986.
American Convention on Human Rights. Signed at San Jose, Costa Rica, 22 November 1969. Entered into force, 18 July 1978.
American Declaration on the Rights and Duties of Man, OAS Res. XXX. Adopted by the Ninth International Conference of American States (30 March–2 May 1948), Bogota, OAS. Off. Rec. OEA/Ser. L/V/I.4 Rev. (1965).
Basel Convention on the Control of Transboundary Movements of Hazardous Wastes and Their Disposal. Done at 22 March 1989. Entered into force 5 May 1992.
Cartagena Protocol on Biosafety. Adopted 29 January 2000. Entered into force, 11 September 2003.
Charter of Fundamental Rights of the European Union. 2000 O.J. (C 364) 1, 7 December 2000.
Convention applying the Schengen Agreement of 14 June 1985 between the Governments of the States of Benelux Economic Union, the Federal Republic of Germany and the French Republic on the Gradual Abolition of Checks at Their Common Borders. 19 June 1990.
Espoo Convention on Environmental Impact Assessment in a Transboundary Context. Done at Espoo (Finland) 25 February 1991, 30 I.L.M. 800 (1991).
European Convention for the Prevention of Torture and Inhuman or Degrading

Treatment or Punishment. Opened for signature, 26 November 1987. Entered into force, 1 February 1989.

European Convention for the Protection of Human Rights and Fundamental Freedoms. Done at Rome, 4 November 1950. Entered into force, 3 September 1953.

European Joint Action on Small Arms. Official Journal L 191, 19 July 2002, pp. 1–4. Council of the European Union Doc. 2002/589CFSP, repealing Joint Action 1999/34/CFSP.

European Social Charter. Opened for signature, 18 October 1961. Entered into force, 26 February 1965.

European Union Code of Conduct on Arms Exports. Council of the European Union Doc. 8675/2/98 Rev 2, Brussels, 5 June 1998.

Geneva Convention for the Amelioration of the Condition of the Wounded and Sick in Armed Forces in the Field. 75 U.N.T.S. 31 (1949). Entered into force, 21 October 1950.

Geneva Convention for the Amelioration of the Condition of Wounded, Sick and Shipwrecked Members of Armed Forces at Sea. 75 U.N.T.S. 85 (1949). Entered into force, 21 October 1950.

Geneva Convention Relative to the Treatment of Prisoners of War. 75 U.N.T.S. 135 (1949). Entered into force, 21 October 1950.

Geneva Convention Relative to the Protection of Civilian Persons in Time of War. 75 U.N.T.S. 287 (1949). Entered into force, 21 October 1950.

Human Rights and the Environment (Ksentini Declaration) Sub-Commission on Human Rights Resolution 1993/32. UN Doc. E/CN.4/Sub.2/1993/7.

Inter-American Convention against the Illicit Manufacturing of and Trafficking in Firearms, Ammunition, Explosives, and Other Related Materials. Entered into force, 1 July 1998.

North American Agreement on Environmental Cooperation. Done at 14 September 1993. Entered into force, 1 January 1994, 32 I.L.M. 1480 (1993).

OAS Model Regulations for the Control of the International Movement of Firearms, Their Parts and Components and Ammunition, Inter-American Drug Abuse Control Commission. OAS Doc. Ser. L/XIV.2.34, 2003.

Optional Protocol to the Convention against Torture and Other Cruel, Inhuman, or Degrading Treatment or Punishment. Adopted 18 December 2002. A/RES/57/199.

Optional Protocol to the International Covenant on Civil and Political Rights. G.A. res. 2200A (XXI), 21 U.N. GAOR Supp. (No. 16) at 59, U.N. Doc. A/6316 (1966), 999 U.N.T.S. 302. Entered into force, 23 March 1976.

Optional Protocol to the International Covenant on Economic, Social and Cultural Rights. Adopted by U.N. General Assembly resolution A/RES/63/117, on 10 December 2008.

Paris Declaration on Aid Effectiveness. High Level Forum, Paris, 28 February–2 March 2005.

Rio Declaration on Environment and Development. Adopted at the UN Conference on Environment and Development, Rio de Janeiro, 3–14 June 1992.

Rotterdam Convention on the Prior Informed Consent Procedure for Certain Hazardous Chemicals and Pesticides in International Trade. Adopted 10 September 1998, 38 I.L.M. 1 (1999).

Stockholm Convention on Persistent Organic Pollutants. Done at 22 May 2001, 40 I.L.M. 53 (2001).

Stockholm Declaration of the United Nations Conference on the Human Environment. Adopted by the UN Conference on the Human Environment at Stockholm, 16 June 1972, A/CONF.48/14.

Rome Statute of the International Criminal Court. 2187 U.N.T.S. 90. Entered into force, 1 July 2002.

UN Conference on the Human Environment, Stockholm Declaration 16 June 1972, A/CONF.48/14.

UN Convention on the Elimination of All Forms of Discrimination against Women. Done at New York, 18 December 1979. Entered into force, 3 September 1981.

UN Convention on the Elimination of All Forms of Racial Discrimination. Done at 21 December 1965. Entered into force, 4 January 1969.

UN Convention on the Law of the Non-Navigational Uses of International Watercourses. Adopted by the General Assembly of the United Nations on 21 May 1997. UN Doc. A/51/49.

UN Convention on the Prevention and Punishment of the Crime of Genocide. 78 U.N.T.S. 277 (1949). Entered into force, 12 January 1951.

UN Convention on the Prohibition of the Development, Production and Stockpiling of Bacteriological (Biological) and Toxin Weapons and on Their Destruction. 26 U.S.T. 583, 1015 U.N.T.S. 163 (1972). Entered into force, 25 March 1975.

UN Convention on the Prohibition of the Development, Production, Stockpiling and Use of Chemical Weapons. 32 I.L.M. 800 (1993). Entered into force, 29 April 1997.

UN Convention on the Prohibition of the Use, Stockpiling, Production and Transfer of Anti-Personnel Mines and on Their Destruction. 2056 U.N.T.S. 241; 36 ILM 1507 (1997). Entered into force, 1 March 1999.

UN Convention for the Protection of All Persons from Enforced Disappearance. Adopted by the General Assembly, 20 December 2006. Opened for signature, 6 February 2007.

UN Convention on the Protection of the Rights of All Migrant Workers and Members of Their Families. Adopted by General Assembly resolution 45/158 of 18 December 1990. Entered into force, 1 July 2003.

UN Convention on the Rights of the Child. G.A. res. 44/25, annex, 44 U.N. GAOR Supp. (No. 49) at 167, U.N. Doc. A/44/49 (1989). Entered into force, 2 September 1990.

UN Convention on the Rights of Persons with Disabilities. Adopted by the General Assembly, 13 December 2006. Opened for signature, 30 March 2007.

UN Convention against Torture and Other Cruel, Inhuman, or Degrading Treatment or Punishment. Adopted by the General Assembly, 10 December 1984. Entered into force, 29 June 1987.

UN Declaration on the Right to Development. Adopted by General Assembly resolution 41/128 of 4 December 1986.

UN Declaration on the Rights of Indigenous Peoples. Adopted by General Assembly Resolution 61/295 on 13 September 2007.

UN General Assembly. Code of Conduct for Law Enforcement Officials. Resolution 34/169, annex, 34 U.N. GAOR Supp. (No. 46) at 186. U.N. Doc. A/34/46 (1979).

UN International Convention on the Rights of the Child. Done by the General Assembly, 20 November 1989. Opened for signature, 26 January 1990. Entered into force, 2 September 1990.

UN International Covenant on Civil and Political Rights. Adopted by the General Assembly, 16 December 1966. Entered into force, 23 March 1976.

UN International Covenant on Economic, Social, and Cultural Rights. Done by the General Assembly, 16 December 1966. Entered into force, 3 January 1976. UNGA Res. 2200 (XXI), 21 UN GAOR Supp. (No. 16) 49, UN Doc. A/6316 (1967).

UN Millennium Declaration. Adopted by General Assembly resolution 55/2, 8 September 2000.

UN Report of the Special Rapporteur (Philip Alston) on Extrajudicial, Summary or Arbitrary Executions. UN Doc. E/CN.4/2006/53 (2006).

Universal Declaration on Human Rights (1948). General Assembly Resolution 217A (III)

UNECE Convention on the Protection and Use of Transboundary Watercourses and International Lakes. Done at Helsinki, 17 March 1992.

UNECE Convention on the Protection and Use of Transboundary Watercourses and International Lakes, Protocol on Water and Health, 17 June 1999, MP.WAT/2000/1, EUR/ICP/EHCO 020205/8Fin.

Vienna Convention on the Law of Treaties. Concluded at Vienna, 23 May 1969. Entered into force, 27 January 1980.

Vienna Declaration and Programme of Action. Adopted by the 1993 World Conference on Human Rights. UN Doc. A/Conf. 157/23 (1993).

World Trade Organization. Agreement on Trade-related Aspects of Intellectual Property Rights (TRIPS). Annex 1C of the *Marrakesh Agreement Establishing the World Trade Organization,* signed in Marrakesh, Morocco, on 15 April 1994.

————. General Agreement on Trade in Services, Uruguay Round Agreement. Entered into force, 1995.

————. Implementation of Paragraph 6 of the Doha Declaration on the TRIPS Agreement and Public Health. Decision of the General Council of 30 August 2003.

Contributors

Judith Bueno de Mesquita is a part-time teacher in the Department of Law, and member of the Human Rights Centre at the University of Essex. From 2001 to 2008 she was a senior research officer in the Human Rights Centre, where she supported the mandate of the first special rapporteur on the right to health, Paul Hunt. She has worked as a consultant for organizations including WHO, OHCHR, UNICEF, the International Planned Parenthood Federation, and MedAct.

Amanda Cahill is currently lecturing in international human rights at Lancaster University, U.K. She is working on her forthcoming book on the right to water in the Occupied Palestinian Territories.

Barbara Frey is director of the Human Rights Program in the College of Liberal Arts at the University of Minnesota. She was an alternate member of the UN Sub-Commission on the Promotion and Protection of Human Rights from 2000 to 2003, and from 2002 to 2006 she served as special rapporteur of the sub-commission on the issue of preventing human rights abuses committed with small arms and light weapons. Frey was executive director of Minnesota Advocates for Human Rights from 1985 to 1997. She is a co-convenor of the Midwest Coalition for Human Rights, a network of forty-eight U.S.-based organizations working collaboratively to promote human rights.

Thomas Gammeltoft-Hansen is a doctoral candidate at Aarhus University and the Danish Institute for International Studies. His research combines legal and political theory, and in particular it focuses on the relationship between international refugee law, sovereignty, and modern state practices of offshoring and outsourcing migration control. He has published on issues regarding refugee law, migration management, EU immigration policy, and the Danish EU opt-outs. He is coeditor of *Sovereignty Games: Instrumentalising State Sovereignty in Europe and Beyond* (2008). Besides his research, he works as a policy analyst with the Danish

Refugee Council and has acted as an expert consultant to the European Council for Refugees, UNHCR, and the Council of Europe.

Mark Gibney is the Belk Distinguished Professor at the University of North Carolina–Asheville. His most recent books include *International Human Rights Law: Returning to Universal Principles* (2008) and *The Age of Apology: Facing Up to the Past* (edited with Rhoda E. Howard-Hassmann, Jean-Marc Coicaud, and Niklaus Steiner; 2007). In addition, he is an author (along with Sabine Carey and Steve Poe) of the forthcoming book *The Politics of Human Rights*.

Paul Hunt was elected by the United Nations to serve as an independent expert on the U.N. Committee on Economic, Social, and Cultural Rights (1999–2002). In 2001 and 2002, at the request of Mary Robinson, then U.N. High Commissioner for Human Rights, he coauthored draft *Guidelines on Human Rights Approaches to Poverty Reduction*. From 2002 to 2008, Hunt served as the U.N. special rapporteur on the right to the highest attainable standard of health. He has lived, and undertaken human rights work, in Europe, Africa, the Middle East, and the South Pacific. In addition to his thirty or so U.N. reports on various aspects of the right to health, he has written extensively on economic, social, and cultural rights, including *Reclaiming Social Rights: International and Comparative Perspectives* (1996), *Culture, Rights and Cultural Rights: Perspectives from the South Pacific* (coeditor, 2000), and *World Bank, IMF and Human Rights* (coeditor, 2003). He is a professor in law, and member of the Human Rights Centre, at the University of Essex (England) and adjunct professor at the University of Waikato (New Zealand). In 2008, the Nordic School of Public Health awarded him an honorary doctorate.

Rajat Khosla is currently working as advocacy specialist with the Asia-Pacific office of the UNMC on indigenous peoples and MDGs. He is also working as a consultant with the UNFPA, APRO in Bangkok. From 2006 to 2008 he was a senior research officer in the Human Rights Centre, where he supported the mandate of the first special rapporteur on the right to health, Paul Hunt. He previously worked as a researcher for the International Environmental Research Centre and as a consultant researcher for the Centre for the Study of Developing Societies in India. He has also worked as an advocate in the Supreme Court of India on several public interest cases involving socioeconomic rights.

John H. Knox is a professor of law at Wake Forest University, where he teaches and writes in the areas of human rights, international environmental law, and international trade law. In the last year, he has advised the Center for International Environmental Law as it helps the Maldives make the case to the United Nations that climate change interferes with their human rights. His recent scholarship includes "Climate Change and Human Rights Law," *Virginia Journal of International Law* (2009), and "Horizontal Human Rights Law," *American Journal of International Law* (2008). Before becoming a professor, he worked from 1988 to 1994 as an attorney in the Office of the Legal Adviser at the U.S. Department of State. He received his law degree in 1987 from Stanford Law School.

Malcolm Langford is a research fellow and director of the Human Rights and Development Research Group at the Norwegian Centre on Human Rights, University of Oslo. He was formerly a senior legal officer at the Centre on Housing Rights and Evictions (COHRE). He advises a number of U.N. agencies on human rights and development issues and has published widely, particularly in the field of economic, social, and cultural rights.

Virginia A. Leary, who died in 2009, was the Alfred and Hanna Fromm Professor of International and Comparative Law Emerita, University of California (Hastings), and Distinguished Service Professor and professor of law emerita, State University of New York (Buffalo). She held the Ariel Sallows Chair in Human Rights, University of Saskatchewan, and the Osler, Hoskins-Wilson Chair in Human Rights at the University of Toronto and Osgoode Hall Law School, Toronto. In addition to her academic work, she undertook human rights missions on behalf of Amnesty International, the International Commission of Jurists, and Human Rights Watch. She received her B.A. from the University of Utah, J.D. from the University of Chicago, and Ph.D. from the Graduate Institute of International Studies. In 2008, Dr. Leary was awarded the Goler T. Butcher Award from the American Society of International Law for outstanding contributions to the development of international human rights law.

Manfred Nowak is the University Professor for International Human Rights Law at the University of Vienna and is the director of the Ludwig Boltzmann Institute of Human Rights. Nowak is presently the U.N. special rapporteur on torture.

Sigrun Skogly is professor of human rights Law at Lancaster University, U.K. She has written extensively on issues of extraterritorial human rights obligations. Among her publications are *Beyond National Borders: States' Human Rights Obligations in Their International Cooperation* (2006); "Universal Human Rights without Universal Obligations?" in Sarah

Joseph and Adam McBeth, eds., *International Human Rights: A Research Handbook* (forthcoming); "Right to Food: National Implementation and Extraterritorial Obligations," in *Max Planck Yearbook of United Nations Law*, vol. 11 (2007). She has also served as president of FIAN International (a human rights organization that advocates for the right to food).

Michael Windfuhr is a political scientist who works as human rights director for Diakonie, the social service agency of the Protestant Church of Germany, and for Bread for the World, a development organization that is part of Diakonie. In addition, he teaches at the Institute for Political Science at the University of Heidelberg (Lehrbeauftragter). His latest publications include the edited volume *Beyond the Nation State: Human Rights in Times of Globalisation* (2005) and *Climate Change, Food Security and the Right to Food* (2008).

Index